FROM HAMAS
TO AMERICA

FROM HAMAS TO AMERICA

MY STORY OF DEFYING TERROR, FACING THE UNIMAGINABLE, AND FINDING REDEMPTION IN THE LAND OF OPPORTUNITY

BY MOSAB HASSAN YOUSEF
AND JAMES BECKET

Forefront
BOOKS

Published by Forefront Books, Nashville, Tennessee.
Distributed by Simon & Schuster.

Library of Congress Control Number: 2024907126
Print ISBN: 978-1-63763-318-2
E-book ISBN: 978-1-63763-319-9
Cover Design by Studio Gearbox
Interior Design by PerfecType, Nashville, TN
Printed in the United States of America

Dedicated to the Arab and Jewish children

CONTENTS

PREFACE

I might never know why I was born at the center of the Palestinian-Israeli conflict, but I know for sure what it takes to get out. Navigating my way out of the spider's web meant breaking bones. My bones.

Trying to solve the elusive mystery of the Middle East is similar to trying to solve the mystery of life: our minds can see or remember events yet find it hard to perceive the chain of events, their order, and most importantly, how these events originated or the forces that created them. Even those who were born into the conflict lived and died before answering all the questions related to its origins. Cursed are those who fall into its web, for it is easy to get caught up but hard to break free.

There are infinite forces at play when it comes to the Holy Land. Some people think it's as simple as two people fighting over territory or religion, a clash of civilizations, the ancient conflict of truth and falsehood, colonizers versus natives, east versus west, and the blame goes on and on. Participants tend to take sides, and driven by personal interest, they become vulnerable to the gravity of an extreme force. The fool tries to exploit the situation, only to be dominated by it. I have seen many try—regardless of their "purpose"—but they were destroyed.

The Middle East conflict is nothing but the eternal conflict between vice and virtue, the lower and higher interest of the self.

Fear, anger, lust, hatred, jealousy, gluttony, pride, guilt, and shame are the dominating forces in this field, while the forces of compassion, tolerance, forgiveness, and love are harder to notice.

Many fight for freedom without understanding what freedom is! They do not realize that freedom is not attained by the rise and fall of conditioned existence or the bringing down of a system or establishment.

Many others seek an external revolution, shedding blood to create quick change, to replace a system or establishment, but sooner or later, we all end up realizing that real change happens from within, and the reality of the external world is nothing but a giant mirror projecting back at us who we truly are.

The entire world now is drawn into the Middle East tragedy. But it is no longer belongs only to the Middle East. It is *our* story, our tale, our nature—our tragedy. The Middle East reality our reality. And each one of us is seeing their individualized and unique image.

In order to solve our conflict in relation to the Middle East or any other conflict on Earth, we must first learn how to be truthful and humble, because our own falsehood, denial, lust, and delusion translate in one way or another.

Before we push the wheel of conflict in any direction, we must ask the questions: Why do we identify with the conflict? What are we seeing? Why is it making us angry, hateful, or compassionate? Do we contribute to the continuation of the conflict as groups and as individuals?

But to be truthful, in our pursuit to neutralize our inner conflict, we need to be ready to drop our interest on material and emotional levels.

As you read through the pages of this book, pay attention to the mental traps—the mind's delusions and inability to see things for what they are because we are blinded by lust or hatred.

Intelligent individuals observe their mental process in relation to the external events of the external world, and once they have learned the lessons, they let go and move on. But others get stuck and are incapable of breaking the vicious cycle of rebirthing and not realizing how reality has been originating.

We are all brought up in a dependent universe where we have to compromise our freedoms in order to compensate for the expectations of family, society, and the rest of our universe. If we don't navigate our way out of a certain matrix or level of consciousness, we could get stuck for eternity without reaching the light at the end of the tunnel. Awareness of consciousness and its fluctuations is the cure. But this requires integrity, effort, discipline, and most importantly, observation of our mental and emotional patterns. Once I recognized these things, my fight in the external world and against its forces took a new shape. Acting with gentleness or with harshness depended on the situation I was responding to. In my case, the vast majority of those around me agreed on the right to practice violence for political and religious achievements. I disagreed. So how was I to get out? How much I was willing to lose?

How did I manage to escape the destructive current of a rigid culture? The flow of the current was so powerful, there was no way to swim against it. So I learned how to dive. Deep enough to reach the bottom and way below the current where I wouldn't be affected by it. Diving was no longer figurative for me but became a literal escape. Deep-water diving required learning buoyancy, pressure equalization, and breath retention for long periods. I had to also train my diaphragm against panic.

Even though diving below the dangerous current was challenging and slow, I eventually made it to my desired destination. Those who tried to beat the current and swam on the surface got tired very quickly and gave up.

It wasn't easy to be born into a death culture, where martyrdom was praised as the ultimate achievement. The perfect escape from human suffering. An ideology enforced by a dominant belief that sees life as suffering and ultimate freedom as found only in the afterlife through death. Instead of fighting the good fight and learning the precious lessons of life and aligning ourselves according to the universal laws of cause and effect, eradicating human suffering through patience, understanding, tolerance, and compassion, many choose to escape through death and suicide. But I believe it takes a lot more courage to *live* and endure life's difficulties.

Going against this death culture is my journey.

I hope that as you read about my journey, you will find answers to important questions regarding the Middle East conflict, but more importantly, I hope you find answers to the many questions regarding human nature.

Unlike my first book, *Son of Hamas*, which focused mainly on my external actions, *From Hamas to America* is my internal journey in relation to the external world.

Navigating my way out of the death culture didn't mean escaping a region or culture or crossing political barriers. I wish it were as easy as that. Crossing borders also doesn't mean transcending conditioning and mental barriers. I may have survived physically when I made it to the United States, but this was just the beginning of the real journey of facing *LIFE*, which is a lot harder than escaping death.

In this journey, I want to give you an eyewitness account of a person navigating the continuous traps throughout a journey and show you how I managed to break free from those traps, in the face of temptation and intimidation.

My life journey toward absolute freedom never happened, for no such thing in the material realm is absolute freedom, because with freedom comes compromise and responsibility. In fact, I have found just the opposite: the more responsibility and relations we have, the more we compromise our freedom. Therefore, we must attain our freedom from freedom.

Every relationship or attachment is a form of imprisonment; in a realm ruled by change, the lines between freedom and slavery can be very fine. And even though we might not achieve absolute freedom, we can still regain control of our lives, eradicate suffering, and create a meaningful life—regardless of external challenges. It simply depends on how much we are willing to compromise.

Conquering our fear of death is essential to unleashing our divine intelligence and creativity and attaining our higher potential in a realm of opposing forces. It's part of the process to clash with opposition. But eventually we learn how to pair opposing forces together so we can work toward progress and creation.

The most important achievement of my life is what I learned about who I am. I learned about the nature of my mind and how it works. Because of this achievement, I was able to defy time and age.

But I don't see a point in living in a realm of repetition for eternity. The current state must come to an end, and integration is necessary in a domain of infinite possibilities. The secret is contentment and nonattachment to the fruits of our work, or success. It is very different when we exit at will, because we are satisfied with what we have witnessed, instead of being forced to exist while still craving more and living unsatisfied.

This journey will take you through many extremes. Try to view this journey through the lens of no condemnation. Don't waste your energy judging the extremes of the journey; instead, pay attention to how the extremes have been managed, balanced, and naturalized. Although this is not a self-help book, think of it as a mirror, where you are capable only of seeing yourself.

There is no knowledge higher than self-knowledge. If we know who we are, we have decoded most of life's secrets. Our knowledge of the external is worthless without the internal connection.

Despite my unfortunate beginning as a rape victim, and experiencing the disadvantages of a child-abusive culture, political violence, and rigid conditioning, I learned how to be a resilient survivor. The traumas and the pains of my journey have been my greatest teachers. Conquering my hatred, lust, and delusions is what has made me who I am today. By conquering the self, the false identities, and my sense of loss and gain, I have found power and clarity.

This book is not about healing. Healing is a great achievement, but eradicating the origins of suffering is what really matters. Everyone has this potential, no matter how difficult it can be to tap into it. If I was able to overcome rape, systematic abuse, torture, sleep deprivation, and beatings, everyone can. This journey is my gift to all those who went through the hell of human cruelty. We can fight, and we can eventually rise above both pleasure and pain.

In a journey into the unknown, I didn't know what to expect next, but this uncertainty taught me the art of walking alone, the art of defying death, and most importantly, the art of contentment. I now have the ability to adapt quickly to any circumstance, any situation. Wealth or poverty, fame or shame, honor or blame, loss or gain—it doesn't matter.

Many of us prefer to live in a zoo, where things are safe and orderly. But few choose to live in the jungle, with no plan or security. Those in the zoo have do have more security, but they also have less freedom. Those who live in the jungle have little security but lots of freedom. I have found that a balance between the two is best, for freedom without discipline can be dangerous; it can bring about our highest potentials or it can destroy us. Rebelling against the source of our security and reclaiming our individuality and independence may sound like a good thing, but without having the power over our senses, it becomes a negative. So developing the skill of withdrawing from the senses is a powerful tool.

Not everyone is supposed to rebel. Some of us are fortunate to be born in a friendly environment. Of course, some people are less fortunate. But all of us have the power to carry on, no matter where we begin.

Life's hardships can be blessings for those who have the power to fight the good fight.

As you read, pay attention to the disciplines I have developed. My disciplines don't always have an order to them, and you might not need all of them. But use what you can and ignore the rest. What worked for me might not be a good fit for you, so choose what is best for you.

Most importantly, learn the lessons that I learned *from my mistakes* so you don't have to repeat them.

The consistent practice of observation, moderation, patience, faith, discipline, physical and mental purity, and breath regulation can get any individual out of any mental or physical captivity, no matter how complicated it may be.

Help might come from the outside, but what is better and more effective than waiting for a savior is taking the initiative and creating the desirable change. Success is great, but what is greater is to overcome failure. In the end, it all comes down to the power of letting go of both success and failure. Those who don't accept defeat will not attain victory.

PROLOGUE

I Am Not Who You Think I Am

As a young Palestinian male living on the West Bank, you never know, when the sun wakes you in the morning, if you'll live to see that sun go down. At no time would that be more true than today, March 29, 2002. Grabbing my M16 and dressed in camo, I mentally put on my persona: a Palestinian freedom fighter wanted by the Israeli authorities as a terrorist. I have to admit that I fit the part. My identity is complicated by anyone's standard. I was born a Palestinian Muslim, the oldest son of Hassan Yousef, a leading Palestinian political and religious leader and one of the founders of Hamas, the Palestinian Islamist resistance organization that governs much of Israeli-occupied Palestine. But the reason I am pretending to be a Palestinian freedom fighter is because I am now serving as a spy for the Israeli domestic intelligence agency, Shin Bet. Like I said, it is complicated.

I head for Al Manara, the center of Ramallah, where fighters from the two main Palestinian militias, Fatah and Hamas, are gathering. Ramallah serves as the major city of the West Bank, about six miles north of Jerusalem. There is a high state of tension after Palestinian terrorists bombed a Passover dinner, killing thirty Israelis. My purpose for going to the center is to gather intelligence on any imminent suicide attacks, which I am desperately seeking to stop. Hanging out with these militias can often produce useful information. Too many militia members are young men ready to become "martyrs" by strapping on a suicide belt, thus guaranteeing a ticket to Paradise and financial security and prestige for their families.

So that is how I find myself on the second floor of an office building overlooking Al Manara Square. Mistake. Big mistake. Little do I know that the Israelis have decided enough is enough, and so the Israel Defense Forces (IDF) have launched a major invasion of the West Bank, assaulting two main targets in Ramallah: Yasir Arafat's presidential compound, Mukataa, and Al Manara Square, where I sit.

Outside the window, flames and flashes of explosions light up the square with tracers like lasers slicing through the smoke and dust from collapsing buildings. The noise is worse: the constant machine-gun fire plus small arms, the roar of 105 mm cannons from the Israeli Merkava battle tanks, the Apache helicopter gunships thumping overhead and firing, with explosion after explosion rattling everything and everyone. It is the scene I've most feared and have done what I could to prevent. My ears ring as I gasp for breath from the smoke and dust and the acrid stench of battle. The building takes a direct hit, knocking me down. I realize I'm in a building that housed Palestinian resistance offices—a prime target.

With me in the same dark room is Hussein al-Sheikh, an important figure in the Palestinian administration charged with coordinating with the Israeli authorities. He pops up, fires a few rounds with his M16, and ducks back. If he happens to hit the steel armor of a tank, I doubt those inside even hear this pathetic retort. He has a satchel full of ammunition and offers me some.

IDF troops and tanks have taken up positions two hundred meters from the square, blocking each of the seven streets that lead into it. There is no escape from this trap. When they spring the trap shut, it's going to be a massacre. The IDF is out for Arab blood.

What a stupid way to die! I'll be one more expendable Palestinian body stacked among militia corpses.

My only chance of escape lies with Shin Bet, and they have no idea where I am. I'd have to call my handler on my special phone. It isn't just the IDF I fear, but my "comrades in arms"; if anyone overhears me, just suspicion will be enough to condemn me to a quick bullet to the head. From my angle looking out into the square, I can see the lifeless body of a collaborator hanging upside down from a pole. The swaying corpse is lit as though by a strobe light with the flashes from explosions. Only Allah knows now if he was innocent.

I have to find a safe place to call from, and so I move into a dark hallway and feel my way toward another room. Light from a flashlight probes the corridor and settles on my back. I hold my breath. IDF? Suddenly the sound of running steps erupts from behind me. Five militia members file by me as I hug the wall. In a moment the light is gone, and in the darkness I hear the clatter of footsteps charging down a flight of stairs. My heart pounds in my chest. I'm scared. Really scared. I smell the odor of sweat and fear that their passage left like a panicked breeze. I know damn well that those militiamen who strut about town like peacocks with their rifles casually slung over their shoulders now realize that today is the day they die. We all die.

I make it into a room with enough light from the window to assure me I'm alone. I take my phone out. *But what if someone comes in as I'm talking?* I open a door; it's a maintenance closet. *If I'm found in there, they'll execute me for cowardice! Now or never; call.* The door smashes open and three figures rush in—a CBS news crew with helmets and flak jackets emblazoned with a large "PRESS." Their interest is to position the camera at the window to get the overhead shot. Even in the faint light, I recognize their Palestinian fixer/translator from my father's endless press conferences. He's Fatah, reporting everything to them. Our eyes meet. I'm not sure he recognizes me, but this is not good, and I slip back into the corridor.

I move into the last room. Empty. I can see figures below running the gauntlet between buildings in search of better cover or maybe a miracle. A film crew hustles across this no-man's-land, only for the last one to be hit and go down. The other two go back and pick him up, at the same time futilely waving at whoever was shooting at them. "Press. Noncombatants." I put my phone to my ear; it's immediately picked up at the other end by my handler, whom I know as Loai.

"Help! I'm trapped at Al Manara Square. Get me out of here!"

I hold the phone out so he can hear the explosions.

"What the hell are you doing there?"

"My job; you didn't warn me—"

"We told you to stay put. All right, all right, I'll see what I can do." He clicks off. What now?

After ten long, long minutes, the phone beeps.

"All right, they'll open up a passage just for a brief moment. You go after the tank has moved."

"Where?"

"Falusteen Street. It will take an hour, two hours; I'll tell you when to go." He clicks off.

Oh my God, two hours. The building shakes like an exclamation point on that prospect. I know those Merkava behemoths take fifteen to twenty minutes to warm up their engines to move. That street, it's narrow; I know it well, but it's on the other side of the square. I'll have to run the gauntlet. *Go now or wait here until the last moment?*

My patience only lasts about ten minutes before I find myself in the doorway of the building looking across a hundred yards of no-man's-land to make it to Falusteen Street. Billows of smoke from explosions and fires offer momentary cover. *My gun? Drop it here?* The IDF was shooting at anything that moved, but if I run into militias, it's my identity card. Black smoke obscures more than half the route.

I take a deep breath, ready to sprint, only to set off a coughing jag. Once calm, I take off running as though my life depends on it. Well . . . out of the smoke, I hit a clear patch; bullets tattoo the paving stones behind me. I make it to a building on the other side, out of their line of fire. *Phew.* I spot a ramp down to an underground parking garage and quickly move down into its darkness. I smell tobacco smoke, and as my eyes adjust to the darkness, I realize I'm not alone. The noise of battle echoes in this cavern, but despite that, I can hear a nearby voice reciting a verse from the Koran. Shit.

It's the longest hour and a half of my life, as I expect the IDF to come charging in, guns blazing. But I'm encouraged when after an hour I hear a Merkava engine revving up; they make more noise than a jet plane taking off. Minutes later, my phone vibrates.

"Go now!"

"Now?"

"Now!"

I hustle up the ramp. In the darkness, I don't see a tank blocking the way. The order had been given to the tank to move, but do the soldiers on the ground know? They are still firing. I can make out what looks like a clear passage ahead. I hesitate. *My gun?* I drop it. I'm certainly not going to shoot at anyone, and it is not going to dissuade anyone from shooting me. As someone whose commitment is to save lives, not take lives, this makes sense to me. Though I often wonder, if it came down to a him-or-me confrontation, what would I do?

I walk briskly down the street and realize a few militia from the parking garage are following me. After a minute walking bent down alongside parked cars, I come to the point where the Merkova has taken up position. All the cars on the narrow street ahead have been crushed into the pavement by this monster. I imagine the tank crew enjoying the destruction like kids, which many of them still are. Making my way through twisted metal and shattered glass and the sharp smell of gasoline, I see no one. I take off jogging into the dark night, with dawn just sneaking in on the horizon.

I make it out.

Once safely back in my hideaway, I shed my sweat-drenched outfit. I've survived. Now my only thought is whether or not my father has survived. Of course, my father, this man I most admire in the world, is not at home. As a top leader in Hamas, Sheik Hassan Yousef has spent some twenty-five years of his adult life in prison or in hiding, where I hope he safely is now. As I am the person he trusts most in a brutal world of deceit and betrayal, I took on the role of his assistant, confidant, advisor, in effect his right hand at the time he became the leading public spokesman for the Palestinian cause on the West Bank. Many of my father's colleagues of the same high-profile status have been assassinated.

My deal with Shin Bet was I would have no blood on my hands; my father would be protected. At the moment he is hiding in the basement of a house in a residential neighborhood populated mainly by foreigners. Shin Bet, knowing where he is, had given the order to the IDF not to go into this house. But you could never be sure. Steadying my already jangled nerves, I call my father. *Ring. Ring.* Finally, his thick voice comes on.

"Son, you will never believe it; the soldiers searched every house on the block except for this one! Our prayers were answered, Allah protected us, a miracle."

Indeed. His life has had few happy moments, moments that confirmed his Muslim faith, but this is one. *You're welcome.* My getting out of Al Manara alive is what I consider a real-life miracle.

His frequent absence over the years has been unbearably hard on my mother, who has struggled just to put food on the table for her nine children. We live under occupation with daily killings in the streets, the IDF bursting into our home at all hours of the night, and the West Bank becoming a lawless jungle. Growing up, we children were deprived of our father's steady presence with his love and example of self-discipline and humility, a man who doesn't give up fighting even for something impossible. We received no support from our extended family nor from Hamas; in fact, we were shunned, a bitter and unexpected reality for me. People are hypocrites. They claim to be freedom fighters, or at least nationalists committed to defending the higher interests of the Palestinian nation. The fact is, fear rules their lives—the opposite of freedom. Fear of the Israelis that helping us would be "helping terrorists."

Whenever my father was let out of prison, he'd be greeted as a great hero and we would no longer be pariahs. But sometimes when he was released and would come home through the front door to be greeted with tears and hugs, at the back door was the Israeli army, arresting him once again and dragging him off to yet another prison.

PART I

1

The Question

How could I—the eldest son of this top Hamas leader and arrested by the Israelis at age seventeen and brutally tortured, like all arrested and then imprisoned terrorist suspects—possibly be working with our most hated and feared enemy, Shin Bet, Israel's intelligence service? What possibly could have motivated me to make such a fateful choice? Even given that it was made in the extreme situation of war, such a choice appears both incomprehensible and deranged.

I have had many diverse labels describing me in my life: *terrorist, spy, traitor, hero, Muslim, Christian, yogi, Buddhist, stateless, refugee, deportee, citizen*. Most of these served someone else's agenda, not mine. My journey is the same as that of all of us who choose to live consciously: to discover who we truly are and what is our truth.

To even begin to understand the impossible, suicidal choices confronting me, it's crucial to know the world I grew up in.

A TOXIC BREW

My parents produced nine children, and, like everyone else on the planet, we were conditioned by our parents and their beliefs and behaviors. We were also conditioned by the particular environment we grew up in, all of which gave us our identity and sense of belonging. The culture established what we should think, how we should behave, and what rules we should obey. Considering this Palestinian culture was located in occupied territory controlled by Israel, these rules we learned would be the bars of my first prison.

My father was a Muslim imam, just as his father was: a man of great devotion and dedication who set an inspiring example for us children. The fact that my father was a respected religious leader, a popular politician, and a founder of Hamas created for me, his oldest son, both expectations from society and possibilities in society. If I was beaten twice as hard in school by the teacher, and then by my father following up at home, for my shortcomings, it was due to the expectations laid on me because I was my important father's son. If Israeli intelligence mobilized great resources to protect me, it was because I was my important father's son. My father, whom I loved and respected during my childhood, was the major shaper of my early life.

This was not a culture that valued individualism as the West does. A person's worth was determined by their place in the social hierarchy and what other people said about them. The family was the most important social unit, and the rights and duties of each member were well defined. The dysfunctional system held together because enough people believed in and followed its tenets. Of all the factors that shaped us growing up in Ramallah—the endemic violence, sexual repression, extreme politics, even Hollywood's influence—the most significant determinant in our lives was religion.

Religion for us was a particular denomination of Islam espoused by my imam father. From the moment we were born, our goal was to please Allah, to be a dutiful servant of Allah. The faith set the standards for a correct life and the boundaries within which we had to live. These were ethical boundaries, sexual and gender boundaries, social boundaries, even political boundaries, as Hamas is grounded in Islam. Our brand of Islam was not the most joyful of practices, as the list of what was forbidden seemed much longer than what was permitted: no alcohol, no drugs, no music, no dancing, no singing. And there were only two religious holidays to "celebrate"—understood more as earnest devotion rather than permission to go wild for a day. Still, growing up with so much forbidden fruit meant there was much I had to explore on my journey through life's orchards.

The reward for good spiritual grades, so to speak, was to go to Paradise. The punishment for failing grades meant burning in the fires of Hell. No chance to make up your grades here; these consequences were eternal. Sadly, it meant that all the humans on the planet who didn't follow Allah and maybe had never even heard of him were relegated to Hell. I must say that this was something that did worry me quite early on as a child. It didn't seem fair. I took comfort in the fact that Islam sought to convert others and thus save them from a fiery fate. Hell is one heck of a concept in that it has had a lasting shelf life in some of the world's major religions.

Some early experiences as a child made me fully trust only what I perceived directly. I was at a funeral in the cemetery next door to our home when the imam gave a fiery speech as the corpse was laid in the ground. He said that after we all left, two angels would come for the man's soul and interrogate him. *Who is your god?* If he didn't know the name of his god, they would torture him horribly and evil monsters would set upon him as he screamed in the worst pain. As a ten-year-old, I was so scared, but so were the fifty-year-olds, so effective was this man of God at instilling fear of his god in us all. All this would happen inside the grave when we left, which was a strong incentive to get out of there. Back home I couldn't help it, but I wanted to go back to hear the torture, even though it was so scary. I asked all my friends to come with me that night, but none of them would. So I gathered my courage and headed for the cemetery. I grew more fearful with each step as I approached the fresh grave, listening for the cries of anguish and pain. But no voices came; it was quiet and very peaceful. I went down on my knees, putting my ear on the ground to hear something from the torture interrogation. Only silence. After that, the cemetery became my playground, as we didn't have playgrounds, and I was no longer scared. This was where I came face-to-face with the reality and truth of death.

Prayer (*salat*) is one of the five pillars of the Muslim faith. Of the five required daily prayers, the first prayer, the dawn prayer (*Fajr*), takes place in the last hour before sunrise. My father would roust us out of our warm beds, then have us wash to ritually purify our bodies. Of course, devoted Muslims like my father and me (from the age of five) would make it to the mosque because praying in a group, as everybody knows, pleases Allah more.

We would walk or drive to the mosque, depending on where my father's job would take him, whether to a refugee camp, a nearby village, or one of the many city mosques. His job as an imam was to lead the prayer, so we had to be there on time. If I was lazy, he would go without me, and my mother would wake me up after he'd left. Ashamed for my laziness and disobedience, I would walk to the nearest mosque to participate in the prayer; sometimes he would be there, other times he'd be somewhere else. When my father was in jail, I tried to keep the morning routine. Going alone took considerable fortitude to get out of a warm bed on a cold morning, to dare to walk alone down an unlit street past the overpopulated graveyard inhabited by jinns (evil spirits and monsters) and real-life predators. The first few times were terrifying.

Hamas leaders and members used to meet before or after the early morning prayers. Everyone would think they were gathering for prayer, yet the fact that so few people were around gave them the chance to conduct political business. As few Muslims made it to the mosque between 4:00 and 6:00 a.m. besides the regulars, it would immediately be known if a stranger sent by Israel suddenly showed up. Attending morning prayers was an adventure for me as a kid. Not many kids showed up. I felt important hanging out with older folks, some real badass Hamas operatives. When I proposed to my friend Samir that we go to pray in the mosque, his response was, "Do you get chocolate there if you go?"

KAROWAN THE BEGGAR

It was a rare person in Ramallah who dared defy these religious and cultural norms, as it was not just the rebel who would pay the price of ostracism. It would be better for Israelis to demolish the family house of a rebel than for a family to have its reputation demolished by its own society. The fear of going beyond the prescribed boundaries maintained the social order. You did not see beggars in Ramallah, despite charitable giving being an important tenet of the Prophet's teaching. Anyone "begging" brought shame on themself, and, by extension, their family members were considered the lowest of the low.

There was one individual who was the exception to this rule. In his ragged clothes, Karowan occupied his spot on the street in the center of Ramallah early every morning until dusk. There was no law to stop him. I felt sorry for him, and whenever I passed him, I'd leave something. Most of his donations were from out-of-towners who felt relief that at least they were not among the lowest of the low. We didn't know if he was deaf and/or blind; he never said a word. Every once in a while, he would emit this otherworldly screech that would stop everyone in the streets. It was never clear what prompted it nor what it meant.

Only later did I learn that Karowan was neither deaf nor blind nor demented. He was an entrepreneur. Finding a niche market, he spent the day "at the office," but he went home at night to a nice area of town and had dinner with the family. It turns out Karowan had joined the 1 percent, becoming a rich man by sitting stoically in the street rather than sitting at an office desk. He built and owned a four-story apartment building. Maybe we could call this a form of enlightenment in that he didn't care at all what people thought of him.

MONEY AND ETHICS

I don't want to give the impression that I was a front-runner for the best-behaved boy of the year award. No, I was a troublemaker. Religions, of course, propagate specific beliefs and sets of rules generally designed to curb human nature and are thus hard to follow, which generates guilt and shame. Religion in that sense held no appeal for me; there was no rule I didn't break. In fact, I did not play by their rules; instead, I *played* the rules.

I worked hard at the mosque, taking care of the three-hundred-square-meter carpet, shouting through the speakers the call to morning prayer (the Azan), and even leading the prayer sometimes. Others were paid to do this, but not me.

After every Friday prayer, people donated cash to the mosque; now and then the imam gave me the task of collecting it. Worshippers donated thousands of shekels; even US dollars were placed on a rug that bore the picture of Mecca. The money was a donation to the house of God. The imam and the mosque-keepers were paid from this money, and the rest was supposed to go to maintain the mosque and renovate and expand it to meet the growing number of mosque-goers. But this was also a venue for Hamas.

The imam there was a Hamas member. In fact, it was rare to find an imam who wasn't affiliated with Hamas. The donors didn't care what the imam or the mosque committee would do with the cash; they just wanted to be seen by others to be giving after Friday prayer. The money was collected in a solid safe, and I had no clue who had the key. At home, my mother barely managed to feed the family, since my father was in prison most of the time.

I thought I deserved a little cash, considering all the hard work I was doing. I needed to buy some new clothes, some new shoes, and possibly the new PlayStation. When the imam gave me the task of collecting donations, I slipped a few hundred shekels into my pocket, giving myself a "gift." And I got away with it, under the eyes of the all-seeing God. Who dares to steal from God? I did.

I even stole from my own mother. She had a women's gathering every Tuesday, a social and religious event. She gave them a little message; they ate sweets; and at the end, they donated.

My mother kept the cash on the upper level in her closet. Even though we didn't have much, she never touched that cash, and the sum grew every Tuesday. I didn't know what my mother wanted to do with the money exactly. Give it to the Hamas women's division? Maybe to Hamas operatives? What was she waiting for?

The money had been sitting in her closet for months. Shekels, dollars, and dinars. We needed money badly. Our asshole Palestinian landlord would wake us up at five o'clock in the morning and demand, in his ugly and angry voice, that we pay the rent, and then he cursed my father, Palestine, and Allah. Well, I thought it was quite okay to take a little bit of that cash. I was aware Mom's stash was donation money, and that by taking it I would be betraying many people's trust and my mother's trust! But I also thought, *A little cash won't hurt.*

Again, I got away with it. Still, there's no escape from karma. My mother would beat me up for any silly reason to release her frustration and anger for the circumstances of her life.

Sexual and gender repression ruled nearly every aspect of our lives. In this patriarchal society, women and men were to be separate;

you rarely saw men and women together. A man could not be alone with a woman in the same room, unless there was a strong reason or they were close relatives. Even in God's house, men and women were to be in separate rooms. Weddings were celebrated separately. And weddings were more often political rallies, with the men claiming, *How can we celebrate joyfully when we're oppressed under the occupation?*

My father's denomination considered itself open-minded, as it did not require women to wear burkas to cover their faces. It did require the hair to be covered, and clothing should in no way reveal the form of a woman's body, particularly the breasts. When my sisters reached puberty, I was not to see any of their flesh from the neck to the knees, aside from their hands. This also applied to my mother. The purpose of women covering themselves was to curtail the lust of men.

When I was eight, my mother and I visited a female friend of hers. She shook my mother's hand and then she smiled and shook my hand. This distressed my mother, who made it clear to me that a Muslim man did not shake a woman's hand. That kind of conditioning is very rigid and can't help but distort one's view of the opposite sex. One learns to look at women as though they're from another universe.

At the same time, teen testosterone flows regardless of race, religion, politics, or, as we say today, sexual preference. I'd have crushes on girls I'd see in the street, but we boys didn't have the skills or permission to interact. When in this repressive culture would we ever learn how to flirt, to gently charm a girl? A sex-ed class would have caused the mosque to shake on its foundations. My knowledge of the "facts of life" came from my equally ignorant peers and their "girlie magazines," which were hidden from parents with the same care a militant would hide a weapon from the Israel Defense Forces.

Fear ruled our behaviors regarding gender and sexual relations. Sex was shrouded in shame. If a girl was seen as outgoing, the gossip mill could label her a prostitute. You didn't see prostitutes anywhere in Ramallah, though I'm sure prostitution existed discreetly somewhere.

We did notice when the Palestinian Authority (PA) returned and brought their foreign "sex workers" with them.

These repressive and distorting values were enforced through shame and fear, the main tools of the politicians and the priests to maintain social control and power. By going against human sexual nature, they contributed to the violent side of human behavior. Based on my experience, this distorted behavior included rape, honor killing, and suicide bombing.

A RAPE CULTURE

When I was an eight-year-old child, one memorable day my family accompanied other families going to the olive groves for the olive harvest. It was a joyful occasion where we had a delicious picnic. As it became late afternoon, one of the families suggested their twenty-two-year-old son escort me home before it grew dark. *Fine.* The others had to stay to collect the picked olives so they wouldn't be stolen.

As we made our way down the path, my escort moved behind me. I felt a menace and started to run, but he caught me, forcibly assaulting me. I struggled and screamed, but to no avail. He anally raped me. Violently. I told no one, as I knew not only would I not be believed, but my accusation would bring shame on my whole family, and the predator would continue on with what by almost any standard was violent criminal behavior. I was a visible wreck, but no one picked up on it or asked me if I was all right. If they did sense it, perhaps they figured it was better not to open that Pandora's box. As I write this, it still haunts me, seared into my cells, and I struggle to purge myself of an event that has both trashed me physically and, I now realize, has probably determined, albeit unconsciously, certain life choices I have made. I'm still healing.

Rape, of course, is a major issue in every society, not just the one where I grew up. For a woman in my birth culture, being raped not only left her deeply traumatized but, if made public, could ruin her life. Also, under tribal traditions, it could set off a cycle of vendetta. This ties in with "honor killings"—in these cases, the murder of the woman by family members for having sex out of wedlock. I don't have direct experience with an honor killing where I knew someone personally, but they were common knowledge.

I did, however, have direct knowledge of a killing that reflected this mentality. My best friend Ibrahim's newly married cousin was shot at a concrete construction site on his way to work. Everyone rushed to the crime scene, and a few men from the mosque managed to take him to the hospital.

Wanting to leave a message, the killer had shot him in the testicles. I saw the fresh, dark blood painting a path where my friend's cousin had managed to crawl across the dusty floor. A handsome man, he'd just married a divorced woman, a beautiful, outgoing, elegant lady. She wasn't satisfied with her first marriage to a rich and powerful man. Women don't divorce men in that culture. The fact that she left him and married another man hurt her ex's ego. He didn't want to kill *her*, because then she wouldn't feel anything. Killing her love would torture her and make her suffer worse than her own death. This is how love issues were settled in our neighborhood.

The investigation of this murder was still open when I left the territories. A man is willing to kill another man for his reputation, his public image. A brother kills his sister for the sake of family honor. A father kills his daughter out of shame. Honor and shame are the constitution of that land.

Most of the Palestinians I knew believed—and still do—that anyone who leaves Islam should be executed. That is not very encouraging for advocates of religious freedom. According to the world I grew up in, *apostate* has become one more of my labels, this one qualifying me for assassination or execution.

I'd be remiss if I didn't mention that before the horror of my rape, I was introduced to sex. Yes, I was an innocent eight-year-old boy, but an eighteen-year-old girl exposed herself to me! When alone, she spread open her gown like drawing a theater curtain open on a holy stage, and she invited me to play on this stage, negotiating the uncharted topography like an awkward though intrepid junior explorer. Part of me realized this must be what I'd been taught was a sin, even worse maybe than a woman shaking my hand. But why was I enjoying this? She seemed to be having fun as well, perfectly happy to offer some coaching from her bemused, older status. There was no violence here. No pain. Yes, pleasure. Maybe this is why people sinned. It could be fun.

SUICIDE BOMBERS

The world I grew up in also revealed its dysfunction by creating a new kind of combatant. A suicide bomber in the contemporary Middle East is the very definition of a terrorist, deliberately seeking to kill as many innocents among "the other" as they can for a political purpose. This act disrupts our notion that every human being has the basic instinct to live. And yet throughout history, humans have been willing to sacrifice their lives for what they consider a greater good.

Recent historical cases are the Japanese kamikaze pilots who flew off to hit American warships and the Iranian child soldiers sent out to clear the barbed wire and mines for their Iranian tanks to cross the Iraqi minefields. As a protection, these Iranian youngsters were given cotton headbands with the inscription *Sar Allah*—that is, "Warriors of God." They were also given a small metal key that Iran's ruler, the ayatollah, said was their ticket to Paradise if they were martyred on their mission. Both cases are a mix of nationalist and religious fervor with volunteers reported to far outnumber the demand. Those heroes who give their lives to the holy causes of the emperor or the ayatollah are celebrated as martyrs.

But that story has some holes in it. It turns out that some of the Japanese pilots, despite "having attained a high level of spiritual training," had to be shoved forcibly into the cockpits. And the Iranian children were roped together to prevent desertion. Both of these examples were in wartime, with the Japanese and the Iranians facing defeat from a better-armed enemy. The suicide bombers in the Middle East see themselves in a war against a better-equipped enemy, thus resorting to "asymmetrical warfare." However, the Iranians and the Japanese were attacking enemy combatants. The suicide bombers attack innocent civilians to sow terror.

As a point man for screening Hamas suicide candidates, I was sometimes sent to prepare them for their missions. My real job was to stop them. Which I did. Why am I mentioning suicide bombers after discussing sexual repression in the world I grew up in? Because getting to know these volunteers, I could see a direct connection between a sick culture and a young person willing to blow themself up. In our Palestinian society, males have to provide a bride price to get married. What young man of twenty-one or twenty-two, brought up and living in poverty, could afford to pay a bride price in gold along with a house (which is what tradition dictated)? The bride's father has to sell off the young daughters to raise the money for the sons to marry. Most sons feel despair over ever being able to marry.

This is not a great deal for the daughters either. Bought as a commodity, the women have no rights. The purchase grants the right for the property owners (husbands) to beat their wives and commit marital rape. Some countries recognize the bride price and unmarried, frustrated young men as a national security issue. There is an incentive to join a terrorist organization to fund themselves and their brothers to be able to afford marriage. In fact, most societies that produce terrorists are bride-price societies. The Saudi government now provides financial assistance for marriage, recognizing that men being married is an effective strategy to stabilize the country and preserve national security. At the same time, Saudi Arabia's Wahhabi fundamentalist Islam encourages suicide bombing against infidels, when the bombing is exported outside Saudi Arabia. The September 11 attack on the United States, led by radical Islamists, was the most disastrous suicide bombing in history, after all.

My land of Palestine has been the crossroads of empires over millennia: Romans, Persians, Byzantines, Arabs, Ottomans, Britons. All have left their mark. America, as today's preeminent world power, is not only militarily the strongest, but culturally its movies, its music, its social media have spread everywhere, which I call "the Hollywood factor," showcasing the lifestyles of the rich and famous. That is seen as the ultimate way to live the good life. Yet these young men know that for them, it's impossible. Add to this that these men have access to internet pornography, which has a pernicious impact and a widespread audience in the Middle East, inflaming the dreaded lust for which they have no acceptable outlet outside the unreachable goal of marriage.

Adding to these issues, too, is that young men are encouraged to become martyrs through Islam's promise that seventy-two virgins await each man in Paradise. Virgins are idealized in the culture. To these sexually starved young men, virgins are like seventy-two brand new cars, not secondhand used cars. Paradise certainly beats the fetid stench of the refugee camp with ten to a small room. And those who don the suicide belt will be celebrated as heroes, bringing honor to their families and a "martyr payment," which might enable their brothers to marry and avoid the same suicidal fate.

The mix of sexual repression, religion, nationalism, economics with poverty and the bride price, and society's applause (postmortem) is a toxic brew that leads to senseless dead-end tragedies. Within the small part I played in halting this madness, I felt equally satisfied by saving untold innocents as well as the prospective suicide bombers who might spend years—alive—in an Israeli prison. They would survive that desperate period of their lives and hopefully, on reflection, reject a death wish for a life wish. I understood them because I also had to go through a suicidal stage fueled by hatred.

2

Torture and Prison

The innocence I came into the world with and the sense of security I enjoyed at my mother's breast was short-lived. I, along with my generation, grew up in a world of violence and bloodshed that indelibly shaped our lives. During the periods of intense conflict, we often wondered if we would survive the day. We saw so much death—people we knew. Our world was a minefield. We began each day standing at the edge of the minefield, and we had to get to the other side safely by the end of the day.

This was a war, a hot and cold war, between Israelis and Palestinians. But there was war at multiple levels, with potential danger and violence from every direction. It's hard to think of a day in my childhood that I didn't get beaten up by someone: father, teacher, IDF soldiers, settlers, classmates, Fatah rivals, Palestinian militias, Shin Bet torturers, street thugs. I've probably forgotten some of the denizens of our jungle, but the point is, if I got home that night without any bruises, it was a good day.

Those physical bruises heal in time. To this day I still work on clearing the psychic wounds from body and soul. Witnessing the horror of what our species, Homo sapiens, can wreak on each other has scarred my soul. As an adult, when I bring my childhood back to memory, it's as though I'm watching it from a height and it all looks like madness. It is ridiculous what people will believe. Call it the human condition; call it insanity; there's no escaping that violence is part of who we are.

As children witnessing all this bloodshed, we could blame those strange soldiers dressed in khaki uniforms, carrying M16s. They didn't speak our language, they looked different from us, and they were angry. We were throwing stones at them, and they were shooting at us. As a young boy, it made perfect sense that they were the oppressors, the aggressors. We were the good guys, and they were the bad guys who would storm into our homes in the middle of the night, take fathers and brothers away, and kill us.

It happened that in the First Intifada (the Palestinian uprising in 1989) when I was nine, all those who were killed in our city, as well as in the neighboring city and in refugee camps, were buried in the city cemetery next door to our home. I think no child in that First Intifada witnessed as much as I did. I participated in every funeral, was there for every mother's tears, and cried with them. I saw what was happening. But I also sensed that one could not blame it only on those IDF soldiers; they were obeying orders. And with people throwing stones at them, they could be trapped where it looked like they wouldn't get out alive unless they killed someone. Do you know how you would act in that situation? Even now, I don't know how I would act today if I had an M16 and a mob was throwing rocks at me. Even as a child I had questions.

TORTURE BY ALL, FOR ALL

On the far side of the Israeli violence spectrum was the practice of torture. This was the "scientific," "doctor-supervised" application of pain—physical and mental—to extract information and confession and to punish. While publicly denying the practice, Israelis made sure it was known in order to instill fear in the population who might be tempted to harm the state by word or deed. In my experience, Shin Bet were expert at the classic methods that left no physical marks. Simple techniques like sleep deprivation can be devastating. Some years later my father and I shared our experiences in the notorious Moscobiyeh Detention Center. Part of the goal of the torturer is to break the will of the prisoner, but my father, even after months, never broke.

On the Hamas side of the spectrum, they were paranoid about collaborators in their ranks. Hamas prisoners in Israeli prisons carried out horrific torture sessions against their fellows they suspected of collaborating with the Israelis. After many years, this practice was finally stopped when it became apparent that horrific torture was more effective in producing false confessions.

On the Fatah side, as a young child, I accompanied my father to a nearby refugee camp that Fatah controlled. I had heard the horrific stories of Fatah torturing those they suspected of collaboration. Accompanying him, often five times a day, allowed me to see what life was like in a refugee camp. Few of us city dwellers had the chance to see, hear, and smell the atrocious conditions our fellow Palestinians were living under. There had been no planning, no infrastructure. What began as tents turned into concrete hovels, often housing ten to a room on narrow, sewage-filled streets. I was able to develop relationships with some of the kids, and I even lived there for a time, which gave me a sense of their lifestyle, if we can even call it a life. When the monster Israeli Merkava tanks periodically invaded the camp, they were too wide for the narrow alleys and simply crushed the homes.

In a situation like this, it inevitably becomes a battle over who controls the streets. It was Fatah that controlled the camp through a person called the Black Panther. This character, a wanted man, had killed some dozen alleged collaborators. The story that was circulating in the West Bank, which really shook me, was when he strung one of his victims up on a tree and cut his throat. All the passersby could see the victim struggling and his blood gushing out. No one went to help him.

So along came my father, who used the mosque as his platform. Within two months, through his eloquence and his message, the once near-empty mosque was overflowing; people were praying in the street. Refugees loved my father and his message, but this did not sit well with the Black Panther. How could this Hamas religious propagandist from outside come and occupy his domain?

He warned my father not to come back, but it was my father's job. So in the blackness of early morning, we would go to the camp for the first prayer. As these were early days for Hamas, my father had no security and was unarmed. We never knew if there, in the darkness, the Black Panther would be waiting, sword in hand. As a child, this introduced me to the internal conflict between Fatah and Hamas. It would become much worse later. In this case the Black Panther never carried out his threat, and my father continued to serve that refugee community.

HAMAS VS. FATAH

As teenage students, this conflict between the two political organizations played out between the two rival student groups. We were organized and engaged in graffiti wars to "control the streets" with our slogans. We kept our painting equipment and tools hidden away in mosques and buried out of town. At midnight we would rapidly strike, erasing all the Fatah slogans and slapping up ours on the city walls. The next night, Fatah graffiti brigades would be out there effacing our graffiti and putting the "correct" messages up. Wash, rinse, and repeat. Somehow we all thought this was part of the resistance to the occupation!

Sometimes the two student groups would engage in pitched battles in the streets, real brawls that could get violent. Not just fisticuffs; we're talking knives, axes, stones, anything at hand to do damage and cause blood to flow. I don't remember anyone in my group getting killed, but I know in other towns there were fatalities. I suppose Ramallah was rather more "civilized."

This wasn't a game where the two teams shake hands at the end of the contest. In the "duty-to-get-even" culture, if someone, say, from Hamas was killed or injured or even humiliated, there was thought to be a bill to be paid by the Fatah perpetrator. This bill could remain outstanding for years. In these clashes we knew the families on the other side, we knew who did it, we knew where they lived, and we had the right to respond at any time. Just as they did. This was the culture, the Sharia-like thinking of "an eye for an eye."

The Israelis, who knew pretty much everything that was going on, regarded this no doubt with a certain bemusement. Though one night, when my paint brigade leader couldn't make it and I was in charge, an Israeli special forces unit was in the area acting on intelligence that a major operation was going down. They observed us coming in and out of the mosque and finally swooped in and arrested those of us who couldn't escape in time. That, at age fourteen, was my first arrest, my rite of passage. We were held without any rough stuff for four days. The rough stuff would come later, when I'd reached a more torturable age and I'd given up the paintbrush for a pistol.

The two major parties competing in elections on the West Bank were Hamas and Fatah. These political parties were not comparable to the Republicans and Democrats in the US or to Labour and Conservatives in the UK. First of all, both parties have armed wings. One metric that highlights the difference would be body count. Character assassination in US politics is standard operating procedure (SOP), but real assassination in Palestinian politics is SOP. In one system it's "Follow the money;" in the other it's "Show me the body count." While we in the partisan youth brigades were pretty violent, the adult version of party politics was in a different league altogether.

Islam itself was born in violence, despite the Prophet's desire to avoid violence. But Muhammad never designated an heir, which led to competing claims. Of the first four of Muhammad's companions to take the reins of power, three were assassinated. The main split claiming to be the rightful heirs became known as Shia and Sunni. Over the centuries tens of thousands died in the wars between these two. And the killing goes on to this day. This is hardly unique to Islam, as history records religions keen to go to war against another religion or eager to stamp out the heretics within the "true faith."

My childhood was not easy. I think that's fair to say. Call it fair, call it unfair, call it a falafel sandwich, I don't care. However, it was rich in experience. Mixed in with the traumatic memories, I have many beautiful memories. I felt like I came from a close and loving family, and I had good friends. Sadly, my journey toward truth and freedom was to mean I sacrificed those.

ARREST

Our beliefs, our behaviors, our choices in life are all shaped by our growing-up years, by our parents, by our peers, by the values of our society. Later when I would be addressing different groups around the world about my experiences, I would tell them that if they had been brought up like I was, they would be terrorists, though in their minds they would be "freedom fighters" carrying out the divine will of their particular god. And their society would celebrate them. So how did I, in the middle of this war, go from hatred and vengeance and the desire to take human life to love and reconciliation and the desire to save human life? This was not an overnight revelation but a decision that unfolded gradually.

In this context it should not be surprising that at age seventeen, my friend Ibrahim and I managed to buy a pistol on the underground market. Why a gun? To kill the enemy. Not only was the gun defective and wouldn't shoot, but we stupidly complained over the phone that we'd been cheated. We were quickly arrested by the Israelis. As it turned out, this was to be to my everlasting good fortune. Imagine if the gun would have been able to shoot and I went out and killed a few Israelis. That would have been the end of any meaningful life for me, not to mention those I killed.

The soldiers who arrested me beat me unconscious with great pleasure, and the subsequent weeks of torture were horrific. Quite naturally, this only fueled my hatred and my desire for vengeance. The torture was interspersed with interrogation. I did not belong to any organization or network; my father was in the political arm of Hamas, not the military wing, so other than telling the truth about the gun episode, I genuinely had nothing of value to offer Israeli intelligence. The interrogator would offer every prisoner the possibility of working with Shin Bet. Just the possibility of easing the excruciating pain of torture made that rather appealing.

Fueled by hatred and the burning desire for revenge, my adolescent mind hatched a plan. I would agree to work with them, and then I would seize the opportunity to grab a gun and kill as many of the motherfuckers as possible. *Wow, there's a plan all right.* So, after Shin Bet had wrung out of me all the useless information I honestly confessed to, the next step in this process was serving my sixteen-month prison sentence.

I was transferred to the Hamas wing of the maximum-security prison at Megiddo. This desert area has been the site of many battles throughout recorded history, from Egyptian times to the First World War. But it is most known today as being the site of the battle of Armageddon, which the book of Revelation in the Bible tells of: "the battle of that great day of God Almighty. . . . And he gathered

them together into a place called in the Hebrew tongue Armageddon"
(16:14, 16 KJV). For Christian evangelicals, the return of Jesus is an
imminent event of the final battle between good and evil. This delusional belief system now plays a practical and policy role in Mideast
politics. Busloads of religious tourists have Megiddo on their itin-
erary. Ironically, a Christian worship hall was discovered under the
prison and eventually, archaeology won out over and the old prison
was demolished.

When I arrived, I was approached by a "commissar" of Hamas
security. They ruthlessly controlled the Hamas contingent in the
prison. I was completely forthcoming with them and told them the
Israelis had made me an offer to work with them. I had a plan, which
I explained. I'd heard of double agents successfully doing it. After all,
wasn't this the goal of our movement? I was sacrificing my own life
with this suicidal plan. I asked for their help. Honesty was definitely
the best policy, as they knew every person arrested was offered the
chance to collaborate with Shin Bet. If they said they hadn't been
offered, then the assumption was they had said yes, and woe be unto
them. I was quickly told my plan was crazy: *We're proud of you and all,
kid, but settle down and serve your time being useful to the movement.*

I was given a job as a writer. Prisoners would write down their
interrogation experiences, which would be gathered, along with confessions of collaborators and secret material from security investigations, into an archive that gave a picture of Israeli methods and how
they played the intelligence game. The eventual goal was to put these
into a manual with limited circulation to those militants who risked
arrest. The challenge within the walls of the prison was how to dis-
seminate this information. It was, of course, all handwritten, and,
like a medieval monk before the invention of the printing press, I was
busy making copies.

We wrote on very thin paper in a minuscule script so one page
included ten normal pages. These would be tightly rolled up and

wrapped with many thin plastic layers so they could be swallowed and transferred to other prisons. The messages were in a numeric and letter code. The key to the code always would be sent with a different prisoner. In the high-security prisons, there were very few prisoner transfers. If there was an opportunity with a prisoner being trans- ferred to a high-security prison, he'd take as much as he could, swal- lowing as many as twenty capsules. The transfer from a prison like Megiddo in the Northern District to Ketziot Prison in the Southern District could take as long as two days.

Several secret reports written for the top echelons of Hamas also went through me. There was one, for example, of some hundred pages that briefed the reader on the evangelical Christian movement in the United States which supported the Zionist project to occupy historic Israel and thus trigger the return of the messiah and the end times. These reports were generally framed as conspiracies, and like all good conspiracies, there was truth in them. I would later have experience with that world in the Bible Belt.

Hamas security took my job away, as they decided they didn't trust me. They were convinced I was withholding information. They were scared to give me access to these secrets. They kept wanting to know about my network. Their view of intelligence work was that operatives had a network. I had no network. I had been completely honest. This was my tribe. I viewed the world through the lens of my father. I had asked for their help, and now I was a suspect in a world where you are guilty until proven innocent. I was still a teenager, an angry and reckless nineteen-year-old, who was freaking them out. Yes, my plan was crazy with the wrong motives. I was a naive kid, and this was a very dangerous game.

I got privileges for who I was because of my father's status, but I was seemingly a loose cannon for Hamas security. On the one hand, they did not want to provoke me, but on the other hand, they kept asking me what else there was that I wasn't telling them. I had told them everything, and to come from being the Hamas prince to a suspect was something I was not prepared for. I told them to go fuck themselves; I had nothing left to say. After that, they did not insist, but that broke the relational bonds between us. They didn't trust me, and I certainly did not trust them.

I began to see the other face of the movement. My illusions were now confronting the reality. A fire had sparked in my total faith and trust in my father's project, which would eventually leave it in ashes. Those "confessions" of collaborators that I was writing down were extracted under torture. On their face, they were absurd, confessing to sexual relations with goats and sheep and every woman in the village.

The brutality of Hamas security was beyond description. Needles shoved under the fingernails and burning plastic pressed on the skin were a couple of their methods. The prisoners confessed to anything just to get the torture to stop. They produced random names of others, which was their "network." Hundreds of lives were being destroyed with this method: the accused prisoners themselves, some of whom were murdered in the prison; those they named as co-collaborators; and all their families living with the terrible shame. And now I felt I was at their mercy. Were they going to torture me to get me to finally tell them what they were sure I was keeping from them?

I had been through Israeli torture and now I was living with the nightmare that Hamas security would torture me. Again, probably the status of my father kept them from submitting me to their violent interrogation, but that hope didn't allay my fears. From the standpoint of the war, Hamas was doing the work of Shin Bet, trimming down their cadres and creating an atmosphere of mutual suspicion and betrayal. Shin Bet knew all of this was going on in their prisons. *So much the better*, they thought.

3

The Bible behind Bars

After those sixteen months, I got out of the hell of that prison, thankfully in one piece. I was naive enough to think that the story of me being a suspected collaborator would stay in prison. But people love to talk. Everything I'd been fighting for, including my reputation, was now in jeopardy. Having the reputation of being a collaborator weighed the same in the public forum as being an actual collaborator. A Hamas security guy came to my home for a follow-up. He was someone I did not like or trust. He didn't like me, and now he was in charge of my secret file.

My sainted father had enemies inside Hamas who were keen to bring him down, and his oldest son being a collaborator could do just that. Once that rumor spread, it would quickly grow from a handful of people to hundreds and then would become "common knowledge." It looked like the only way to clear my name would be to become a suicide bomber.

Then, as one more point of irony in this crazy situation, the Israelis offered me a way to save my ass. Eventually, they would offer to build me up as a number one terrorist threat. My sworn enemies would offer me a way to save my life, while my people, my tribe, were offering me a rope tied to a pickup truck, which would also drag my father into disgrace. But this rescue would only come later.

After two months the Israelis got in touch with me, suggesting a meeting. I didn't think I'd go, but then I thought it better to meet and tell them I wasn't interested; I wanted to concentrate on my studies. My Hamas handler came to instruct me on how to behave in the meeting. One of the ironies was that these "handlers" often got trapped themselves. They were behind the curve, and the Israelis knew what they were teaching and simply worked around it.

In the meeting at the Ofer military base, I asked the Shin Bet agent, Jabir, why they didn't do anything to stop the torture and killing of those who had worked for them. Here they were trying to enlist me, and they had done nothing to intervene to help the others, even though they controlled the prison.

Jabir said he'd been in the agency for eighteen years, and in all that time, out of all their assets, only one actual collaborator had been exposed. I knew Hamas was full of shit. If what Jabir said was true, that meant all of those accused and murdered were actually innocent! Hamas security—angry, vengeful men—were engaged in a sadistic and fratricidal purge of innocents. And the Israelis at least were sounding rational. They weren't pushing me to suddenly become James Bond; in fact, they told me to continue with my studies. In time I would hear from them again.

Who was I to believe? What were my options? I was living in an insane world, a world of fear and hatred, a world of killing and death. Still, there was something deep inside me, perhaps an illusion, but one not yet poisoned by disillusion, and that was, as pretentious and naive as it might sound, the desire to save the world from its madness, to stop the killing. If we value human life, if human life is sacred, then saving human life, vowing not to take a human life, is an unassailable choice. I couldn't articulate this clearly at the time, especially not with Jesus' words, "Love your enemies." Still, at some level, I knew I could be uniquely placed to make a difference, to save lives.

So here I was, recently out of prison with the label of *suspected Israeli collaborator*, the result of my being honest with Hamas and honest with Shin Bet. I was caught in the middle between these two forces. Hamas didn't trust me, and I didn't trust them. Shin Bet didn't trust me, and I certainly didn't trust them. Yet it was Shin Bet, with their smarts and their resources, that managed to convert my public label of *Israeli collaborator* to *big-time Hamas terrorist*.

It's not hard to imagine the tension I was living under. One slip of the tongue in the wrong world and it could mean my premature demise. I had no friend to confide in, no pillow talk in my celibate world (the Israelis were adamant about this: no women, no honey trap), no therapist, no referee in the Great Intelligence Game. I was very lonely. This was a recipe for depression, but like a tightrope walker, all my attention went to keeping my balance so as not to fatally fall.

A CHANCE ENCOUNTER

An incidental encounter in 1999 would completely change the trajectory of my life. Since I felt like I did not belong to either of the worlds I lived and worked in, I decided to try hanging with people who were not part of either the Muslim or Israeli worlds. I decided to attend a Christian Bible study.

This was before the Second Intifada, when it was still possible to travel from Ramallah to Jerusalem. We met mostly in private homes, not in a church. The attitude of these missionaries was, "We're here to help," and their job was to invite people to Bible studies and bring them to the Lord.

I enjoyed it, finding the discussions stimulating, not just about the Bible, but getting to know something about American culture, like football and basketball and learning some spoken English. English was my worst subject in school, taught with a very dry grammar by a teacher whose pedagogy was child abuse—beating us—which was not a great way to learn. It was much better to hang out with native English speakers who preached love.

The start of my life journey could not have been more bleak, more monochromatic. We, in effect, lived in a prison, a prison of body and mind. We could not travel abroad to see the wider colorful world, and our minds were in thrall to rigid belief systems. However, as human beings, we had the curse and blessing of our imaginations, stimulated by our natural desires and influences from outside the home. As I came of age, I could imagine the forbidden fruits of sex, drugs, and rock and roll, aided by clandestine copies of *Playboy* and the infiltration of Hollywood. But what I never, ever could have imagined was that in a few short years, I, who had never stepped into a church, would be addressing thousands upon thousands in the megachurches of America's Bible Belt with the believers clamoring around me to sign their Bibles! A rock star of the evangelical movement? Come on, get real.

Thus began my journey with Isa, known today as Jesus Christ, for whom I was to feel a strong affinity. This was to be a turning point in my life and the beginning of a long, public misunderstanding about my relationship with the man Jesus and the religion of Christianity. But this gets us way ahead of our story. There had to be many miracles on the road ahead to allow me to survive the countless life-or-death situations to come.

Ramallah, as it turns out, is known as a Christian town founded by Christians many centuries ago. Though today Christians are the minority to the Muslim majority, this reflects the mass exodus of Christians from the Middle East. In 1948, 30 percent of the population of Palestine was Christian; today it is 1 percent in the territories and 2 percent in Israel.[1] With both Jews and Muslims involved in ethnic cleansing, it would turn out that three was a crowd in this land holy to the three Abrahamic religions. Many Christians fear there will soon be no Christians living in the Holy Land where their religion was born.

Growing up, I was familiar with the presence of Christians, particularly the clerics in their black robes, tall hats, and distinct plumage to signal rank and distinguish themselves from each other, whether Greek Orthodox, Lutheran, Roman Catholic, Maronite, Armenian, or countless more. They seemed overly ostentatious, especially compared to my father, the embodiment of the modest Muslim who dressed like everyone else and who was a role model for me. I was familiar with the Christian celebrations of Easter and Christmas, with their symbols of the cross and the manger. Our celebrations, like Ramadan, were not about joy but deprivation to please Allah. Those who worshipped this Jesus were aliens to me, part of an alien world I thought I could never bridge.

Later I did come to realize the essence of their customs and traditions. Just like other religions, dress code, code of conduct, and language define who is religious and who isn't. It's a lot about appearance, little about the essence, but the followers buy into it and have no choice but to respect it. In Muslim societies a man with a long beard and a long white dress and proper prayer beads to keep count of the chanted prayers is given status by these things. Even Israeli special forces use religious customs in pulling off a badass operation. And when a criminal decides to drop their criminal life, the quickest way to gain social recognition is to become religious. Better a hypocrite than a criminal.

My learned father often served as a teacher. All schools in the territories were required to teach Islamic studies, though not Christian studies. My father taught at a Christian school, so I managed to get a glimpse of it. It was like going into a whole different dimension, a foreign country. In the Christian school boys and girls were in the same room! And they had subjects like music and art. These Western schools were limited to the wealthy, foreigners, and Christians. For me, it was always an adventure, something completely different.

My entry into the Bible study would lead me to become close friends with a young, handsome couple from Southern California, Tawfik and Yvonne. Tawfik's father was one of those many Palestinian Christians who had left, emigrating to America. Tawfik spoke some Arabic, so it made sense that their church, the International Church of Christ, would send them as missionaries to the benighted Middle East. It was through Yvonne that I got a job with the United States Agency for International Development (USAID) village water and sanitation program—water forever being a key issue in this water-deprived part of the world.

This wonderful opportunity seemed to make everyone happy, most of all me. Even my generally anti-American father was pleased, as he was grateful the program was working to give his constituents safe drinking water and sanitation. Shin Bet was pleased, as it meant my new ID card would allow me to travel more freely, and my salary would account for my spending money. Those working there became my friends. USAID wasn't supposed to employ anyone who was politically active, but the head guy liked me and kept me on.

Because of the intifada, the US policy was that their people could only go to the West Bank for the day and return to Israel at night. The IDF would warn the Americans to stay away when they had planned an operation, which would turn the West Bank into a war zone. But Shin Bet's operations were secret and did not get broadcast ahead of time. I was able to warn my American manager to stay away—"Don't ask me any questions; just stay away." They did, and he was grateful, as the next day all hell would break loose in Ramallah.

My close friendship with Yvonne and Tawfik continued, and my family warmly welcomed them. Yvonne sometimes stayed at our home, and my father went out of his way to help her, even driving her

• where she needed to go, not the proper protocol for an imam. This was again how informal person-to-person "diplomacy" can work without all the garbage. Yvonne didn't think my kindly father was a "terrorist"; he didn't think she was part of the Central Intelligence Agency (CIA) conspiracy to promote Israel's takeover of all of Palestine.

After September 11, 2001, which came to be known as 9/11, and the Second Intifada, terrorism became the focus 24/7. With the daily violence, foreigners were being pulled out of the West Bank. Yvonne and Tawfik were to return to the sunny beaches of California. We promised to stay in touch, and I said I would visit. This was more a fantasy than a realistic plan, since reality for me was heading to prison.

The irony was, I was going to prison because I had saved human lives, including, in one incident, four not-so-innocent lives who knew my identity as the person who "ratted" on them before they could carry out a suicide bombing. Shin Bet said, "The only way we can protect you is to sentence you once again to prison as a major terrorist." This was all part of the crazy logic of the Great Game, but it did mean saving my life as well as my father's.

BACK IN PRISON

So, if I wanted to stay alive, which I definitely did, the only real option was to go back to prison for supporting terrorism. Irony of all ironies. Included in the package deal was my high-profile father, as keeping him incarcerated was the one semi-assurance that overzealous Israeli authorities, anxious to emblazon their résumés, wouldn't send him to his Paradise. (It is interesting that out of the three Abrahamic religions, only Jews—at least many whom I have interacted with—do not believe in the afterlife, whether above or below, but emphasize life here and now.) I say "semi-assurance," as there were always incidents when Israelis' desire to brandish a scalp was greater than honoring the deal. A notorious case was that of a Palestine Liberation Organization (PLO) leader who returned from exile and honored his side of the bargain by not engaging in terrorist activities. He established himself publicly in an office. From a distant helicopter, the Israelis shot an American missile of awesome accuracy that went through his office window, took his head off, and left his unsuspecting body still seated in his chair. This headless photo made the front pages.

This time around, my loyal companion was a Bible, and my opportunity was months of reading time. Throughout history, reading and writing have been one of the rare benefits of prison time for the so inclined. My treasured Bible had one side in Arabic, the other in English, so there was the added bonus of improving my English. Fortunately, the Prophet considered the Bible part of the canon, though he departed theologically when the notion of Jesus being the son of God was espoused. Muhammad always insisted that Jesus was a human being, not a deity. I hoped this semi–stamp of approval quelled any suspicions my fellow prisoners had. I was also devouring any other books I could get my hands on, and I had the blessing of an English dictionary.

There were no Christians in this prison, mostly Islamic extremists like Hamas and Palestinian Islamic Jihad and PLO factions. They were the kind that, if they found out what was going through my questioning and seeking mind, including how this Jesus was influencing me, that would be enough for them to kill me. Now with this chance to immerse myself in the pages of the Bible, I felt I was having a direct encounter with this Jewish man; there was no distance between me and Jesus, no two thousand years. A friend. I felt a total affinity with him, a kinship given our life situations even across the centuries. He lived his own truth, awakening his inner intelligence, living by the cosmic laws, not man's laws.

First, he had this powerful message of "Love your enemy," which spoke directly to my situation, to my struggle to put that message into practice with my Israeli enemies. His message of love was like a breath of fresh air in my known world of dogmatic Islamic hatred. And the belief that human life was sacred confirmed my commitment to do all I could to stop the killing and not to have blood on my own hands. That conviction and my insistence that potential suicide bombers be spared meant I was now spending twenty-seven months in jail.

My experience of Christianity as a system of beliefs up to this point had been through my new friends. Now isolated in prison for months with no denominational middle man, I was fascinated by the human journey of this great master. My focus was on the events and milestones in the journey of Yeshua, or Jesus Christ. The number of words in the Bible attributed to Jesus adds up to only a few pages. Here was a young man well-versed in the Jewish law who went against the flow of society and confronted the religious authorities with intelligence and courage, and at times with spirited anger. I was so fed up with the Islamic religious authorities for their hypocrisy, arrogance, and a righteousness designed to protect their power and position that I felt totally in sync with Jesus' attack on the hypocrisy of the Pharisees and the teachers of the law. They bent the scriptures to serve their selfish desires. They desecrated the temple and the mosque. Jesus was not one to go along to get along, to opt for the agreeable to remain in his comfort zone. He comforted the afflicted and afflicted the comfortable. His friends were the rejects of society: the tax collector, the prostitute, the fisherman; not the wealthy, the socially prominent, the 1 percent of the day. He knew perfectly well that by taking this confrontational position he would pay with his life; the "Hosannas" of the crowd would become the "Crucify him" of the mob.

This Bible-reading experience in prison would be a turning point for me. I became ever more aware of the difference between this avatar Jesus Christ who walked our earth and what was to become the religion of Christianity incorporating his name. This gap for me would only widen, particularly in the United States, the more I had contact with the Pharisees and teachers of the Christian law. Having strongly rejected Islamic religious dogma, I was not about to embrace Christian dogma.

I never signed up for a particular denomination nor described myself as a Christian. I said at times I was a follower of Jesus, though he felt more like a companion or a friend. At the time, perhaps, I followed the guidelines of a master, but I was not limited to his guidelines. I had my own individuality. I could not copy Christ. But this is the reality of everyone on a journey with masters and teachers, as we have to find a way to transcend them.

The Christians' narrative for me was that I was a Muslim terrorist who saw the light, accepted Jesus Christ, and became a Christian. In other words, I was a bad guy, and now I was a good guy. Praise the Lord. In my early days seeking asylum in the US, I did enjoy the support of a Christian community and am grateful to those who helped, though that did not last when I challenged them. I certainly acknowledge the social utility of religion, the good works of many in the name of religion, but for me on my journey toward higher consciousness, I came to see the whole theological scaffolding of these religions based on delusion, products of the human mind.

I recently came across a quote from Kierkegaard, who himself was a believer:

> [Christ] did not want to form a party, an interest group, a mass movement, but wanted to be what he was, the truth, which is related to the single individual. Therefore everyone who will genuinely serve the truth is by that very fact a martyr. To win a crowd is not art; for that only untruth is needed, nonsense, and a little knowledge of human passions. But no witness to the truth dares to get involved with the crowd.[2]

4

Playing the Great Intelligence Game

onths of being in prison meant I was on hiatus from my role as a valuable Shin Bet asset. Did I miss it? Yes, to a degree. The excitement, the tension, the risk of death around every corner did have an addictive quality. But now with my adrenalin at normal levels, I had time to reflect.

I knew I was lucky to still be alive. This was a testament to my caution but also to the extraordinary lengths Shin Bet went to protect me. The resources they devoted to this effort had to be a dent even in their sizeable budget. Clearly, their cost-benefit analysis considered my efforts worth it. On the positive column of my balance sheet, I had directly saved human lives. And that was personally very satisfying. I was acting on my beliefs.

Being the son of Hassan Yousef, I was perfectly placed. I knew the culture like no Israeli could. I knew hundreds, if not thousands, of people in the community, many of whom were to play a part in this war. From Shin Bet's standpoint, having me as an asset was a great coup. From my standpoint, it gave me the opportunity to save lives. I had my own moral compass, which shaped my consciousness and enabled me to play and live these different roles. I understood that right and wrong are beliefs; how the world works is cause and effect. Again, if your belief system holds that human life is sacred, this collaboration was the opportunity of a lifetime to act on that belief in a world riven with hatred, fear, and killing.

On the negative side of my balance sheet, taking the untraveled road would mean losing family, friends, home. As it turned out, I was gifted for the Great Intelligence Game. The results speak for themselves.

My first book, *Son of Hamas*, gives a solid account of many of the anti-terrorist operations I was involved in over a ten-year period. Before I became committed to this endeavor, I had a Hollywood James Bond view of the intelligence world. There was derring-do, for sure, but not the glamour. Like police work anywhere, it was more shoe leather and tedious detective work, though in today's world technology plays a major role. While I am not a fan of Shin Bet, one can only admire the resources, the intelligence, and the Machiavellian dedication—and, yes, the track record—they bring to the Great Game. As this was one of the worlds I immersed myself in, let me review this world in a way I did not recount in *Son of Hamas*.

Intelligence agencies operate in the netherworld hidden from society. They serve the state and the politicians in power. They have their interests, yet like any organization, they have to produce results. The Israeli-Palestinian conflict is not a two-state conflict like the Cold War with Communist Russia and Capitalist America, where in the best of times captured spies were exchanged and in the worst of times were simply eliminated. Showing some linguistic delicacy by avoiding the words *killed* or *murdered*, the CIA went with *terminated with extreme prejudice* and the KGB with *wet works*. With the end of the Cold War, the rival old warriors of the CIA and the KGB could meet in an upscale restaurant and with vodka and whiskey talk about the "good old days." This was a *symmetrical conflict*, to use today's phrase, while the intractable Israeli-Palestinian conflict is asymmetrical warfare between one state actor, Israel, and a stateless population with rival fratricidal political and military groups. In this shadow intelligence war, it's all about information.

What to do when the information is locked within the brain of your prisoner? How far will you go and what means will you use to unlock that information? It depends on the urgency and how tough the prisoner is in resisting your effort to get him to talk. Those who have never been in Israeli prisons cannot fully understand this world. The basic rule hammered home by Palestinian movements and terrorist organizations is *Trust no one*; do not give information to anyone, as they could be a potential collaborator or informant. For the terrorist organizations, the challenge is to keep abreast of Israeli methods to get prisoners to talk and to warn their cadres, while for Shin Bet, the challenge is to constantly come up with new methods, new tricks unknown to their adversaries.

If the prisoner is naive and not very intelligent, Shin Bet can play the normal small game: checkers, not chess. They put in the prisoner's cell a collaborator posing as a prisoner. He sports an abundant beard, constantly prays and praises Allah. For a secular prisoner, this might be effective in getting on his nerves, but the point is to inspire the prisoner's confidence in his new devout cellmate. Even if our prisoner resists for a couple of weeks, finally the need to share with a fellow human being, a believer, can loosen the tongue. For those posing as prisoners, it has to be one of the most peculiar and specialized job descriptions, though, if they really are religious, they can have both the paycheck and get their five prayers a day logged in.

Then there's the reverse psychology ploy, effective with those who have the fatal flaw of being brought up to be polite. The recalcitrant prisoner has been alone in a cell for a long time, has lost track of the days, but still is not talking. A new prisoner is put in with him. Our prisoner greets him, but the newbie doesn't answer. As the hours go on, it's clear the newbie is very suspicious of our prisoner, if not hostile. After some twelve hours, he gets why the newbie is withdrawn and uncomfortable. He wants to make him feel comfortable.

"Don't worry, brother; I'm not a collaborator. We're on the same side here."

"Look, no offense, but I was told to trust no one."

"I was told the same thing. I understand, don't worry; I'm not going to ask you any questions. Relax. I trust you. Maybe at least you can give me some news from outside. Before I was arrested, I was working on an operation and I hope it happened, as I haven't said anything to these bastards."

"I don't know; there have been some bombings in Ramallah. Where was yours?" And so on.

A method one notch up from this, for a more resistant prisoner, is to isolate him in solitary confinement. No matter who they are, after one month, two months, or three months in which they haven't spoken their language or had any human interaction, when suddenly they're put with a "comrade" from their culture, there's a good chance they'll open up and start talking. This is how they sometimes extract information that they cannot extract from traditional torture, though the United Nations (UN) recently has classified solitary confinement as torture.

There is, of course, the timeless method of extracting information through torture, which is the deliberate infliction of physical and/or mental pain. There is now a universal catalog of "scientific" torture methods used by intelligence services, and regardless of whether their lawyers decide, like the Americans, that waterboarding, sleep deprivation, electroshock, being locked in a stress position, being drugged, or being exposed to extreme temperatures do not fall under the "legal" definition of torture, it is torture. That's speaking from my own experience, though I did not have the worst of it compared to my father. Handcuffed, he was hung from the ceiling and given electric shock until he passed out; when he revived, he was then kicked again and again. For months my father did not break, did not talk.

What do you do if you're Shin Bet and you have a prisoner who won't break after six months of unrelenting torture, and an Israeli judge, acting under Israeli law requiring charges to be brought after six months of detention, won't give you more time? This law is an attempt to maintain some semblance of "the rule of law" in a democracy, but there are ways around it. It is, after all, a very dirty war.

My father would enter the front door of our home, released from detention, only to have the IDF waiting at the back door to talk to him for "only five minutes"—and he would disappear for months. And there was the notorious case of Saleh al-Arouri, who was held almost eighteen years without being charged. I knew him, and he was the last Hamas person I spoke to before leaving. He was finally released, as this indefinite detention without a charge undermined Israeli's claim to be a democracy. Their suspicions of him turned out to be true, as he had been a founder of Hamas's military wing. In 2018 the US State Department announced a $5 million reward for him.

THE BREAKING OF HAMZA

Let's take the case of one of the toughest prisoners, whom we'll call Hamza al-Turi. For six months Shin Bet interrogators tried every known method to get the information, and he didn't say a word. He's a rock, just the kind of operative a terrorist organization can trust with its secrets. Shin Bet is under pressure, convinced their mute prisoner is someone directly responsible for suicide bombings, and without his information more people could die. With the approval of high-level generals, they drive the blindfolded Hamza for some hours to a secret air force base. Upon arrival, four or five guards dressed as civilians beat him and release dogs on him. He has no idea where he is. He can't tell the Red Cross where it was, and if the Red Cross goes to a likely prison, the prison authorities will say, "We cannot take responsibility because the prisoner wasn't here."

Finally, they tell Hamza that he's too dangerous, that they can't keep him here, that they can't release him back on the battlefield, and so they're exiling him to Lebanon. While Israel rarely sends someone to Lebanon, they know Hamza is connected to the Hamas military wing and has Jewish blood on his hands. Hamza figures that he's better off in exile than he is being tortured here.

Hamza appears in the military court, and they've given him a defense attorney. The sitting judge approves the exile request. Within three hours, Hamza is sitting handcuffed in a van headed north. His spirits lift from the horrors he's been put through as he gazes out the window at his first sight of nature after six months of cell walls. He feels a growing sense of pride that he beat the motherfuckers; he held fast, an example of the Islamic warrior who was right never to give up, never lose faith. They arrive at the Lebanese border gate, where a sign announces, "You are now entering Lebanon."

During this period of civil war and turmoil in Lebanon, the southern part of the country formed a security belt, ostensibly controlled by the mainly Christian militia, the South Lebanon Army (SLA). The SLA received funding, weapons, and logistics from Israel. This security belt was for Israel's security. The threat was from the Iranian-supported Hezbollah ("the Party of Allah"), which was waging a guerrilla campaign in the security belt.

Hamza is shoved out of the van, and the border gate is opened for him. His guards remove his handcuffs, give him some food and water, and point him in the direction of a narrow path that snakes toward the foreboding mountains. Signs with skulls and crossbones warn that the area is heavily mined. He's never been out of the territories, and here he is in a war zone peppered with lethal mines. And it's freezing cold. He hesitates, as though afraid to plant his foot on the ground. They shove him, and he stumbles ahead. The last words he hears as he walks into the unknown are, "Don't ever even try to come back."

One kilometer, two, and no sign of a village or any humans. The months of torture, bad food, and confinement have left him weak, and he's dangerously tiring. Was this their way of killing him, setting him loose in the wilderness? Suddenly, a half dozen armed men jump out of the bushes, pointing an impressive array of AK-47s at him.

A frightened Hamza raises his hands and cries out, "Don't kill me! I'm Hamas! Exiled!"

Whoever they are, their response is to grab him, blindfold him, and bind his wrists. They lead him heaven knows where, urging him on with kicks and blows. When they remove his blindfold, he finds himself in a camp, an active camp with fighters, some scanning the skies for planes, others tending to equipment, including ground-to-air missiles. A Hezbollah flag flies over the camp, which Hamza recognizes.

A heavyset, fierce-looking man dressed in combat camo confronts him. He speaks with the heavy accent of South Lebanon. "You're a spy here to collect information on the resistance."

"No, no, brothers, I'm Hamas."

"You're busted and we're going to kill you."

"I swear by the Prophet, honor be his name, I'm Hamas."

"What are you doing here then?"

"I told you, the Israelis, our enemies, our enemies, drove me to the border and told me to walk. I'm exiled."

"In the last twenty years, they haven't sent anyone to exile."

Others have now gathered around, pointing their guns at the unnerved prisoner. Hamza holds his breath. If he's going to survive this, he has to prove himself, validate himself to another militant organization, though they share the same god and the same enemy. He understands their hostility; it is logical not to believe this stranger.

"My name is—"

"Don't fuck with us. You could say you're Abdullah Barghouti. You show up pretending to be Hamas. You better convince us with some real information we can check. If you don't, we shoot you and leave you for the dogs."

With that, everything, all the information he's kept behind the wall of his iron will against the worst of tortures, pours out of him. With his life on the line, this man who said nothing vomits forth his story.

His Hezbollah listeners become more and more fascinated as he recounts operations, names of those still in the battle, names of comrades who died, the imam who recruited him into the struggle. He's on a roll, finally free to tell someone and claim his honor once again. As he gains confidence, it comes across more and more as boasting, justified after all he suffered. Most are caught up in his story: how he killed Israelis, the celebrated martyrs he worked with, how he never said a word to his torturers. Most appear convinced. But the skeptics keep up the questions, demanding more. More names. With more information, he might make a mistake and his lies will be uncovered. Finally, such a torrent of detailed information has to be the truth, as no actor could pull it off with that depth of sincerity. The skeptics are convinced. No room for acting out here in the wilds.

"We believe you."

Hamza nearly melts into the ground with relief.

In a few minutes, a Southern Lebanon van appears and he's helped into the back. Next stop, Beirut. Thoroughly wiped out but relieved, he closes his eyes, soothed by the van swaying over the dirt road and the music coming from the van's speakers.

The van heads south, not north, and brakes at the border gate. Hamza jolts awake, opens his eyes, and sees the gate as the van heads back into Israel. Dazed, he tries to make sense of it. The music fades out and a voice comes over the speakers. A familiar voice. A frightened voice. His voice.

Momentarily confused, he realizes it's his recorded voice telling everything, every secret, every name to his "Hezbollah brothers." He can't control the hot, acrid tears that stream down his cold cheeks. An earsplitting scream empties out his soul. His identity and his honor were tied to his not breaking, not talking, not betraying the tribe. Now, his self-identity is that of unforgivable shame.

This shows the lengths the Israelis are willing to go to get information and what extensive resources they're willing to commit. Shin Bet always has to stay ahead of their enemies, keeping them ignorant of their latest stratagems. This was one they hadn't used before, so none of their prisoners would have been briefed. The creative Shin Bet brain trust, along with their staff of psychologists, is constantly at work to come up with fresh ruses to gather information.

On the Palestinian side, the effort was to keep up with all the Israeli methods and tricks they use so militants, when arrested, knew what to expect and how to resist. For example, once the exile ruse made the rounds of the prisons, there was considerable risk using it again, especially committing such a hefty budget.

Again, this is an asymmetrical situation: there are thousands of Palestinians held in Israeli prisons, while no Palestinian prisons hold Israelis. In the rare event of the capture of an Israeli soldier, the interest of the captors is not to extract information but rather use the captive as a bargaining chip in an exchange to release Palestinian prisoners.

When Yasir Arafat returned to Ramallah in 1996, the Palestinian Authority took responsibility for security and arrested hundreds of Hamas militants and leaders, putting them in PA prisons. My father was among them. So Hamas was getting it from two sides.

THE ONE WHO GOT CAUGHT

As I noted earlier, Jabir from Shin Bet said that in his eighteen years with the agency, only one collaborator had been exposed. Who then was this actual collaborator who'd been caught? Jabir said his name was Khadr Tannus, a Christian working with Fatah. I had never heard of him or this story. I went back home determined to find out if this was true.

I quickly found out that Tanus was a leader in Fatah, born into a wealthy Palestinian Christian family. He held the position of File of the Wanted, which meant he was responsible for those the Israelis were searching for, the most wanted. He put them in safe houses, providing them with weapons and money. Weapons on the West Bank are extremely expensive. For example, an assault rifle like the M16 cost around $10,000 or required capturing or killing an Israeli soldier—an unlikely event.

What distinguished Tanus from his fellow Muslim leaders in secular Fatah was not that he had been born a Christian, but rather that for twenty years he'd been working with Shin Bet. The Israelis provided him with the weapons and the money. The weapons worked, but they had GPS built into them, and this was before people knew what GPS was. How to explain where this money came from? "Follow the money" can be an effective means to uncover a traitor. Khadr was able to say it was family money he was contributing to the cause.

For close to twenty years, Shin Bet knew everything about Fatah's system, where the safe houses were, who was in them, what operations were being planned, what their individual weaknesses were. Knowing this, why didn't they just sweep in, arrest, or kill them all? That would be the response of an army, but intelligence is a different game; intelligence is playing the long game. The lifeblood of intelligence is information—accurate information. If they swept in and took that group of leaders out, they would lose their source. A new group would inevitably rise, and Shin Bet would have no source. You can barbecue the golden chicken and feast on the meat for a day, but no more golden eggs, no more reliable information from a trusted plucked chicken.

Another challenge was that your man in a key position has to deliver the goods for the enemy organization Fatah. If he doesn't, that could be suspicious in itself, and he could be demoted and kept out of the leadership loop. Rather than arrest the wanted men, Shin Bet kept an eagle eye on them. Shin Bet or the army would go on a "search mission" for the wanted men. They would search the mother's house, family homes. They knew all the time where the targets were and even would search houses very near the safe house. This created a great sense of relief when the danger passed, and the safe houses organized by Khadr added to his standing with the leadership.

The Shin Bet goal was to weaken the Palestinian organizations while maintaining an attrition rate that would be "normal" for Fatah or Hamas, accustomed to arrests and killings. And to protect their source, they always had to have a figure who could be blamed, not the source. They would often take out the number two, who would be from the military wing. Taking out the number one, generally a politician like my father, risked creating a split producing two terrorist cells to deal with. But if the military wing was neutralized, that meant the politician lost power and could mean he was more open to negotiating.

Once upon a time in this story, someone in the leadership got suspicious and told his colleagues that he had a bad feeling about Khadr. The others dismissed it. They said, "This guy knows everything about us, our safe houses, our weapons, our military wing's operations. If he's a traitor, we wouldn't be sitting here; we'd be six feet underground for eternity; the Israelis would have killed us and destroyed our organization a long time ago. A feeling's not proof, comrade. Think about the operations that succeeded; it can't be him."

Undeterred from his gut feeling, the accuser came up with an idea that posed no risk or cost to them, so they reluctantly agreed it was worth a try. Paranoia, after all, was a required job skill. The plan? *Give Khadr false information, not about Fatah, but about Hamas, so they won't be as careful and might make a mistake.*

The most wanted terror suspect in the territories was Yahya Ayyash, known as The Engineer. In 1992, while studying electrical engineering at Birzeit University, he joined Hamas's military wing, the Izz ad-Din al-Qassam Brigades. He was the first to develop explosives for Hamas and was the originator of the first suicide attacks. Israel held him responsible for the death of hundreds of their citizens. Everyone wondered how he could escape capture for so long. Israel wouldn't hesitate to move if they knew this terrorist's location, even if it meant sacrificing all the sources they had—that's how bad they wanted this guy.

The Fatah cell called a small meeting, including Khadr. A variety of subjects were discussed. One member casually reported gossip from his neighborhood. The Hamas hero bombmaker Ayyash was staying there; the local Hamas operatives were helping him as he trained potential suicide bombers. But he was only going to be there for a couple of days. The five people in the meeting knew that if the Israelis acted on that, it was 100 percent certain Khadr Tannus, their comrade, was the rat. Khadr couldn't wait to get out of the meeting; this offhand comment was a golden egg—a jumbo golden egg.

The excited Khadr went to his handler and said that he knew where the most wanted of all the most wanted was hiding but that he would only be there for a short time. Immediately, a decision was made at a top-level meeting in Israel to send a special forces unit to arrest or kill this mass murderer. The starving mouse was so mesmerized by the sight and smell of the cheese, it didn't see what the cheese had been placed on. This is a case where if you give such a powerful temptation to an intelligence service, they will abandon their entire protocol: the source, the motive, the context. If it was a Hamas informant's source, they might be more careful to protect their source, but this was a casual conversation originating from another organization. Khadr was just lucky to be there. When this all went down, Hamas would try to find out who in their organization was the rat. This could be one of those deals with two knocked out of combat for the price of one.

Within thirty minutes, Israeli forces landed. With such a show of force, so quickly, no escape was possible this time. Some generals showed up to share the glory of this historic arrest. Generals on the scene require forces to protect them, so with the added numbers, it was a highly visible operation. The house was thoroughly searched, the concrete walls smashed, in case there was a place in a wall that hid a cowering Ayyash. Before the raid, Fatah knew there was no Ayyash there. Now, both Shin Bet and Fatah knew Khadr was an Israeli agent, and neither knew where Ayyash was. This was a major failure for Israeli intelligence.

I spoke with a Fatah friend who told me he was given a pistol and told to kill Khadr. He, in fact, had been one of the five who set up the sting. He confronted Khadr, his best friend for years, but couldn't pull the trigger. He couldn't get his mind to make the switch to see him as a traitor.

This botched operation by Israeli intelligence coincided with Arafat's return in 1994 under the Oslo Accords after long years of exile. The newly established Palestinian Authority immediately arrested Khadr. They were eager to interrogate him, as he knew a lot after twenty years of working with Israeli intelligence. Certainly not a process Khadr would be looking forward to.

Within hours Israeli Prime Minister Shimon Peres called Arafat, his fellow Nobel Peace Prize laureate. He said, "Whatever you want in return for this guy, I want him out before he's killed." I don't know what Arafat got in return, but Khadr was quickly driven out of Ramallah to Ben Gurion Airport. I heard he ended up in San Francisco. The Fatah cell, the five, were all rounded up and put away.

Khadr Tannus escaped with his life, but he paid a price only too familiar to me: his family was left behind—a traitor's family.

In January 1995, Yahya Ayyash escaped to the Gaza Strip after a deadly terror attack on Tel Aviv's Dizengoff Street. A year later, he had his last phone conversation when his bomb-laden cell phone exploded in his ear.

My handlers always referred to the Khadr incident to show that they had my back. They insisted Khadr was the only person ever discovered. "If anyone is discovered, we will get them out no matter what price we have to pay." Of course, this was not simply a humanitarian motive, but that guy would have a lot of information about how Shin Bet works.

5

My Chaste Romance and
Keeping Father Alive

When I was twenty-three, I met a gorgeous girl in the relatively free city of Jerusalem. And we began a secret relationship which went beyond any fantasy my stunted imagination could come up with. Miriam was tall and had light-brown hair and white skin; her stunning looks made all heads turn. She was a Muslim, spoke not only Arabic but also Hebrew and English, and worked for a nongovernmental organization (NGO) connected to USAID, where I was working at the time. She was an only child; her father was deceased and she lived with her mother. She didn't wear a headscarf, and I wasn't sure how she fit into my repressive society. Though she knew my father was a conservative imam, she saw me as someone completely different, not a typical Arab male. And I was not a hypocrite. My respect toward her was absolutely real. I had interacted with Americans at work and at the gym, as well as with some Christians, so my approach to her was not the typical one of an Arab man to an Arab woman.

Over the following months, we developed a weekend routine. We were both making good money. We both had USAID IDs, which enabled us to pass through checkpoints, and we both had cars. She had a convertible BMW, and I had my father's Audi, which Hamas had provided him with to enhance his prestige, even though he disapproved. Miriam and I drove our separate ways to Jericho, and there we stayed in a bungalow at a resort on the Dead Sea. This was an Israeli resort in an isolated area forbidden to Arabs, but this was during the time of the Second Intifada, and the resort business was suffering. The female owner figured we weren't terrorists, we'd paid, and what could be more normal than an attractive, clearly unmarried couple arriving in two separate luxury cars?

So here we were. She had no father who would normally blow the whistle on a wayward daughter, and my father was securely in prison. It was guaranteed no other Palestinians would be there. We were on the shores of the Dead Sea with perfect weather. Still, we were in hiding, bungalow bound, with no strolling on the beach holding hands nor moonlit dips in the sea. All the chaos, the bloodshed, the hatred, the war, we left outside the bungalow and created a magical zone of wonder and beauty. This was the first time in my life that I'd held in my arms the naked body of a woman. What an amazing blessing to be introduced to the loving warmth of a woman in this way.

And yet I was still a creature of my culture, fortunately. We cuddled, we kissed, we fondled, but there was never penetration. I respected her virginity, as I knew in our culture what that loss could mean. It would dash her hopes of marrying if it were known. Surgery to replace a hymen was an option, but I certainly didn't want any part of that. And Allah help us if she became pregnant. What could be more selfish on my part than that? And marriage? No. I cared for her and did not want to hurt My Jericho Girl.

We were crazy, since the price of discovery could be a death sentence. The stakes in our culture were that high. Breaking that taboo by any form of sexual relationship outside of marriage could be cause for bloodshed. This is why parents freaked out and drove those lessons home to their children: not only would the family's reputation be ruined, but the man or woman—or both—could be killed.

I must admit that part of the thrill of it all was the fact we were breaking the rules. This was the forbidden fruit, which made it all the sweeter. Those days are still among my most powerful memories of this cherished human experience, even though—and maybe because—the relationship was never consummated.

But as they say, all good things must come to an end. Were we discovered? There were no fathers, families, or busybodies to find out. But there was Shin Bet. As a Muslim, I was born to make Allah happy; as I spy, I was nurtured to make Shin Bet happy. They were not happy at all.

They read me the riot act. I was to end this relationship immediately. They said they hadn't made all this effort and spent all this money to create a credible cover, only to have me to throw it all away for a few hot weekends, especially since I'd put Miriam at risk as well. I was told I must behave the way a model Hamas member should. They did not like it that I was going to a Western gym, hanging out with foreigners, perhaps with CIA agents pumping iron next to me. They also did not like my contact with Christians or that I was not going to the mosque. The last thing they wanted was for Hamas to start doubting me.

They were not the only ones upset. My father returned from prison only to learn that his son was driving to work and going to the infidel gym. He took the keys and the car away.

What was I going to tell Miriam? As usual, I tried to stay as close to the truth as I could. I was putting her at risk. It was selfish of me and dangerous for both of us. We knew the rules of our society. I respected her as a woman in that society. Maybe she was thinking that I was the man she'd like to spend the rest of her life with, but that was mission impossible. Still, I couldn't fully answer her question of why. I had this beautiful, marvelous woman weeping in front of me. Sadly but safely, we parted, both still virgins. Wiser? Perhaps.

And Shin Bet was happy. Very happy.

I did learn more of Miriam's story, though. Her father, it turns out, was murdered as a collaborator with the Israelis. Shin Bet told me he had nothing to do with Israeli intelligence. There was no way I could share this with her, and the subject of her father never came up. So this only child and her mother were deprived of a father and husband and blacklisted as collaborators. Go figure.

KEEPING MY FATHER ALIVE

My priority now was to keep my father alive. Not an easy task, as his priority was to maintain his public image, his status, which was to get us both nearly killed. It's difficult to exaggerate how easily he could have been killed. My father had no sense of the danger he was in. His two best friends were Jamal Saleem and Jamal Mansour. They had gone into exile with him in Lebanon, and they spoke every day to each other on the phone. The three were at the same leadership level in the political wing of Hamas. As members of the respected older generation, they set themselves up in offices, received journalists, and led public lives as spokesmen for the organization. One morning, as my father's two friends were giving an interview, guided missiles came through the window, killing them, their bodyguards, and two journalists.

I told my father, "If they're targeting people at this level who are from the political wing, not the military wing, you've got to hide." He believed he was well protected with a security detail brandishing AK-47s and the Palestinian Authority security agencies giving him a heads-up if there was a threat. But that wasn't exactly effective against a missile coming through your window.

From my point of view, the safest place for him had always been prison, but as I wasn't about to propose that, I urged a safe house. However, we were in the labyrinthine game of intelligence where nothing is what it seems. First of all, I was betraying my father in order to save him—treason and heroism in the same sentence. Given my importance to Shin Bet, I assumed they had every interest in keeping my father and me alive. That's the one card I held that gave me some confidence in his survival.

When I asked Shin Bet if they were intending to kill my father, they, of course, said no, but they said he could be killed by someone from Hamas or another organization. They explained that my father, a wanted man, was not taking precautions, walking around carefree. He was the object of celebrity spotting, like a movie star; people would go back and tell everyone, "I saw Hassan Yousef today." People began to wonder why he hadn't been killed, since he was in the same role as the others whom the Israelis assassinated. The rumor mill went into gear: "He must be working for the Israelis." So Shin Bet was trying to protect their major enemy from himself!

My father loved to give interviews, especially to Al Jazeera, which reached the whole Arabic-speaking world. He felt obligated to represent the cause, and being on the airwaves enhanced his status. As a wanted man, he did not give interviews in the same place—ever. Shin Bet had said that to maintain his "wanted" bona fides, he had to keep changing cars. At the time of the intifada, Al Jazeera sought him out because he was emotional on TV, which appealed to their audience.

I managed to put him in a safe house, with only Shin Bet and I knowing the location. The IDF was after him and, as usual, were led to look in all the wrong places. To always have a different car, I'd use rentals or go to friends who were not affiliated with Hamas to ask to borrow their cars. Even my Christian friends loaned me their cars, knowing I was the son of "The Most Wanted Celebrated Media Terrorist"; they were quite intrigued by it all.

I'd pick up my father at the safe house, put him in the back of the car, and cover him with a blanket. I'd even change my appearance at times—for example, slapping on a mustache. I told him that this was a fucking serious game and when I told him to lie down, he had to lie down. I didn't care if he was suffocating in the back of some smelly car. He would complain, "Where's my Audi?" I had to remind him how many times an Israeli helicopter had targeted a specific car.

Shin Bet also engineered a ploy to enhance his standing. The IDF laid siege to Yasir Arafat's compound, Mukataa, the Fatah head-quarters, blaming him for a series of devastating suicide bombings. Through the Americans, a deal was proposed by the Israelis to lift the siege, if five leaders were turned over to be jailed. My father was on the list, thus giving him another cover with the Palestinian Author-ity. This orchestration was again by his worst enemy protecting him from himself. Eventually, the siege was lifted and six Palestinian lead-ers who were holed up in Mukataa—not including my father—were turned over to be jailed in Jericho.

As always, this was three-dimensional chess. There were other players on the board. Shin Bet was not the ultimate authority in the Israeli system; the ministers, the prime minister, the politicians were. As an example, let's say the defense minister sees this grubby Arab character all over the media challenging the authorities and the army. "What the hell," he says. "Put a missile on his head; what are you waiting for? Get rid of him. This is a political issue; I'm being criticized."

So Shin Bet then has to explain to the defense minister why they're not killing him. They will have to reveal their sources, in effect reveal-ing me. It's against agency protocols, but they have to do it. It's not that the defense minister doesn't know secrets and can't keep secrets, but he's still a politician and might make a slip. A journalist might ask him about Hassan Yousef. Can he keep a poker face? Does he know how to hide the truth? It's a potential mess. Even the prime minister at the time, Ariel Sharon, would get reports across his desk that stated I was behind the information, though I was also coded "GP," for "The Green Prince" (*green* because of the Hamas flag and *prince* because of my father's status as a top leader in Hamas).

It was important for the agency that my father was outside and gave us access to the movement, preserving all those leads. However, every time he appeared in the media, it broadcast a failure of Israeli intelligence to catch him. Some Israeli newspapers could make an issue of why this terrorist demagogue wasn't being shut up. The media is one player on the board, and they affect public opinion, which affects the politicians. Good for democracy and all that, except when it comes to the intelligence world, whose currency is secrecy and misinformation. We're in the world of shadows—ain't no sunshine.

Ah, my father. How can I criticize him, even when I profoundly disagreed with him? I saw the entire reality from a completely different angle. He became a popular leader entirely through his own efforts, sustained by his implacable Islamic faith, ready to die for Allah. He came from a small family in a small village. He did not attain political power through international connections, money, or belonging to a powerful family. He was a founder of an organization that was to dominate the indigenous population of Palestine. He was to survive the high attrition rate for Palestinian leaders and countless years in Israeli prisons. He was not just my father. He befriended me. He trusted me when other Hamas leaders would not. This trust was his way to express his love, as he was always busy. He wanted to get me involved, help me to know everything about him, and share his life with me. We were very close.

It was very hard for me. But I was protecting him, like it or not. Betraying him and saving him simultaneously. Crazy.

At some point I asked Gonen Ben Itzhak, my Israeli handler for a time, why the agency didn't kill my father, or, alternatively, why they killed those other two who, like my father, were in the Hamas political wing. He said the difference between my father and those guys was in the last few months, they had gotten heavily involved in the military wing. With the Second Intifada, things got mixed up, and those two were involved not just in mentoring terrorists but in ordering attacks.

THE HUNT FOR IBRAHIM HAMED

My handler, Gonen, who I knew then only as Loai, disappeared from my life without explanation, and I was assigned a new handler, whom I knew as Tamir. Gonen, with whom I would remain friends even after I left my service to Shin Bet, not only respected me but encouraged my independence, as I had ferreted out terrorist cells when Shin Bet had failed and discounted my insistent evidence. He treated me as a fellow human being engaged as a partner in the same righteous cause. I did not find out until much later the sad story of why Gonen was no longer my handler. Tamir was a devout Orthodox Jew, and right from the get-go, it did not go well between us. He looked upon me as the hired help, and it was hard not to sense his anti-Arab racism. He disapproved of the independence I enjoyed working with Gonen. The help should be put in their place, he thought; the high-flying hawk should have its wings clipped. With this new sheriff in town, everything was more at risk.

At this time, the number one hunted terrorist in the territories was Ibrahim Hamed. Eloquent, arrogant, and elusive, he took pride in blowing up buses and pleasure in the scores of Israeli dead, no matter the dead Palestinians who were collateral damage. Hamed was also skilled at neutralizing his rivals in Hamas. It can be argued that in times of peace, those who devoted their talent and education to the death cult of nationalism could be constructive leaders in society. The success of Palestinians in the diaspora is proof of this. However, this son of a bitch would be a criminal mob boss in utopia. When Israeli forces closed in on his collaborators, hoping he was there, those collaborators were following his order to go down fighting to the last bullet. But his body was not amid the scattered body parts from the shoot-out and tank assault. It had been my task to attempt to identify the bodies as I knew them. He had fled.

I was bending my brain to find any clue that would lead us to where Hamed was holed up. Shin Bet knew where his wife lived, and the house was bugged. But that led to nothing; only once when the youngest child asked where his father was, the mother replied, "We don't talk about that." Actually, Shin Bet's Jerusalem district had an informant living in that house, a piece of information they did not share with the Ramallah district, which was looking in all the wrong places. Credit for an important arrest was important to each district fiefdom. For the district chief, the credit, deserved or not, could lead to promotion and perks on the climb up the ladder. Even though they were in the same organization, Shin Bet members made mistakes, violated protocols, and covered up evidence of wrongdoing in the black hole of "classified." Or, as in the situation with Gonen, those responsible for mistakes found a scapegoat.

Who was the real leadership of Hamas on the West Bank? It was not known who was directing the terrorist operations, channeling funds and weapons, coordinating Hamas activities. The Israelis kept on arresting and breaking up cells, sending suspects to prison and assassinating leaders, but this didn't slow down Hamas terrorist activities. Who deep in the shadows was in charge? I thought my father might be one of the leaders who would know, but he had no idea who the leaders of the military wing were. He could deliver a coded message to a drop box with a request, say, for emergency funds, but still had no idea who he was reaching out to. We knew that there was an important Hamas headquarters in Syria, but that was beyond the reach of Shin Bet.

We also knew that coded messages were going to this hub via the internet. Shin Bet determined they were going to Damascus from an internet café in Ramallah, and they told me to check it out. I went and found some twenty men intently hunched over computers. Clean-shaven, no one stood out, except somehow my instinct drew me to one man, and I have no idea why. Whoever it was communicating with Damascus had to be trusted by the leadership and was also dangerous and super aware if he was being followed or watched. Later, I was showing a property for sale at an open house and was just closing up at the end of the day when a man called wanting to see the property. The man who appeared was the man from the internet cafe. *Coincidence?* He said his name was Aziz Kayed and he ran a center for Islamic studies in Al-Buraq. Well-spoken, he came across as a professional, and I dismissed him as the possible liaison with Damascus and thus didn't share this encounter with Shin Bet.

Later, when I accompanied my father to Nablus, where he gave one of his fiery speeches, we met with the local council, the Shurah. One of its seven members suggested that my father meet with a man named Aziz Kayed. *Hello. These are just too many coincidences. Could this man be the real leader, or at least the key to lead us to Ibrahim Hamed?*

Back in Ramallah, I excitedly contacted Tamir and asked them to do a computer search for "Aziz Kayed." A number of "Ramallah Aziz Kayeds" came up, but none of them were close to the man I'd met. I persisted in my hunch and told a reluctant Tamir to run a search on the whole West Bank. *Bingo.* My Aziz Kayed showed up: he was born in Nablus; he had been a member of the Islamic student movement ten years before but had given up all activities; he was married with children; his friends were secular, open-minded. Nothing suspicious.

In a meeting I explained all these coincidences. Though Shin Bet trusted my instincts, there simply was not enough to go on.

As we were talking, a bell went off in my memory bank; his résumé was very much like three others I knew who were passionately active in the student movement, had advanced university degrees, and then dropped out of sight: Salah Hussein from Ramallah, Adip Zeyadeh from Jerusalem, and Nejeh Madi from Salfit. Shin Bet then followed them. It turned out they all knew each other—and Aziz Kayed. And they all worked together at Al-Buraq! *This was way too coincidental. Could these be the real guys running Hamas?* It turned out, yes, the more they were monitored, it was discovered they had total control over the money that came from outside, which was used to buy arms, produce explosives, recruit, support fugitives, everything, all under the cover of an innocent research institute. Even my father had no idea of their existence.

One day, as we were following Nejeh Madi, he walked to a commercial garage, lifted a unit door, and disappeared inside. *Why would he be going there?* We kept a close eye on it. Two weeks later the door opened from inside and, stepping into the sunlight, was none other than terrorist mastermind himself, Ibrahim Hamed. Waiting until he returned to his hideout, special forces surrounded the building, preparing for a shoot-out, a fight to a martyr's death, as he had ordered his companions to do. Ordered first to strip and come out, there was no answer. Given ten minutes and then the building would be blown up, he emerged and stood naked before the soldiers.

Of all the anti-terrorist operations I was involved in, this was the most significant, as it led to the capture of Ibrahim Hamed and it uncovered the real leaders of Hamas on the West Bank who directed and financed the carnage. I had the advantage that no Israeli working for Shin Bet for a limited period of time could have, as I had known the players and the terrain over my lifetime. Hamed was sentenced to fifty-four life terms in prison as the court heard the murderous results of attack after attack. He certainly was responsible for many more deaths than that. He offered no word in his defense, only that he did not recognize the authority of the court.

Tamir took full credit for the operation, which greatly enhanced his career. He called me only to say he'd been ordered to call two people, one of whom was me. It was a strange call; there was no word of thanks or acknowledgement of my contribution.

6

An Ominous Phone Call

It was early morning, and I was with my mother, who had taken the freshly baked bread out of the oven and was preparing breakfast. My phone beeped.

My mother said hopefully, "Maybe it's your father." I knew it wasn't. He was in maximum security with other Hamas leaders, and part of the punishment was to have no family visits. Yet where there's a will, there's a way. We could exchange brief words on cell phones. Even in maximum security prisons, cell phones are smuggled in by approved visitors or by prisoners transferred from minimum security prisons. The transfer is no small feat, as the cell phone is secreted up their anus. For sure not an iPhone. The transfer can take as long as two days, bouncing around over bad roads on a steel bench locked in a stifling van in which prisoners have vomited hundreds of times. In the prison, each prisoner will have a turn for a quick call until the battery runs out.

"Hello."

"*Assalamu alaikum.*" An Arab voice. *Peace be unto you.* "Is this Mustafa Hamid?"

"You have the wrong number." I clicked off. Code meaning, *I'm unable to talk.*

My mother was visibly disappointed; I could only shrug. Excusing myself, I climbed to the second floor, which was my space under the roof, my "penthouse." The most striking décor of my simple room were the walls riddled with bullet holes and a hole in the floor from a missile that came through a balcony window, exploding a sofa and the concrete floor. My interior decorators were the IDF. For some reason, my family never wanted to repair the hole or the wall, perhaps keeping it as some kind of memento of our particular family history. At the time, I was allegedly a top terrorist the IDF was determined to kill. They'd surrounded the house with Merkava tanks and American choppers and ordered me to come out. I'd escaped a minute before when Shin Bet called urgently to warn me to get out. The IDF fired away. They were furious that they'd failed to kill me. Little did they know that this was all part of the Great Intelligence Game.

I returned the call and the Arabic voice answered.

"Assalamu alaikum."

"This is Abdul Karim." We constantly changed code names; this would put me through to a middle man who would check what number the call was coming from before he would put me through to my handler, Tamir. Ever since the invention of the telephone, which allowed the human voice to travel over great distances, an adversary has sought to listen in. A kind of technological arms race resulted to keep communications secure. Shin Bet was particularly concerned with the security of our line, as the Palestinian Authority had obtained the latest technology from the CIA.

It's not always about the latest technology, but simple human brain power. For example, in one case a Palestinian group would get cheap cell phones and use them to text in code only once or twice a month, for a matter of seconds; they'd receive a message and then turn them off and take out the batteries. A foolproof idea. Right? Wrong. Someone in Shin Bet whose job was to think like the terrorists got the idea to ask the phone company, "Are there any numbers out there, any phones that are used for a couple of moments a month and then turned off?" Well, yes, there were. Okay, what person gets a phone, uses it to text for a few seconds a month, gets a return message, and shuts it off for the rest of the month? Certainly not teenage behavior, nor normal innocent behavior. Okay, it could be someone cheating on their spouse. With that insight the group was caught— and for all I know, maybe some errant spouses. But the Shin Bet are not the Saudi moral police.

"Hello."

"Yes."

"We need to meet today. You'll be met at the North Gate."

"All right."

Normally, we arranged all the details of the next meeting when we finished the last one. Our next meetup had been scheduled for next week, but there were times either I or they felt it important to meet right away. Why they felt the need to meet then, I had no idea, but I felt a sense of unease. Even after ten years, the great lesson in the spy game remained *Trust no one*. I had to trust that in Shin Bet's cost-benefit calculation, I was worth more alive, continuing to prove a benefit to them in our common goal of stopping the terrorists.

I would have to get moving and skip the breakfast my mother was preparing, a combination of lamb's liver and testicles chopped and fried in olive oil with a whole range of mouthwatering spices.

The meetings always took place somewhere in Israel, though I never knew where it would be. After the Second Intifada, when moving around became problematic, the trip would take three to four hours, though Ramallah was only six miles north of Jerusalem. The fact that it takes that long is a testament to the precautions Shin Bet takes. I had to pass through four zones, each with their own specific risks where one slipup could cost me my life. The zone called Red in Ramallah is the most dangerous; then they proceed to Orange, Yellow, and finally safe Green, which was inside Israel where no Palestinian militias could move.

Israelis don't come into Ramallah unless they come in force. The closest Shin Bet would normally come would be to a suburb five miles outside the city. So that meant that in the Red Zone I was on my own with no backup from them. I headed downtown to catch a shuttle north. The risk I was running in Ramallah was that someone would recognize me and wonder, *How is it that Mosab Hassan, a wanted man, is walking around in the center of Ramallah?* Those who are wanted are underground. In the fear-ridden, paranoid atmosphere of Ramallah, suspicion is a reflex that only grows as one person tells another, and so on. I wore the most nondescript clothes to blend in.

At the taxi stand, I got into a yellow van, the shuttle north. So far I'd seen no one I recognized, though I wouldn't know if someone in the street had recognized me. I didn't know the three people already in the van. We headed north, the opposite direction from Jerusalem, which was the point: to be spotted heading south toward multiple checkpoints could sound a fatal alarm.

We were now in the Orange Zone, which was territory where Shin Bet could operate. I got out near the North Gate, crowded with students, and was directed over the phone toward a gray Toyota car, indistinguishable from the hundreds of others. I knew that within five minutes of the pickup point there were two IDF vehicles with Shin Bet agents in IDF uniforms ready to intervene if there was a problem. They were armed but wanted to avoid any incident.

I slipped into the passenger seat. The driver was a Bedouin working with Shin Bet. His Arabic was native. Even though the Shin Bet personnel I worked with spoke Arabic, they were Ashkenazi and had Israeli accents, which, if we were stopped by the wrong people, could mean real trouble. The driver was someone who had picked me up before but didn't know who I really was. He handed me a wig. Sometimes it was a mustache. We had a cover story of why we were together in case we were stopped by the Palestinian militia. We took a circular route that would start to take us more southward.

In this Orange Zone, the challenges were checkpoints. If we were going through a major checkpoint, where there were often long delays, Shin Bet would arrange it so some forty vehicles would be allowed straight through and our vehicle and our backup would be in the middle of those forty. The Border Police couldn't be trusted for this kind of operation, and one of them might recognize me from being on TV with my father. On the more remote, less traveled checkpoints, Shin Bet would take them over completely, and their people would wear Border Police uniforms and let us through while checking the other traffic. However, before getting to known checkpoints, there were the risks of arriving at a spontaneous checkpoint set up by the IDF or running into patrols or an accident blocking the road with Palestinian police. Only once, at a surprise IDF checkpoint, did our backup intervene when it looked like we were held too long.

This time we drove a longer distance in order to go through a remote checkpoint taken over completely by Shin Bet. As we got near, the driver gave a heads-up that we were approaching. It was an odd experience, as I recognized some of the faces of the "commute team" who specialized in these operations. We played our parts. I'm not sure how many have put two and two together and know my true identity rather than knowing me just as "The Green Prince."

Soon we were approaching a busy major checkpoint into the State of Israel. Another Shin Bet unit would be there and take over one or two lanes. They knew which car I was in. They let through, say, ten cars without a search, then we passed, and then ten cars more along with our backup were allowed through without a search so none of the Border Police would know which car was important. In a way, this circuitous journey became routine for me, but I was always aware of the risks; I didn't doze off out of boredom.

We passed through easily. Now we were in the Green Zone in Jerusalem. But in no way did this mean they would ease up on their rigorous security protocols. The Bedouin driver let me off in a designated street. I was told on the phone by my handler to walk in a certain direction. *Am I being followed? Any cars with Palestinian plates?* I hadn't been searched up to this point. *Do I have a gun? Am I wearing a suicide belt?* Agents were looking through special devices that could detect any of those. *And what about the beggar on the street, the woman at the newspaper stand?*

Here's how it worked. My handler was in touch with the driver, who gave him constant feedback about the situation at street level. My handler then gave me instructions based on the commute unit reports and other sources. For example, he would tell me, "Walk down King David Street." Sometimes I'd be walking a kilometer until he'd say, "Turn right on King Solomon Street and keep walking."

I had yet to see the van that was due to pick me up, but I knew it was close, probably following me in the traffic. I didn't look for it. There could be more instructions. Then, suddenly, the van was alongside me, the rear door automatically shooting open. I leaped in and the door slammed shut, all in a couple of seconds. I disappeared into the world of Israeli intelligence without a trace.

I was alone in a space with curtained windows so I couldn't see out, though there was a light inside. There was air conditioning, which was a relief after walking in the noonday sun of Jerusalem. The space was armored on the inside. They'd learned their lesson. Earlier, a Palestinian working for them had gotten in the back with two guards. He was wearing a suicide belt and blew himself and the two guards up. Now, anyone being transported like me rides alone in the back and can only blow himself up—not the driver or Israeli civilians in the busy streets of Jerusalem.

The drive could last as long as an hour. Soon I would lose all sense of direction. Finally, the van pulled into a basement garage that could be anywhere. I got out and they did a thorough body search along with metal detectors. They led me upstairs to a room. It looked like many of the others I'd been in, like an average living room. I couldn't see out the glazed-glass windows. The only ominous sign was the same kind of chair that was in every such room, a chair where the subject is placed for the polygraph, the lie detector test. Over the ten years I'd gone through that many times and always passed, I suppose because I always told the truth.

My previous handler, Gonen, the one person in Shin Bet who showed a sincere interest in me as a human being, didn't pursue this option. He trusted me. No one else in the organization trusted me, nor did I trust them.

Tamir greeted me. He didn't like me, and I didn't like him. I believed we at least had a common interest in tracking down terrorists, but that was it.

He told me that we were going to do a routine lie detector test. *Routine?* Normally, they gave me a heads-up beforehand and even gave me the questions that would be on the test. That took me by surprise, as a small man with thick-rimmed glasses walked in toting a black case. The polygraph expert. I hadn't seen him before in previous sessions. Tamir exited, leaving me alone with him.

I sat in the chair. We went through the familiar drill of wiring me up: an electrode on my right thumb, pinkie, heart, left lung, right lung, and one on the belly to gauge emotion. He was all business, reminding me that only yes and no answers were permissible.

I couldn't see his monitor with the pens tracing their wiggly lines across a scrolling roll of graph paper. The AC had the room cool; I wasn't sweating.

"Have you ever carried out a terrorist attack against the State of Israel?"

"No."

"Have you ever planned a terrorist attack against the State of Israel?"

"No."

"Have you ever been in contact with any other security agencies like the CIA?"

"No."

Three more questions; he repeated a few to see if there was a different reaction.

He quickly took the electrodes off, packed up without a word, and left me in the room alone. I wasn't worried. I didn't like being left waiting, but I supposed he had to consult with his manager as they analyzed the squiggles.

After half an hour he returned, wearing the same passive expression.

"Well?"

"You failed."

"What?"

"You failed on two questions."

"That's not possible. I've never failed a test before in ten years." I thought it had to be a mistake.

"The machine never lies."

No machine is perfect. "Which questions did you interpret that I failed on?"

"One was, Have you ever planned a terrorist attack on the State of Israel?"

"No, of course not. I have no plans."

"If you have something to tell us, it will be okay."

"No, I have not and am not plotting any attack," I said with strong conviction, but I realized now all they were left with was this infallible machine reading I was lying.

"You're not cooperating."

"I'm telling the truth, no matter what that machine says."

"I'll leave you to others."

He left the room and I was alone.

I got up from the cursed chair. I felt like the building had collapsed on me, pinning me under the rubble. I was in shock, shaking.
Alone. Left with my mind running wild. I grasped onto the hope
that they were only playing with me, that this was one more of their
games. I hadn't failed their "test." But that's like holding on to the
edge of the cliff by one finger, which gave way to the realization that
I was terrified.

*For ten years I've lived on the edge, with many brushes with deaths;
this is just one more.* I got a hold of myself. My number one priority
was, *How do I get out of this?*

I didn't know it at the time, but it seems so obvious now: that
room was covered with cameras, and every sound and move was being
observed and recorded from another room. Every TV cop show has
this scenario. So I was being observed now. Every move, every expression, was being scrutinized to determine how I responded to this news.
Any amateur observer would see that this person was really scared.

Two hours later, having left me to marinate in my fear, Tamir
and his manager, Rolli, with whom I had clashed before, came into
the room.

They confronted me, their expressions hard. For them, if I was
not a terrorist, I was always a potential threat to flip. After all, I was
the son of a Hamas leader, whom I loved and respected. When would
that conditioning flip me?

"We can't let you go tonight."

"What? How do I explain where I've been?" This would put me
at considerable risk.

But I knew how they thought. The lie detector, if they believed it,
said I was lying about a terrorist attack. If they let me go, I would tell
my fellow terrorists that we had to attack now, tonight. How would
they explain after the resulting carnage that they had let me go?

They led me down a level into a windowless room close to the garage. Bed, chair, bathroom.

A woman brought me dinner, followed by a man with a TV. The TV didn't work, and I had no appetite.

I lay on the bed, alone in the silence of the room with only my noisy mind to keep me company. *Who do I call for help? My father? My family? Friends? What authority can I appeal to? The United Nations?* The handful of people who knew the reality were all Shin Bet, and now they were treating me as a dangerous enemy. My previous handler, Gonen, the one Israeli who understood me and cared about me, was long gone.

How do I get out of this? I was in a tiny cell within a bigger cell within a larger prison. I'd survived many deaths in those ten years, but that was either when Shin Bet had had my back or I'd been unbelievably lucky. Strong images of those ten years flooded my mind. *What are my options? They're all shit; all the cards are in Shin Bet's hands. What are their options now that they believe I'm lying and their fears that I would flip have apparently come to pass?*

They could kill me. They had so many methods, especially if they wanted to make a public statement. An unforgettable image that was front-page media content was the headless body of Abu Ali Mustafa, sitting at his office desk. For that hit, the American-made death machine was more than five miles away in the "safe zone" at a high altitude, out of earshot. There were only two seconds of the weird sonic *whoosh* of the missile as it flew over the city, through the office window to its target. Asymmetric warfare; each one of those missiles cost $100,000, not to mention the chopper, all courtesy of the American taxpayer. I had been very close to the operation, and I knew Israel did not have any evidence of his involvement with terrorist attacks. But Rolli, who ordered it, got his promotion; the politicians were "doing something"; and Arafat was sent a message.

In my case, killing the right hand of Sheik Hassan Yousef would just be one more killing without any political gain, though it would leave my father without protection. For them, now that I was seen as a liar and thus a threat, disappearing me could have a certain appeal. All the secrets I knew would go to the grave with me. As a bonus, that left the way open to kill my father, for which there was considerable political pressure. Grim scenarios clamored in my mind.

Another option to get the "truth" was torture. They could send me back to the Slaughterhouse, the Moscobiyeh Detention Center in West Jerusalem. The mere memory of the torment made me tremble. My fear had not been Shin Bet turning on me but Hamas catching me. I had been prepared for that, prepared for their torture and prepared if it was the Palestinian Authority. But I hadn't been prepared for the Israelis torturing me or turning me over to the Palestinian mob. Just thinking of that brought up a horrific memory. One day, looking out my window, I saw down in the street a group of Hamas thugs beating a young man and then shooting him. Not yet dead, they tied his feet to the back of a pickup truck and dragged him through the streets of Ramallah, the fate of a "traitor." Ramallah was under curfew with Israeli tanks, but that didn't stop this demonstration. They hung his body up in the town center. I saw it the next morning. Shin Bet said he was innocent, having nothing to do with them. I always felt in some sense he died for me.

What about calling on God to save me? Not Allah, not Yahweh, but God, the Christian version; after all, I'd even been informally baptized in 2005. I was doing God's work for peace. Yet I realized, lying there in that room, that praying was not my first reaction. It was more practical: trying to figure out how to get out of that seemingly hopeless situation.

As the long night wore on, I began to accept that this was probably the end, and there was no way to avoid asking the existential question, *Have I made the right choice to take this lonely path?* I had paid a high price for playing this role. *Regrets? What have I achieved?* Reflecting on this, my spirits began to rise. Yes, I not only had kept my father alive, but I had saved countless lives, both Israeli and Palestinian. I did not have blood on my hands. My involvement had been limited to stopping the suicide bombers from killing themselves and killing innocent people.

Where is there hope? The good news, I realized, was that all the resources they devoted to me getting to a meeting reflected my high "market value." The commute teams consisted of some twenty-five agents who were tied up all day with my coming. Surely they weren't going to throw this asset out because of one test. That's what I was to them; I was an asset, not a particular human being, but an intelligence asset I had to believe was worth keeping.

They came to get me in the morning. They did not have to wake me, as I hadn't slept.

"You can go back now." That was hopeful, but I waited for the "but" part. "But you must come back tomorrow for another polygraph test."

ROUND TWO

I took this as good and bad news. Good, as I was able to go back home and take stock of what to do; bad, in that if I hadn't been nervous on this last test, now the nervous pressure was sure to move the needle.

Back in the van, we did the elaborate journey in reverse to get me back home. With the swaying of the van and my previous lack of sleep, I dozed off until we got to the major checkpoint for those leaving Israel and traveling into the territory. The last five miles to Ramallah could be tricky. Sometimes I would be dropped off and would walk, which did have its risks. This time they let me off at the North Gate and I took the shuttle back.

I slept well that night. The next day I found myself in another room somewhere in Israel, all wired up and facing a different expert. He asked me the same questions. This time I tried to suppress my nervousness, which then made me worry that the results would come out that I was lying.

I was left alone for only fifteen minutes before my handler and his manager, Rolli, came in without the expert. They were smiling.

"Congratulations! You passed."

At one level I felt relief, but at another, I knew it was over. I was done. Ten years. I owed them nothing with all I'd done. I wanted out of this prison. Gone from Palestine, from the Middle East. I wanted to do the impossible: go to America.

I went back home and shut myself up in my room. I would not answer the phone, especially if Shin Bet was trying to reach me. I was incommunicado with the outside world and hardly communicado with my own internal, unmoored world. I was adrift in the ocean, far from any shore.

It's interesting how years later, information can come out which casts a whole different light on a transformative event in your life. My former handler, Gonen, later told me that he was in the supermarket when he was approached by the head of the government's polygraph department. This was an important post, as the Israelis used the polygraph not only as a tool in intelligence but across the broad spectrum of government. The Israeli Polygraph Examiners Association was known to maintain the strictest code of ethics in a controversial field. He told Gonen that he had strongly advised against using the polygraph in my case. Why? Because there was no way in hell I could ever pass it, so what was the use of it? I would fail because of the many identities I was juggling, having to play each 100 percent. My conflicted subconscious would send signals to my body's vital signs that the machine would read as lies. The head of the department said they didn't listen to his recommendation. *And, by the way, say hello to Mosab for me!*

It had all been a charade. I hadn't passed the second one. The purpose, engineered by Tamir, had been to break me, to bring this independent spirit, this Green Prince, under his strict control. Well, it had the opposite effect. It was his decision to put me through this and so humiliate me that was the straw that broke this proverbial camel's back.

A FATHER'S DREAM

Some six months before I was able to leave, my father called me from prison and said he was very concerned. I wondered what that was about. He had no idea about the chaos of my life at that point. He said, "I saw you in a dream last night. Our entire house was on fire. And your mother was trying to put out the flames but couldn't. No one from the neighbors was able to put out the flames. I came into the house, and you were in the middle of the living room, crucified. Crucified, and I could not help you."

I was shocked. I didn't know what to tell him. On one hand, I was involved with some Christian groups, and I had an idea of the crucifixion and the Son of God dying and the painful journey of Christ. My father was telling me the truth in prophecies. So was this a warning? My father, out of his love for my other brothers and the family, had to "sacrifice" one of his children, even though he gave me the promise that I would always be his son.[3] But I had created this reality. I am aware of the choices I made, and I don't regret them. I take responsibility for them. I'm okay with the discomfort my choices will and have caused.

NEGOTIATION WITH SHIN BET

When I finally emerged from my torpor and opened negotiations with Shin Bet, they went on and on, month after month, but they realized I was determined not to work for them ever again unless I could take a break. They finally said okay to Europe, but I insisted on the States. They relented, stipulating that my trip would only be for a few months. I had to go through the whole genuine military tribunal hearing to approve my departure for medical treatments that were not available in the territories. This finally was approved, and things became urgent, as my US visa was running out. I had to clean up everything I could, including liquidating my assets, as my intention was never to come back.

With the money I'd been making from different sources, such as my computer repair company, I bought a new penthouse apartment in a good area of Ramallah. I installed everything in that penthouse: a supersized bathroom, a big kitchen. I hadn't moved in yet. When my travel permission came through and my American visa was running out, I immediately put an ad in the newspaper asking for $60,000, which was what it had cost me so far. It was easily worth $80,000, but I didn't have time to dicker; I had to make sure I got cash quick, as I was not coming back. My maternal uncle, Abdullah, saw the ad and said why not sell it to him? That made perfect sense: he was family; he knew the property and knew it was a great deal at cost. I told him I was going abroad for surgery and study and probably wouldn't be back for a couple of years. In a very complicated Middle Eastern–style deal (complicated because we don't have banks and mortgages to do this), we made a three-way deal between the building owner, myself, and my uncle's elevator company. My uncle would buy the apartment for $45,000 and send the money in two months.

So now, somehow, perhaps with some form of divine intervention, all the seemingly insurmountable obstacles had been cleared, and I had permission to leave. Jordan had been a year and a half and forty kilometers away, but now my journey into the unknown was truly to begin. I had thirty days left on my passport before it expired. It was good that my knowledge of international travel was so limited. I was certainly aware that what I held was the flimsiest of all the world's travel documents and the clock had been ticking down against its imminent demise. Little did I know that it was crazy to travel on any passport that would expire in thirty days. Not that I had a choice. Later I would come up against the travel requirement that your passport had to have more than six months before expiration, or else airlines acting on the requirements of your destination country would refuse to issue you a ticket. But that was all ahead of me. Right then, the road ahead looked clear. So, with hurried goodbyes, and unstated wondering on both sides if we would ever lay eyes on each other again, I departed with promises to talk often on the phone.

PART II

7

A Nomad in America

I was at the historic Allenby Bridge spanning the water-starved Jordan River. This was the only entry-exit point for West Bank Palestinians like me traveling abroad. More than a simple boundary, it divided two different worlds. I had no idea what awaited me. In the maelstrom of the Middle East, intelligence agencies from the US, the UK, the French, the Turks, the Iranians, the Egyptians, the Saudis, the Israelis, and of course the Jordanians had their presence in the listening post of the territories. The Jordanians had a very competent, long-standing intelligence operation. They taught the Israelis a lot with their emphasis on human source intelligence, or "HUMINT."

Will the Jordanians arrest me? Send me back? Will I ever make it? They certainly knew who I was. My father was a figure on TV with me at his side, and the Jordanians were wholly opposed to Hamas. I felt like an insignificant pawn in this game of big players, subject to the arbitrary whims of any insignificant official.

Somehow, I was waved through. This relieved a considerable weight from my shoulders. I was less apprehensive, but there still were many more steps before I would make it to my ultimate destination—America. The one certainty I had in this welter of doubt and uncertainty was that I was never going back.

Miraculously, all went according to plan. I took a bus into Amman, Jordan's capital, which was humid, dirty, and noisy. At the airline's office I handed over $1,500 in cash for a round-trip Air France ticket to Los Angeles. They hadn't balked at my passport expiring in thirty days. The Queen Alia International Airport in this post–September 11 world was chaos. Milling about were uniformed American soldiers in transit for combat duty in Iraq and a mix of international passengers. Once I was buckled in on the Air France flight, I was able to breathe easier. We landed at Charles de Gaulle Airport outside of Paris to transfer to the LA flight. Next, I found myself flying over North America and approaching Southern California. I could see below the vast urban sprawl of the LA Basin and the Pacific Ocean stretching to the horizon. My taut nerves signaled the final obstacle, getting past US customs and immigration.

We left the plane in a fast-moving herd, past "Welcome to LA" signs, down a flight of stairs, and into the vast hall with immigration officials sitting behind their computers. I was in a line for foreign passport holders. The uniformed officer took my document, did a double take on the unfamiliar document, leafed through it, checked the photo against my semi-smiling face, and found the visa.

"What is the purpose of your visit today?"

"I've been invited by good friends that I worked with at USAID," I managed to get out.

He rummaged through the document. "You know this travel document expires in thirty days?"

"Ahh . . ." What could I say? I knew this official had the power to refuse me entry and send me back on the next flight. I was mentally prepared to refuse to board and stay in the airport, taking up permanent residence there.

There was a line waiting behind me. The official's stamp hovered over the page with the visa for what seemed like an eternity. *Whack!* He handed my passport back to me.

"Welcome to the United States; enjoy your stay. Next!"

FIRST STOP, SAN DIEGO

I floated to the baggage carousel, picked up my small bag, walked up a ramp, taking my first steps in America, and emerged from a tunnel into a sea of expectant faces. I scanned the crowd and there was Yvonne, as beautiful as ever, with a broad smile as though greeting a family member. We embraced. She was super excited; it seemed hard to believe for both of us, though she had no idea what it had taken for me to be standing there with her.

In her monster Mercedes SUV, we drove down to the upscale beach community of La Jolla outside of San Diego, where Tawfik was waiting. My first time on an LA freeway. My first American meal—at an In-N-Out Burger. Welcome to everything fast in laid-back California. They had a condo that overlooked the Pacific Ocean. As a real estate agent, Yvonne had sold some high-end properties and leased the condo and the car. Breathing in that fresh ocean air, clearing my lungs of the smog of war, I thought it couldn't get any better than this.

California! The place I'd read about, seen in the movies (when I could; during the intifada, the Hamas militias burned the theaters down), and listened to its music (though not in the house, as my father considered music a sin), with beautiful people like Yvonne and Tawfik, a constitutional democracy with free speech where everyone was free to practice their religion. Left behind were the politics and trauma of a war zone. I was free from my double life with death around each corner; call it a triple life, as I'd kept my Christianity a secret, except from a few fellow Christians. Here I was, this Ramallah boy, in an exciting new culture populated by gorgeous bikini-clad women and tanned Adonises with six-packs. Like it had for so many refugees who had come before me, looking for a new life and opportunity, it all looked as bright as the sun shimmering over the pounding emerald surf below.

The first step of my plan to stay in the US was to line up a good immigration lawyer who would submit an asylum request when the six-month stay allowed by my visa ran out. Fortuitously, Tawfik's divorced father, Hani, a Palestinian Christian nationalist of the Popular Front for the Liberation of Palestine (PFLP; a designated terrorist group), was eager to help a fellow Palestinian. He was part of the mass exodus of millions of Christians from the Middle East. Like the Jewish diaspora, Palestinians were spread throughout the Western world. When I was in an Israeli prison with thousands of inmates, only a couple of them were Christians. Hamas didn't accept Christians.

Hani had a lawyer he used, and because Hani vouched for me, the lawyer agreed to take my case without charging me. He assumed that I was another Palestinian activist come to the country. So it was a bit of a shock for him when we filled out the application based on the fact that I'd gone against my family and left Islam.

HELLO FROM LA JOLLA

I was able to call my family and report I'd safely arrived. When I was finally able to reach my father, he was relieved I'd made it and asked if I was happy. I said I was, and I was staying with Yvonne and Tawfik. My father was the wisest of sages about the ways of people. His wisdom had been honed over many years of listening to and counseling those who had come to the mosque and also the hundreds of prisoners whose tortured lives he had comforted. He then said, "As a friend, when you love someone, love them in moderation. They might become your opponent."

Tawfik and Yvonne loved each other, yet they often fought, and it would escalate when Yvonne drank. I couldn't understand why they were fighting so much, since they had everything: family, material comforts, a home. Yet their condo was like an emotional war zone. They had quarreled in Palestine, but not like this.

Their American Dream was falling apart. I was also learning more about their church, the International Church of Christ, founded in 1979. They only had around 110,000 members, and they had numerous strict rules, such as no kissing before marriage, and were very male-dominated. And all rule-breakers, as well as Muslims, Jews, Catholics, and all except the faithful of their cult, were going to a literal Hell. This version of Christianity didn't sound good to me. In fact, it sounded like the religion I'd just left.

I noticed Tawfik wasn't following all the rules. Of course, impossible rules are designed to implant shame and guilt in the minds of the faithful. We were back to the Pharisee rule-makers and their means to maintain control and power. My reaction to these rule-based exclusionary religions would later lead to exploring Eastern religions like Buddhism, Hinduism, and Zen, which did not grow in such barren desert soil.

Tawfik had a job in Mexico, so he was often away. It seemed like I was Yvonne's only friend. Two weeks into my stay, when Yvonne had been drinking, as she did every night, she and Tawfik had a fearsome row. She turned to me and said, "Come on, I want to walk on the beach." I wasn't sure what to do, but I thought it best to accompany her to keep her from harm.

We walked along the cliff area with the rocks and pounding surf below. She went tottering right up to the edge. I begged her to come back. She had told me she'd been having suicidal thoughts. She tended to be overdramatic, but this really frightened me. I finally pulled her back. I could see the media headlines: "Arab Terrorist Throws Beautiful Young La Jolla Woman off Cliff!"

We went back to the car, but she drove in the opposite direction from the condo. I said Tawfik would be very worried and that perhaps we should go back. She drunkenly insisted she had something to show me. We pulled up at an empty condo she was showing to potential buyers. *Why were we going here?* Once through the door, she reached out to hug me. *Oh my.* She was both drunk and hungry for the love and affection she felt she wasn't getting from Tawfik. I drew back. Yvonne was like a sister to me; she'd stayed at our family house in Ramallah. I had enough sense to know this was crazy. It would destroy not just a friendship. I was loyal.

The next morning she apologized, but it was evident to me, especially when Tawfik was away in Mexico, that this was not a sustainable situation. I was getting a crash course in the reality of middle-class America. In debt on the condo's mortgage and the leases on the Mercedes and Tawfik's BMW, still owing on their student loans, and with the real estate crash in the offing, it was a high-anxiety time for the couple. That only fueled Yvonne's insecurity. It was no wonder she was drinking, and the couple were taking their angst out on each other. My idealized version of America was inevitably being tempered by my direct experience of a money-oriented society.

But what were my options without this safe harbor? Fortunately, I had one: the family card. Like the millions before me who emigrated to this country with family who had arrived before them and had successfully resettled, I had a cousin, Yousef, and his father, my uncle Douad, who lived in the Midwest. As it turned out, my missing favorite sister, Tasneem, also lived there.

MISSOURI AND MICHIGAN

I flew off to Columbia, Missouri. Yousef and I were very close, as we had shared time on the streets and in prison. In terms of new immigrants living the American Dream, Yousef was an apparent success: he had a home with a mortgage; a job where his hard work and skills were rewarded; a wife; and kids who attended the local public schools. Unlike my family, his family was not a conservative Muslim family that regularly went to the mosque. Yousef, in fact, was a Marxist, and had been a member of the secular Popular Front for the Liberation of Palestine. Back in Jerusalem, he had often worked construction and had Jewish friends; he also drank alcohol—not the approved Islamic profile.

Yousef was my partner when, at almost eighteen, we purchased that stupid defective pistol. He married his half-American wife when she was fifteen. They waited until she was eighteen to apply to come to the United States based on her citizenship. One of the questions on the exhaustive visa application was, "Are you a member or representative of a terrorist organization?" There also was still a staple from Cold War days: "Have you ever been a member of the Communist Party or a Communist front organization?" Yousef, though no longer a member of the PFLP and a lapsed Marxist, had a twofer going to disqualify him. So he checked the "no" boxes. That was not the strategy I was going to follow.

Since I was now in the Midwest, my priority was to search for my sister Tasneem. Thanks to the internet, I tracked her down in Dearborn, Michigan. From the day she had left Ramallah with her new husband, we had not heard from her. This was a heartbreaking story for our family.

Tasneem was the middle sister, always very special, her beauty stunning. When we were both in school, it was my duty to go to her school and walk her the two miles home. Once, we were caught in a sudden, violent hailstorm, a rare event in our part of the world. There was nowhere to shelter, and we were pelted with large hail. It was both painful and freezing. My sister was crying with pain. The only thing I could do was shelter her with my body as best I could and take the blows from Mother Nature. We had a special bond, and I felt a responsibility for her. I can picture her now, asleep on the sofa, an innocent and compassionate child, with her tears still not dry from when the IDF came and took our father away.

My father, with most of his friends killed, knew he faced an uncertain future regarding his daughters. A father with three sons appeared in Ramallah from the States. He was an engineer who worked for Ford in Detroit. He'd known my father some forty years ago when he'd lived in Jerusalem before emigrating, but they had not seen each other since. He would hear my father give speeches in the Al-Aqsa Mosque. His children were brought up in the States, well educated: one a dentist, one an optometrist, and one an MD. The father sought out the leading families in the city from the religious class. He targeted young women between eighteen and twenty. The sons were in their late twenties and early thirties, all with attractive smiles, perfect teeth, and good eyes. Qualified brides were easily found, among them the tall and slim Tasneem.

They all got engaged in one big party. Tasneem was now engaged to the doctor, and the plan was she would finish her last year in school and then they would get married. The three bridegrooms came back a year later, and they all got married. I was at the wedding, and they seemed like nice guys who would provide a good life for their new wives. My sister received her papers from the consulate and was granted a green card. And off they went to the States.

We awaited news that she'd arrived safely, but no news came in the first week. Nor the second week, nor the third. We realized we had no phone number, no address, no way of reaching them. Months passed. It was clear they'd cut off all contact with us. The other two families experienced the same ominous silence. I went to the village the father was from and talked to their friends. No one had a phone number or any way to contact them. This was before Google. Where was my innocent nineteen-year-old sister? I didn't know if she was alive or dead.

The family finally allowed my sister to send us an email. She said her new life was fine; she was well. "My husband doesn't want me to talk to my family or anyone else." Though I continually sent emails to her address, I never received a reply. My mother was heartbroken. We had given her away to strangers, but this behavior was not the way of our culture. Families helped each other. The émigrés would come back each summer to their roots, to their grandparents, aunts, and uncles. But these guys had no roots; they were accountable to no one. It was shameful for our family. For five years, we didn't hear anything else, and then came an email from her saying she was fine and was pregnant again.

When I arrived in the States, I at least had their names and looked them up on Google. I found a clinic in Dearborn with an answering machine. I left a message saying that I was in America and wanted to come see my sister and the children. I received an email from my sister saying welcome. I wrote back saying I was glad she was alive and asking whether we could talk on the phone. She wrote saying she couldn't. No one in the family had seen her for six years. The crazy part was that this family posed as religious people.

The situation must have become too ridiculous even for them. I heard back asking when I would come. This didn't sound like a visit but an appointment. Her husband sent me his cell phone number. I called him and he gave me the address and an appointed time in the afternoon to appear.

I showed up at their house in Dearborn, the city with the largest Muslim community in the United States. It was the first time anyone in our family had seen Tasneem since the wedding. She looked yellow, with no life force. She was not allowed to drive. She could not go anywhere without being accompanied, usually by her mother-in-law. Once a week the whole family got together. The only friend she had was a neighbor, a sixty-five-year-old white woman whom she talked to through the fence. She introduced me to her. The garden was the one pleasure that Tasneem was allowed to pursue. The children played in the basement where there was a TV. I played with the children and had dinner, and in two hours my time was up.

The culture approves this kidnapping. It's not ISIS; these are God-fearing citizens, and they'd cut my sister off from her family and the world. Even in Saudi a married eleven-year-old can still see her family. In six years she's been conditioned: her way is the husband's way. Her husband exploits it both ways: as a doctor, he enjoys the respect of the larger community; as a Muslim, he enjoys the respect of that community for following their rules—though in the larger American community, his behavior is criminal.

I could not rescue her. She was happy to see me, but our moment was clouded, knowing it was only temporary. Asking questions was awkward. *Are you happy? Does he beat you? Why can't you at least speak on the phone with your mother and father?* With a heavy heart, I took my leave from my beloved sister living in a form of slavery in a basement in Michigan, the land of the free.

AIMLESS

Going back to my cousin and his family, I had no particular plan other than waiting out that six months before the attorney would submit the asylum application. Who knows how long it would be before an appointment could be made? So my days in the heartland of America were aimless.

The days in Ramallah had been lived with such intensity, though the skills I'd honed in the cauldron of that war zone were unlikely to be employable here. I was not a musician or an artist or a writer, so this free time could be spent creatively. What I did back home could not have been more creative—*there*; hence I was still alive. Under the terms of my visa, I couldn't have a job.

Yousef worked for a multimillion-dollar high-flying real estate company. He supervised construction and would travel around the Midwest to building sites. The company had a small plane, and sometimes I'd fly with him to properties in other states. His job was to see how the construction cost on a site, like an apartment complex, could be cut in half. He came up with good ideas and hired the right labor. The bankers and this highly leveraged company were making out like the bandits they were. Yousef at least would get generous bonuses along with a $100,000 annual salary. He was justifiably proud of his accomplishments after only being in the US five years. And then came the 2008 financial crisis, precipitated by greedy companies like his, and he lost his job.

I soon discovered that Columbia, styled "the Athens of Missouri," was a partying university town hosting the University of Missouri. I soon pursued "night classes" in the local bars crowded with pretty coeds. I was definitely an undergraduate in these matters, despite my age. I would get back to the house intoxicated around one or two in the morning. I didn't share with Yousef my Christian experience where alcohol was okay.

Now that two months had passed, it was the time for my uncle to pay me what he owed for purchasing my condo back home. I got through to him, but he gave various excuses about how he didn't have it now; it would be later. Eventually, he stopped answering when I called. I called other people to put pressure on him. They said he owed them money too. This did not bode well for me.

Yousef began to worry that I was setting a bad example for his son. Yousef was conflicted over issues of cultural identity and specifically over alcohol. Back in the village where his grandfather was the imam, Yousef didn't go to the mosque, didn't pray, and didn't fast during Ramadan; yet for some reason, he was always afraid of alcohol. For the religious, alcohol was a worse sin than not praying, but here was Yousef, liberal and open-minded, constantly repeating, "Religion is the opiate of the people" and believing drinking alcohol would sully his reputation. Despite his departure from the cultural norms, he still craved respectability.

There is an existential fear of losing identity when one is thrown into an alien environment. The Muslim community in Kansas City found itself in a culture afraid of Muslims. That encouraged many to reignite their religious practices in order to hold on to their identities. Yousef wrestled with this issue of identity, including what he was leaving his sons growing up in this environment. There were certain lines he didn't want them to cross.

As time went by, Yousef's behavior toward me became weird, and it was evident we were both growing more uncomfortable. As family and because of tradition, he couldn't just tell me to move out, but it was clear to both of us that the time had come.

BACK TO CALIFORNIA

I'd been talking to Tawfik, and he urged me to come back to Southern California. Yvonne, who I also was talking to, also proposed I come back. My aimless extracurricular "college life" no longer had an appeal, and my one goal of asylum was to be played out in Southern California. Thanking Tawfik and Yvonne, I flew back after nearly three months in Middle America.

So I landed for the second time in Southern California. This time all was not shiny and new, nor full of hope. I was glad to see Yvonne again, but it was clear her relationship with Tawfik had not improved. I settled back in the condo, my only goal to pursue asylum, which would at least give me the right to work and thus provide a constructive focus to my days.

And then a completely unpredictable incident happened. Yvonne got into the files on my laptop and found that I had been watching pornography! "I thought you were better than that!" She didn't let up on shaming me. In a nice bit of irony, Tawfik confessed that while in Mexico he watched porn and masturbated. For her, this was equivalent to cheating with another woman. She made it clear she had lost all respect for me. My free seaside condo days were numbered. Counting what money I had left, I took my leave and headed into downtown San Diego.

HOSTEL HOPPING

San Diego, the beautiful oceanside American city, like so many California towns has a Spanish name, as it was once part of Mexico and, before that, the far-flung Spanish Empire. To the south, over the border fence, is Mexico and the teeming city of Tijuana. The fence was built to keep people from the south from venturing north, most in search of work as economic migrants.

One of the major industries of this sun-drenched city, with its nearly 1.5 million residents—a confusing mix of legal and illegal—is tourism. As a result, downtown San Diego has more than its share of hostels, where I could find a bed for twenty to twenty-five dollars a night, which would keep me off the street. Though it was dormitory-style with ten to a room, it was fun, and I met and made friends with travelers from all over the world—though it wasn't so much fun when my stuff was stolen. At least my tattered travel document was still in my possession. I think I still entertained an idealized version of America, part of the baggage I'd landed with. I got to know this city of beaches and skyscrapers by walking everywhere, this America of the tents of the homeless and the mansions of the wealthy. To live the good life here you had to be either a surfer or a millionaire or, best of all, I suppose, both. I was neither.

It was in a hostel that I met Daniel, a young Californian who would turn out to be my closest, most loyal friend in this difficult and at times lonely chapter of my journey. Daniel had just arrived in the US to go to college. He was being supported by his grandmother. I told him I was from Israel, not Palestine, and he was very interested in how I'd come to be in San Diego. As he was new to the city, I showed him around and we explored together, partied together, did all sorts of crazy things together. Hostel stays were limited, so we had to keep hopping from one to another. We'd eat together and hang out at the hostels. My fading finances didn't allow me to do anything more. The hostels were a place to meet cute girls and just be part of something. Daniel was doggedly chasing a Mormon girl and went so far as to go to a Mormon church. His interest was seduction; hers was conversion. So for me, it was both fascinating and amusing to be introduced to one more version of those declaring they were following Jesus, styled here as The Church of Jesus Christ of Latter-Day Saints. This version had its angels and possibly a talking salamander and the traditional talking snake of Genesis. Everyone needs a good creation myth.

My lifestyle was unsustainable. Math was math. The $7,000 I'd brought with me had nearly run out and would run out long before I applied for asylum, and it could be months before I got an appointment. I had already exhausted the family option. I was very grateful to be in America, as I felt safer here, certainly, but my anxieties were different. Instead of being anxious about torture or death, here I felt financial worry.

I was not the typical legal immigrant who came to America from the old country penniless, seeking economic opportunity and a better life. I was a refugee escaping life-threatening persecution, seeking refuge and a different life. I desired the freedom to be who I was, not trapped into playing various roles dictated by others. I had been financially successful in Palestine. With my various gigs, I had been making more money a month than the Israeli prime minister's official salary. (Who knows about the unofficial?) I was giving up an affluent lifestyle and, to all appearances, respected social and economic status.

Now marooned in San Diego and literally hungry, I gave my penthouse uncle another determined try. He did answer the phone. As a reflection of my desperation, I said, "Okay, just send me $2,000 through Western Union" instead of everything he'd promised to pay me. He said he would right away. I paced back and forth in front of the Western Union office and kept going in to ask if the money had arrived. The sympathetic clerk checked each time, shook his head, and said it hadn't arrived. My phone had run out of credit. After a few days I realized all attempts to reach my uncle were futile. He never sent a cent, and he told my parents that he had sent it all. I learned he was making big bucks as the exclusive dealer for a big German company producing elevators, and he had a penthouse built with all my savings in the best neighborhood of Ramallah where he could sit on the terrace and overlook the city.

On every street corner in California, illegals were looking for day jobs. Ironically, I was "legal" and so could jeopardize my case if I was caught working. Plus I had no identity card, no real passport; I couldn't get a Social Security card, a credit card, or a driver's license. If you're not making money in this society, you're not respected. I couldn't even say I was being treated like a second-class citizen, as I wasn't a citizen.

There was another factor that worked against me. The shadow of September 11 still hung over the country when I arrived in 2007. I came from the West Bank, where people were gripped by fear, only to discover Americans lived in fear as well. The demon for both was terrorism, real and imagined, propagated by the press, the preachers, and the politicians. For Americans, terrorism had replaced communism as the official bogeyman of the times. Islamophobia ruled the day. Though I did not wear any foreign clothes or headdress, instead sporting Levi's and a T-shirt, I did have brown skin and black hair. I had that third-world look that could place me in many countries, but since the Middle East was at the top of the news, many took me to be an Arab, which I was.

I would sit peacefully in a café, drinking my coffee, when someone would confront me and shout, "Hey faggot, go back to your country!" Once when I was shopping at Whole Foods, an enraged man put a fist in my face, yelling, "You son of a bitch, motherfucker, bastard," evidently wanting to fight. I did what I always did in those situations, which was acting as though he weren't there. No one stepped forward to help; rather, they went about their business as though we weren't there. Finally, the man grew tired and left.

8

The Wait

I was rescued again by Tawfik. He had had enough battling his wife, and he moved out, renting a small high-security apartment in a historic building in downtown San Diego. Yvonne stayed in the La Jolla condo. He invited me to join him, share the rent, and have my own room. Somehow I would make the finances work. Tawfik was having a hard time with his job in Mexico along with his marital crisis. So he was happy I was there to talk to.

Tawfik was a nutritionist working with cancer patients. He had a mail-order business for superfoods, and I became his partner. I ran the phones and made some money for us. He was into raw food—not just raw vegetables, but everything raw: raw milk, raw cheese, raw red meat, raw fish. I adopted the same diet, which also included juicing. Very California. Besides this diet, Tawfik taught me three things: Christianity, marijuana, and gambling. None, fortunately, turned out to be addictive.

We'd get high on marijuana and go out and gamble, in Las Vegas or local casinos, betting one hundred dollars for the night on blackjack or roulette. I was also introduced to poker. I enjoyed it all, but thank goodness it was small amounts. With real money, I could see it becoming an addiction. I was not risk averse, after all. Here I was tasting the forbidden fruit proscribed by the strict Islam I was nurtured on, not to mention the danger of music, dancing, and other fun. I was having a second chance to experience the youth I'd been deprived of in Ramallah. It was hard for me to believe that the Prophet Muhammad thought that joy is only to be found in Paradise by forbidding it in this earthly life.

At last it was June, the long-awaited six months from my arrival and time for the lawyer to file my application for asylum. I was going by the book—no overstaying my visa as many did and disappearing into the nooks and crannies of mainstream America. The granting of asylum was fully justified in my case, given that my forced return was a death sentence. The next step was an interview with Homeland Security, where they could either approve my asylum request or reject it, which would mean facing deportation. Thanks to the American justice system, however, if my case was rejected, I could appeal to an immigration judge for a final determination. Scheduling the interview could take months, which gave me breathing room.

CALLING JERUSALEM

I was following my plan of never going back to the territories. And with my application filed, I thought it appropriate to tell Shin Bet I was not coming back. I was done.

So I tapped in my special Shin Bet number and was promptly put through to my handler, Tamir. After exchanging a few formalities, I think he expected me to report that I was coming back. I gave no details about what I was doing nor that I had applied for asylum.

"I'm not coming back."

"What do you mean you're not coming back? You promised. What about your father? What about the important things you were doing here?"

That struck a note within me, making me feel guilty. When I didn't reply, he took a different tack.

"How is life in the United States? Pretty pathetic, no? Have you crossed the line between fantasy and reality? You are too small there; here you are big; you can make the change you want. We can help you help your people. Come back. Don't be selfish. If only for the sake of your mother, come back."

I didn't respond.

"Think about it; I'll call you back."

We rang off.

No way in the world was I going back. My financial situation was dire. I owed them? Give me a fucking break. They were a stone on my chest. They owed *me*, big time. Okay, they'd played me, and I'd played them. They'd played me with all their false promises and bullshit. They had no respect for any Arab who collaborated with them. They were racist and tribal, not an uncommon feature in our species. The "wisdom of the Palestinian street" had it right: the Israelis would squeeze you dry like a lemon and throw you in the trash. So many collaborators were thrown onto the streets of Israel. You could find them living the life of junkies in the suburbs of Tel Aviv; they would never fit within Jewish communities. Nobody would accept them and nobody would defend their rights. Some of them successfully filed lawsuits against the agency, created some attention, and received very small amounts of money when the government or the judge had no other choice. But there was still plenty of juice in my bitter lemon, and they would no longer be squeezing me. But they still owed me.

Two weeks later, as a sign of my real desperation, I called them again asking for help. I was due an oft-promised pension, which I could have taken before I left but hadn't.

"Can you help get that money I was promised?"

I remember very distinctly the laughter at the other end of the line.

"You want us to help you, and you're there. It seems you have no clue that you have a big problem with us right now. Not to mention you've said you're not coming back. And you're asking us for help!"

Basically, he was saying, "Go fuck yourself."

Okay.

"I'm going to write a book and put everything in it. Everything."

"What book?"

Actually, this was years before I wrote any book; it hadn't even crossed my mind, but I wanted to get across that they were not the only ones with power in this imbroglio. I was a threat to them because I knew a lot about their operation, their assassinations, their killings, and their brutality. I was in a whole new chapter of my life, and it did not include them. Yes, I knew I could be assassinated by Shin Bet after I bailed out with a head full of state secrets. I was familiar with their varied methods, from a simple bullet to the head to sophisticated killing machines. At this point in my journey, my death would be little mourned and only celebrated by a few in Shin Bet, as all the knowledge I held would accompany me to the grave. Still, I did not have many options.

AN UNEXPECTED ATTACK

I remained close friends with Yvonne and saw her from time to time. This two-state solution of separate homes did not mean peace. I did my best to act as a mediator for Yvonne and Tawfik to get back together, the one-state, one-home solution, as I knew they loved each other.

One day she called, saying she'd like to drop by the apartment that evening. I replied that would be great, as Tawfik would be back from Mexico. I told Tawfik she was coming, and he was angry with me, so I texted her that it was not going to work out for that evening. Tawfik; his dog, Simba; and I spent a quiet evening watching TV and having a couple of drinks. Then we went to bed.

At 1:30 in the morning, the doorbell rang insistently. This was a high-security building. You did not get in without a key and passing checkpoints. I went to the door and peered through the peephole, seeing a woman I didn't recognize. I opened the door. Suddenly, the door was shoved into my face by Yvonne, who pushed past her friend, who fled. I backed up as a shouting, cursing Yvonne beat me with her purse across my head and face. It hurt. Simba went berserk barking. Tawfik appeared in his pajamas and dragged Simba into another room. I wasn't used to a woman hitting me, to say the least. Defending myself, I tried to block the blows and then pushed her away. Drunk and in high heels, she fell back onto the floor. Shouting, "You son of a bitch!" she got up and jumped on me. Tawfik reappeared and got between us and grabbed her, trying to push her out the still-open door.

Appearing in the doorway was the president of the building. He shouted at Yvonne, "Get out of my fucking building!"

"He's a terrorist!" she screamed. "You don't know. He's a terrorist!"

The president, with whom I had a cordial relation, was not in a good mood at two in the morning, "I don't care—terrorist, not terrorist—get the fuck out of the building!"

She retreated.

Tawfik looked at me. "What happened?"

"She attacked me, hit me in the face, the head; you saw."

"I was in the bedroom; I didn't see what happened."

"I didn't hit her."

"I know you didn't beat her." I could see he mostly believed me, but there was doubt. He wasn't the ideal witness.

I was very shaken. *Why in the world did she blame me?* I thought it was her husband she was angry with. I had always acted to bring them together. *Why did she want to kill me?* She was the best woman friend I'd ever had. She was a sister to me. Back in Palestine, the three of us had had such fun together. Love had turned to hatred, a dark, pure hatred—but why? I never would figure it out.

And to shout out that I was a terrorist? She knew nothing could hurt me more than that. Terrorist? Yvonne had no idea about my work with Israeli intelligence to defeat terrorism. Nor did she know how many times I'd been there to protect her and her colleagues from entering the territory at dangerous times. She knew my fragile situation here in the States. That was no casual name-calling.

This time there was no morning-after apology from her. Both of us were taking damage-control measures in this stupid war. I went to the police and filed a complaint to cover myself, as I didn't want any misreported incident on my record that could jeopardize my staying in this crazy country. Tawfik agreed to be a witness.

She was showing bruises on her arms, along with photos, to her family, claiming I'd beat her. The only way I figured she could have gotten those bruises was from Tawfik trying to restrain her. But this could be serious; her brother was part of a Mexican drug cartel, and her father thought his daughter had been beaten up by this "terrorist."

I was hurt and angry. I wrote her a nasty, angry email—not my best moment.

That day Yvonne's mother called me, distraught. "My husband went out and bought a gun, and he's come to kill you. I tried to stop him, but he said he'd already lived long enough. He's downstairs." *Oh great.*

I looked out the window, and sure enough, Yvonne's father was standing there in his wide sombrero along with two other men. I was alone. I looked for something to defend myself with, but against a gun, there was nothing except locked doors and hopefully a security guard.

My phone rang. Yvonne's father spoke with his Mexican accent. "Hi, amigo; I'm outside. We have a situation; why don't you come down and we'll talk it over?"

"Yes, it was a very unfortunate misunderstanding." No way was I going to go down there and get shot. Maybe this craziness was genetic.

"Amigo, come on down, just a friendly talk."

"Why do you need a gun to talk?"

He then turned and spoke rapidly to his two *compañeros*. My phone signaled that he'd hung up. They didn't leave until a while later. *Does this mean I'll risk being ambushed if I venture outside?* Ending my life so ignobly after all the times I'd escaped my demise would be one more case of cosmic irony on my journey.

Two days later the police called and asked if I wanted to press charges. I said no.

If I stayed here with Tawfik, that eliminated the option for Tawfik and Yvonne to get together again. Tawfik didn't say straight out that I had to get out. He knew I had no money and nowhere to go. But he started to behave strangely, as though looking for a reason for conflict. I was careful not to do anything to escalate the situation.

I often cooked for both of us. He loved my cooking, as I made a lot of the dishes his mother had. One day I had the pot boiling on the stove and was putting in garlic that I'd chopped.

Tawfik hovered over me. "My mother didn't chop the garlic."

"Well, sorry, it's chopped."

"You're not doing it right."

"You won't taste the difference, believe me."

It escalated into a real argument. He grabbed the boiling pot and deliberately threw the scalding water on me. I got some pretty serious burns. I'd never seen violence like that from him, particularly directed at me. That was it. There was no way I could stay.

Somehow the gods were smiling on me. Once again friendship would rescue me from the street. I called Daniel. Supported by his grandmother, he had rented a small apartment. He enthusiastically invited me to come stay with him.

When I moved out from Tawfik's apartment, I had to leave behind some items that I still needed. I gave Tawfik my address, and he came by. He was filing for divorce from Yvonne, and they'd left the church. He handed me a box of my things.

As he was getting ready to drive off, he rolled down the window. "Did you ever hit on my wife?"

"No, I told you I never hit her; she was the one who hit me."

He struggled to explain what the slang expression meant. When I understood, I was shocked.

"I had a dream the other night," he said. "An angel came to me and said you were having an affair with my wife."

"Dude, absolutely not. Your angel must have been the devil. Sleep with the wife of my best friend? Never. I always respected both of you. I know my truth." There had been times when I was practically invited to take advantage of her loneliness and her neediness. But I could not as a matter of integrity.

He seemed to accept that. He rolled the window back up and drove off into the sunset. That would be the last time I saw him.

I'll always be grateful to Tawfik and Yvonne, my first close American friends. They welcomed me, took me into their home, shared the fellowship of their Christian community, and never really asked anything in return. Do I consider their subsequent behavior a betrayal? We're all trying to survive in this life. They were caught up in the stresses and unrealistic expectations of American life—marriage falling apart, heavy debt, leaving their Christian faith community. While going to Hell was not a major worry for them, earthly cares like bankruptcy were. But, yes, to be honest, I did feel betrayed by Yvonne, hatred replaced love for no reason I could fathom.

LIFE WITH DANIEL

I moved in with Daniel. It was a small apartment, ideal for a college student, with one bedroom and a living room/kitchen. With the generosity he always showed me, he wanted me to take the bed. I told him I loved sleeping on the couch. My first day there, he wanted to give me $1,000. I refused to take it. He put it in a bowl and said if I needed more to just let him know. Eventually I did. He said someone like me, with all I had contributed, should never be homeless and should be able to buy the things I wanted. He always kept the fridge well stocked for me. That was Daniel.

I settled in, waiting to hear back about my asylum appointment with Homeland Security. At least now I had a fixed address so I could be reached. I had heard that moving too often had made some asylum seekers miss their appointment and their chance to stay because they never saw the notice. Meanwhile, I kept perusing the internet looking for some work, no matter how humble, in the illegal job market. At one point, Daniel asked me to hold $30,000 for him, as he trusted me to keep it for him. I don't know where he'd gotten the money (an inheritance?), but I declined. He was the only true friend I had at this point; he trusted me, and I was not going to violate that trust. He still left $2,000 in case I needed it.

I told Daniel some of my story, and he was to be the only one who fully believed me. Actually, Daniel's belief in my story would contribute in part to his future undoing.

On one of our forays into the city, we met Melanie, a beautiful young woman who was an exotic mix of Irish and Filipino. She was an army vet, married to a white soldier deployed to Iraq. Melanie worked as a part-time model. She was very lonely with her husband gone, and so we became an unlikely trio of friends, like the three musketeers. We went everywhere together: we'd go to the beach, eat together, listen to music, dance, lift each other up. We made a nice team in diverse California: the white college kid, the Arab refugee, the Filipina veteran. For the not-so-diverse conservative Christian community we became a part of, they tended to see us as the druggie, the terrorist, and (later) the prostitute.

Sometimes when we'd go out dancing and drinking, Melanie would get drunk. No way I could let her go home alone. I'd take her back to our place and give her my bed, and in that sleeping hierarchy, turn down Daniel's offer to take the couch and sleep on the floor, a location I was not unfamiliar with. It was a lot cleaner than the cells in the Israeli Slaughterhouse. I could only be grateful. Anyway, my relation with Melanie was one of pure friendship, again a matter of personal integrity. My experience so far in this culture was women were treated as objects, though at least with more independence than the women from the culture I came from.

One of the pleasures of this time was going to visit Daniel's grandmother, Laura, in Ventura, an hour north of Los Angeles. Ninety-four years old, she was all there, a lot of fun, a great hostess, super generous, and completely independent despite walking with a cane and living alone. She was one of the nicest Americans I had met. She adored Daniel, and Daniel adored her. She had worked in the movie business as a sound librarian. You need a gunshot from a particular gun, you need a volcano erupting, she had it. She was set financially; she owned and rented two houses in Port Hueneme, and she received her Social Security every month. Her grandson was not left wanting, as she financed his education, living, and bouts of rehab from his being overly fond of drugs. She loved our visits. We would stay for a couple of days and were well fed and entertained. I remember once I fell asleep on a La-Z-Boy and at night, she came and gently put a blanket over me. That gesture touched me since I was a motherless child in an alien land.

She certainly sensed that I was having a hard time financially. She offered to give me $1,500 to allow me some security. I turned it down. I think she felt, "I'm ninety-four. What the hell am I going to do with all this money besides help people who need it?" Daniel was her only grandchild. His father, Bob, was a successful sound editor in Hollywood, but Laura did not get on at all with Bob's wife. Laura also did not pay attention to Bob's warnings that I was a bad influence on his son. On a later visit, she framed her offer to me another way. Daniel had never had a brother; he'd never had any friends, she said. "You've been a real friend to him; he respects you and listens to you. So please, I would like you to take $1,500 a month; and as you share his life, give him advice, since you seem very wise." I turned that offer down as well, since I was already doing what she had asked.

9

Speaking My Truth

Through Craigslist, I got a job in La Jolla at a high-end sports club. My job was making smoothies and salads and washing dishes. The clientele of the club was into health food, and here I was with an unexpected knowledge in this field from my work with Tawfik. Part of the job became shopping for the food. I would go to Whole Foods but soon figured that the fresh fruit and vegetables at the farmers market were a better deal and were of higher quality. My boss, Minh, was happy that we were saving money. The members were happy with the vittles and the service. I was able to use the gym to work up a sweat, and I had access to good food. I was very happy with my first job in America.

The only downside was I had no car and there was no good public transportation to get to the club. I had to take two to three buses, and if I missed a connection, I had to wait some forty-five minutes for the next bus, which meant I was late for work too often. But Minh was understanding, and as an immigrant and refugee himself, he knew how difficult it was to land in another culture. In fact, he made me the manager, passing over a few employees who had been there much longer.

This first job did not change the direction of my life, but the people I met at the club did. Foremost among them was the charismatic Matt Smith. He was a personal trainer at the club. We were close to the same age, with me a year older. We could not have had more different upbringings. My greatest childhood achievement was surviving. Matt, a navy brat, had an idyllic upbringing. He grew up on Coronado Island off of San Diego, surfing, playing water polo, and playing in a punk rock band. His parents were not religious. Through high school and college, he considered himself an atheist. After attending college in Santa Barbara, he set his sights on making the 2004 Olympic rowing team. He felt being an Olympian would give him value and help him become somebody. His life completely changed at a bar in New York in 2002 when he met his future wife, Rebecca, a student at Columbia and a born-again Christian. Soon after, Matt had his moment of grace, inviting Jesus into his heart. Later he was to realize, as unlikely as it would have seemed, God was calling him to become a pastor. The couple moved to California, where Matt enrolled in the Southern California Seminary and pursued several degrees. When I met Matt, he had a fledgling church, Barabbas Road Church. He invited me to join, but at that point, it was not for me.

In fact, we were heading in opposite directions. I was leaving the strict fundamentalist version of Islam that I'd been brought up in, and while I had studied the teachings of Jesus, I was not eager to dive into another set of rigid dogmas. Matt, on the other hand, was fully embracing a strict fundamentalist version of evangelical Christianity. Brought up in a secular California lifestyle, he welcomed a religion that had strict rules of behavior and a belief system that had a monopoly on truth. Also, he liked being a pastor, which to him meant self-fulfillment and power. Matt's ambition was to become a recognized member of the religious establishment of his time, a powerful megachurch preacher. From my point of view, this placed him on the wrong side of the table that Jesus angrily overturned in the temple.

Although we were not on the same page, we did enjoy a genuine friendship. Matt even suggested that I date his sister, which certainly was a sign of approval. We spent time together debating religion, him full of what he'd just learned in seminary, me speaking from my own experience. We also discussed our personal issues, the way friends do. Still, he had converted his parents and his sister to the faith. I had rejected the religious laws and duties enforced by society, and it cost me every comfort and security I knew. It was difficult for Matt to grasp this. I was living with the threats of Shin Bet, deportation, the American government through the Federal Bureau of Investigation (FBI), and potential Hamas assassins. Aside from Daniel, Matt was the only person with whom I shared the fact that I had been working with Shin Bet.

For Matt, this was exciting, not only for the James Bond side of it but also the Israeli side, where he saw as my work as helping Israel draw closer to fulfilling the biblical prophecy of the Second Advent of Christ. He continued to ask me to join his church, but I had more on my mind, as the crucial meeting with Homeland Security was coming up in a few days. He took my turning him down to mean I was losing my faith. He would throw various biblical verses at me to convince me to join his church. Growing his church was his goal. In his mind, this was the way to save the world.

OFFICE OF HOMELAND SECURITY, FEDERAL BUILDING, ANAHEIM, CALIFORNIA, SEPTEMBER 11, 2007

The bright sunlight of a Southern California morning streamed into this corner office. A portrait of President George W. Bush smiled from the wall. An American flag drooped on a pole in the corner. Across the desk from me sat an overweight Homeland Security officer. After nine months in the land of the free, this was my first encounter with an official of the United States government. And he was angry.

On the desk was a single file, almost a foot thick. The Homeland Security officer wetted two fingers and leafed through pages. I assumed the file was mine, but I had no idea what was in it.

"How did you ever get into our country?" He shook his head in disbelief.

It seemed prudent not to answer. His undisguised hostility has thrown me on the defensive. And my English was not good. I was afraid both of misunderstanding and saying the wrong thing.

"How in the world did we grant you a visa?"

From out of the file, he took my pathetic travel document. As a stateless Palestinian, I had no real national passport.

"I had a job with USAID on a water project."

"Did they know who you were?"

I managed to look puzzled.

"That your father was one of the founders of Hamas and a leader of the most notorious of terrorist organizations?" His impatient tone said, *Don't play dumb with me.*

"Yes."

"Did this woman at the consulate in Jerusalem know your background?"

A rhetorical question; I didn't answer.

"Did she know you'd served time in prison?" He pulled out a paper. "Six months, then nine—that's nearly two years. Hopefully, for her sake, that was after she issued the visa." He scanned the paper.

"They were for administrative detention. I was never convicted of a crime."

He snorted. "Two years they lock you up, and you're not a terrorist. Come on, the Israelis know what they're doing."

That indeed was true. In fact, Shin Bet had orchestrated all of those prison terms to protect me. This line of questioning highlighted the dilemma I faced. If I told the truth about my ten years working with Israeli intelligence and saving countless Israeli lives, that would surely get my asylum application approved. *But who would believe this preposterous fantasy? How would I prove it?* Only a handful of Shin Bet agents knew of my involvement. And Shin Bet, when questioned, always stuck to their mantra: *We neither confirm nor deny.*

My application for asylum was based on religious persecution. A Muslim who converts to Christianity is subject to death. As a bonus, my family would be ostracized, with little choice but to disown me. But that would not heal the pain of my apostasy, particularly for my father. On the other hand, this terrible price I was personally paying was one more testament to my commitment to Jesus Christ.

This man across the desk with the authority of a gatekeeper had hung over my head the label of *potential terrorist*, not *sincere Christian*. That file told him where I'd been born, who my parents were, what they did and what they believed, and what religion I'd been brought up in, and with all these details, at which he'd only given a cursory glance, he'd made a judgment about me. I fit a profile. His job in counterterrorism was to ferret out terrorists. He didn't see me as a human being; he saw me as a probable terrorist asking for asylum in his besieged country. Before September 11, there were a few applicants who lied and were granted asylum and then committed terrorist acts. He needed to probe and find something he could nail me on. Ironically, he was doing the same job I'd done for ten years. He homed in on the key question from the statutory language that could put you in prison for a long time.

"Have you ever given material assistance to a terrorist organization?"

"It depends on what you—"

"To Hamas! Hamas is a terrorist organization." Rising blood colored his gray face.

"It depends what you mean by material assistance." I wasn't trying to be a wiseass at all. He'd gotten me wrong-footed, scared. This was not what I'd expected.

"All right. Have you ever filled your father's car with gas?"

"Yes."

His face softened as though he'd hit his *gotcha* moment.

"That's material assistance. Have you ever given him money?"

That made me think. When I was earning, I'd certainly been provided money to keep the house going, especially when my father was in jail. I finally answered, "I don't remember exactly, but yes, probably."

A flick of a malignant smile crossed his features.

I might have added that some of my income was coming indirectly from Shin Bet and, in that sense, Shin Bet was providing material assistance to Hamas, a terrorist organization. That might have had its fun moment, but then the proverbial can of worms would be opened. And the officer was even providing financial aid through his taxes to my terrorist father. The US government gave aid to the Palestinian Authority, which gave my father $3,000 a month as salary for being a member of the Palestinian parliament.

"Do you talk to your family on the phone?"

"Yes."

"Do you send them money?"

"No."

"What do you talk to your father about?"

"I haven't spoken to him for a long time; it's not easy, as he can only talk for seconds at a time."

"And your mother?"

"Yes, she's worried about me and wants to know how I'm doing. When I'm coming back." I immediately regretted that last phrase as he perked up.

"Does she work for Hamas?"

"Ask her."

"Your siblings, brothers, sisters?"

"Maybe a few words, just 'How are you?' kind of exchanges."

He looked exasperated. "I still don't know why the hell you didn't bring a lawyer. Don't you realize—" He stopped himself, but I could finish it: *Don't you realize you're in deep shit?* The answer was yes, I did.

"The letter just said an appointment at Homeland Security, the date and the time. I didn't know it would be like this."

His expression said I was being dumb. But I'd done the math. The lawyer charged $500 an hour, and this session would go seven hours.

"And I don't understand," he said, pointing to the file, "how the Israelis ever let you leave the country."

"Palestinians can leave for medical reasons if that medical treatment is not available on the West Bank."

"What was yours?"

"Surgery on my jaw."

"Did you have it?"

"Yes."

"So, mission accomplished. You can go back."

"If you send me back, I will be killed. It's as simple as that. That's why I'm seeking asylum, to stay alive to freely practice my religion."

He studied me carefully. He didn't speak. This was not a brief bureaucratic meeting; this had been an interrogation.

We held each other's gazes.

Finally, I said, "You don't believe me, do you? I am not a terrorist. I've never killed anyone. I've never hurt anyone. I believe life is sacred."

"It's irrelevant whether I believe you are not. I do have the authority to grant asylum in clear cases, but I'm not approving yours. Your status is no longer refugee; it's deportee. You will be going before a judge before being deported."

I sat there stunned. *Deportee.* I knew things had not gone all that well, but this? I'd spoken the truth. What else could I do? My case had seemed clear to me. Jesus said, "The truth will set you free,"[4] but I knew from experience that did not always work. I'd faced many angry interrogators before who had thought I was a liar and a terrorist. At least this confrontation had not come after days of torture. This was the United States of America, where I knew that under the Constitution, once I was on US soil, I had rights. And it was that fact that made the angry man across from me frustrated, as he no doubt felt resources were being wasted on someone seeking to take advantage of the system.

He slapped the file shut, a gesture of finality. Interrogation over. I stood up on shaky legs. I didn't know what to say or do. *Do I shake his hand? Do I say thank you?*

I made it to the door and into an empty hallway. I looked for somewhere I could sit down and take stock.

I sank onto a bench, trying to quiet my rapid breathing. It was all black. Perhaps Shin Bet was right: I couldn't make it here in the Wild West. *Who am I really, anyway?* At this darkest of moments, I felt like a child who, unable to swim, had been thrown into a turbulent sea far from a distant shore. Out of all the darkness and confusion, the one clear point of light was that my survival depended on my being able to stay in this country.

THE SHEPHERD AND THE SHEEP

The church can be a perfect place for someone going through a crisis to find support, so I finally joined Matt's church. Under Matt's zealous direction there was religion and dogma with Sunday services and Bible study, but also time for fun. We played sports together—a lot of soccer, even surfing; we played music and had swimming parties and barbecues. This was theoretically a network of people who shared the same faith and the same beliefs. These were people you could talk to, become friends with; meet the girl, make a baby, build a home. I met some wonderful people. They were very supportive and particularly wanted to encourage me in the development of my faith.

While I was not a newcomer, as I'd had seven years of study and attempting to follow Jesus in my dogma-free life, I was still grateful for their help, as I had lost family and friends back in Palestine. And as a new immigrant struggling to survive, I was at the bottom of the socioeconomic ladder.

People wanted to be kind and supportive, but I was able to see that my story was largely irrelevant to them. Many only focused on the part where I'd been a monster who now saw the light. Like any community sharing a belief system, they had expectations. All members had to trade in their freedom and put on the mask that makes you fit in. Breaking those expectations and rules leads to confrontation. I'm not against this aspect of the church, because there are so many wounded people who are confused and in desperate need of the pastor's leadership and the support of a strong community. Trading in one's identity for a new one and a temporary sense of security can be necessary and healing for some.

As an Arab and a foreigner, I stood out in a congregation that was mostly white Republican. Matt shared with me how much he wanted his church not only to grow but to be diverse, which would be good for the church's image. At one of our church meetings, an African American couple attended. After we were all sitting around, I piped up, "Matt, you must be very pleased; you have white members, Melanie and I are brown, and now you have Black." The place went stone silent. *Did I say something wrong?* It seemed a perfectly normal observation, and I was just expressing what Matt had put in my mind as a positive goal for the church. You had to be brought up in America to know how to negotiate this ugly third rail of American life: racism.

Another cultural mishap was a result of my stupid Arab pride. I had gone hungry for days and was in a Bible study class. My fellow church members had brought food to sustain themselves through the discussion. Did anyone offer to share their food with me? No. Did I ask anyone to share their food? No. In my Arab culture at such an event, I would have been offered food multiple times. Pride is a huge barrier to a higher level of consciousness. When in Rome, go ahead and ask if someone will share a bit of his pasta with you.

During this period there were certain ideas Pastor Matt came up with that left me dumbstruck. One was that members of the church should go out in the evening to Pacific Beach and cover the area with charcoal graffiti promoting Barabbas Road Church and God. He invited me to come along.

"Matt, how will anyone come to the church when they see some scribblings on a wall? In fact, it could be a real negative."

"The plus is to build teamwork among us. So come, it'll be fun."

Pacific Beach is a celebrated San Diego spot that attracts beautiful, bikini-clad women from all over the world, along with hot local college girls. The tactic seemed silly. It also rang the bells of memory: back in Ramallah, when as teenage students we participated in the graffiti wars between Hamas and Fatah. This, as you might recall, had been the occasion for my first arrest. In retrospect, our graffiti efforts were certainly ineffective—and worse, as we Palestinians were fighting among ourselves. Comparatively, Matt and the faithful were risking, at most, embarrassment and a fine for effacing property.

Though Matt was now my pastor, we still did not see eye to eye. Once, when he was giving me a ride in his car, I told him there had never been and there will never be a person more liberal than Jesus Christ. He said he wasn't sure what I meant, that perhaps it was the language barrier, but that I shouldn't mention it again since it could be misunderstood in a bad way. I didn't want to argue with him.

I asked him to stop at a liquor store. When I got back in the car, I was holding a paper bag. He asked, "What did you get?"

"Some Johnnie Walker Black Label."

He was incredulous: "You drink that?"

"Now and then, yes. Do you want to have a drink?"

Matt thought drinking alcohol was a sin, one that could merit excommunication. Of course, I came from a religion with that same prohibition. I think he realized then that I was going to be an embarrassment for him and his church.

It was becoming more and more evident to me that I was not living my true identity. The identity that I had inherited from my parents, from my society, from their conditioning in this Islamic paradigm, was no longer my identity. What was my truth? Where was I at this point in my journey?

I did not want to let go of a possible creator, God, the source of existence. Many people at this point would have embraced atheism, but I did not want to cancel out the possibility that there was something out there. I was certainly in total admiration of the master, Jesus Christ. It is against the Islamic religion to make anyone or anything equal to Allah, which is called *shirk,* the one sin that cannot be forgiven. One can drink alcohol, commit adultery, or betray someone and still be forgiven. But to say that Jesus Christ is equal to Allah eliminates any chance of recovery. At that point, I was able to see God within Christ, but I was still blind to seeing God within myself. Departure from Islam is not easy, but I could take one step and say, "I'm out"; that set an intention and disconnected me from its people and its conditioning. By announcing my departure, I knew I was losing the comfort and security that came with Islam.

This was not a conversion to the religion of Christianity. It was a rejection of the religion of Islam and all the denominational stupidity of Sunni, Shia, Salafist, and jihadist, which are all nothing but human delusion. I was expanding my understanding to other possibilities. I continued to be fascinated by the persona of Christ. I saw his power, his divinity, his behavior that rose above our conditioned existence. He was someone who conquered hunger and thirst through forty days of fasting, and finally conquered death. For me, he was a very daring, inspiring individual. He was able to rise above the material, and we, in our stupidity, ignorance, greed, and fear, killed one of the greatest masters of all time.

My admiration for Jesus inspired me to act on my own authority for the first time, not to be a follower, not to be just a sheep, not to just go with the flow to the slaughterhouse. Christ could not do it on my behalf. He inspired me to do it for myself, knowing I would be the one to pay the bills for it. I decided to walk into the unknown, to lose my security, my family, and my relationship to everything that I knew. In renouncing Islam, I had to reveal I was a follower of Jesus Christ—whatever that meant. I had to trust that, even though I was going against the flow of my society, I knew this was my birthright: to do what I wanted to do, even if I was making a mistake.

It was Jesus' message of love and compassion and gentleness that drew me closer to Christianity, though I found few churchgoing Christians who saw within this belief system what I saw in Christ. My experience would be that the teachers of the law and the religious authorities might preach the words but convey a different message through their actions. Still, one thing I knew: if I had stayed in Ramallah, my crucifixion would have been certain.

Determined to go ahead, I called my friend, the Israeli journalist Avi Issacharoff, from Israel's oldest newspaper, *Haaretz*. He had interviewed my father many times. I had seen him relatively often, as he covered the West Bank and Gaza for the paper. I told him I wanted to go public with the fact that I was rejecting Islam and was attending a Christian church. Knowing well the culture, he immediately saw that this was a big story, that the oldest son of Hassan Yousef was rejecting his father's faith and becoming a Christian. He said, "Give me a couple of weeks; I'll come to the States, and we can talk face-to-face."

He came to San Diego, and we sat down to dinner. It was good to see him: bald, those big ears, and a ready smile. I gave him the story.

He knew a big story like this could have real consequences, not only for the father-son relationship but for the political implications in a culture where this action was tantamount to a death sentence.

After the interview, he told me, "I want you to know, if you change your mind, I will not publish it, and nobody will ever know about this."

"I want to go ahead."

"Take your time; think about it. I'm going to take a week or two before I publish it."

For him there was also a risk. He was constantly going to Ramallah, the West Bank, and Gaza to interview people, and he could be afraid someone would cut his head off.

Avi, working on the piece, later called me up to ask what denomination I was with. I was very uninformed about all this. My interests were not in researching the varied denominational landscape. I hadn't studied the history of evangelical Christianity or any denomination. My interest was in the actual practicing; for example, *What does it mean to love your enemy?* I certainly knew with Islam there was a wide spectrum between Sufis and ISIS, with countless denominations in between. But I didn't know about the differences between Christian groups. As I happened to be with Matt at that moment, I handed the phone to him as I asked, "What denomination are you?" He said, "Evangelical Christian, Southern Baptist." I asked Avi if he had heard of that, and he certainly had. I wished I would have known better. But this is how, when the piece came out, people would discover I was in San Diego and that everybody who wanted to reach me could do so through Matt's church.

I felt I needed to explain to the church community the consequences of my decision. I was also looking for their understanding and support, thinking they would welcome my public announcement of seeing Jesus as my companion. I met with a core group. Matt's parents were there along with many from the community I had gotten to know fairly well. Even though they had known me now for a few months and I had known them, we still were coming from two different planets, two different realities.

Their reality had been shaped by Islamophobia and the war on terrorism and their default emotion: fear. When I explained that the consequence for a Muslim rejecting Islam in favor of Christianity was a death sentence, this triggered their fear that my presence in their midst could lead to others being killed. Added to this fear was the fact that Homeland Security had decided I should be deported. They trusted these authorities. As they say, I was losing my audience.

I saw doubt and disbelief on their faces. Would the FBI come down on them for harboring a terrorist in their church? Perhaps my anxiety was infecting them, as negative energy permeated the room. I couldn't appeal to them that their faith obligated them to help me. It was evident they didn't want to take the risk. This was not a group I could count on for support. I was personally hurt and disappointed. I'm not saying all turned their backs on me; some kept their relationship with me, calling me and texting me. But in general, there was a crack in the relationship.

So Minh, my boss at work, who was in the meeting, heard all of this, and he talked with other people. He had to ask himself how long it would take the government to realize that he'd illegally hired a "terrorist" who was being deported. Minh felt he had to let me go. I understood and didn't take it personally, but it did mean I was out of a job as well as my primary source of income.

The church was having a Fourth of July barbecue at Matt's parents' home on Coronado Island in that soft, white world bleached of the hard truths lived by many not so far away. Despite my recent disappointing meeting with the core church group, we still had our invitations for the party. Melanie, Daniel, and I arrived at a party already rocking in the holiday spirit of American Independence Day: music, firecrackers, children racing about, the aroma of meat cooking on the barbecue. Here we were under the hot Southern California sun, but soon to be met with a chill. Melanie and Daniel were lying on towels on the grass lawn when Matt's mom came and took the towels away. Bizarre. One aspect of the life of Jesus that I admired was that he hung out with the outcasts of society. It was clear our host considered us outcasts and did not want us there. We left early, before the annual fireworks display over Glorietta Bay.

After this treatment, I could not continue attending the church. I told Matt that his parents acted as hosts of the church, standing at the door Sunday morning. "How can I come? I know they're scared of the situation I'm creating." His parents wanted to protect their son and his business—his church. I proposed that I take a break for a time from the church. Matt jumped on that, as it gave him a nice way out. He framed it as my being concerned about my own personal security, and it made sense for me to decide to withdraw. In reality, he did have justifiable concerns about his church's security.

As the wheel of fortune spun to the negative side, Daniel's father called him. He declared that Daniel would no longer be subsidized in San Diego and cut him off financially. Daniel had to return to Ventura. Part of this could be attributed to me. Daniel had apparently told his father about some of my exploits. Bob's view was that my people committed acts of barbarism. I was well accustomed to *terrorist*, but *barbarian* was a new one. Earlier, Daniel's grandmother, Laura, had asked Daniel to write up a legal document that would give Daniel two of her houses. Daniel asked me what he should do, since he wasn't feeling comfortable about it. In my "wisdom," I urged him to accept the offer. "Come on; your grandmother wants to help you." The last thing Bob's wife wanted was to have two houses go to Daniel.

Bob owned eight houses already and had his eye on his mother's other houses. The wheel of fortune would now spin in Bob's favor as a result of a freak accident. Daniel was visiting Laura, and as he was coming back from shopping, he opened the door just as Laura was heading out. Her cane got caught in the door, and she fell, breaking her hip. Bob said he didn't believe the story. He believed that Daniel had beaten up his grandmother. Laura confirmed that it was an accident, but Bob believed she was lying to cover for her grandson. Bob called in the police, and they bought Bob's version. Daniel was thrown in jail, charged with elder abuse, and forbidden from seeing his grandmother. Daniel was crushed.

I spoke to Bob, who said his mother had $500,000 in a bank account that had somehow all but vanished. "Daniel was stealing from my mother, his own grandmother. And you've been stealing from my mother."

"Hold on right there, Bob. I have never taken a penny from your mother. The most I received was a good meal and a night's stay. She's one of the finest people I've met in this country, and I never took advantage of her generosity." Father-son relations are not always easy, but here was real hatred.

Bob's next move was to have his mother warehoused in a "retirement home" outside of Los Angeles. When we finally found out where she was, Daniel and I went to visit her. She was there in a wheelchair, completely drugged. She didn't recognize us. This was to be the last time we ever saw her. Bob put us on a blacklist, forbidding us to see her, and so the next time we came, we were turned away. In terms of that popular American capitalist game Monopoly, Bob now owned twelve houses on the board while Daniel waited for a Get Out of Jail Free card.

Here was this handsome young man with a nice apartment in a great city enrolled in a good college, supported by a loving grandmother. Five years later, he would be homeless, living on the streets of Ventura, California, with stops in jails and mental institutions a part of his downward spiral. Yes, the good-hearted Daniel was a drug addict. Despite his advantages, he was trying to escape his father. It was meth that was to ravage his body and destroy his mind. And it broke my heart as I tried to do what I could to help, but drug addiction, as we all know, is too often well beyond the abilities even of those who care deeply about the addict. But I'm getting ahead of the story here.

With Daniel returning to Ventura, no one in the church was clamoring to put me up. The only person who would let me in was Melanie. She had just been in a fight with her ex-soldier husband. Her blood was all over the small studio. The place was a complete mess: dirty clothes everywhere, bed unmade, dirty dishes. A visual picture of chaos. When I arrived, she was so beaten up and drained, she hadn't had the power to even attempt to clean up. Why this brutal beating? He was trying to force her into prostitution, and she had refused. He went berserk. He wanted her to hit the streets so he wouldn't have to work and so her body could support his drug habit. Here was this gorgeous woman who had worked as a model, now sitting bloodied and bruised. This was the lower depths of America: drug addiction, prostitution, soldiers traumatized by war, domestic violence against women.

I was back to sleeping on the carpet, this time a bloodied one, which somehow was an apt metaphor for this phase of my journey. As I lay on my back, staring at the ceiling, my mind had one thought: *Nothing will stop me. I am going to publish this story. There is nothing to be ashamed about. I am not going to feel guilty.* The only thing that I worried about was my family. I loved my family, and I came from a culture that placed family and their reputation above any individual freedom. *But you know what?* my interior dialogue was saying, *I cannot lose myself for the sake of my family. I have to move on. I have to tell them the truth, and I have to be truthful about who I am. I don't want to be wearing the mask anymore.* I knew I was alone. I couldn't count on Matt and his people. I was going public, no matter the consequences.

Now it was just a matter of waiting for the *Haaretz* article to see the light of day. Daniel, bless his soul, visited from Ventura, and he bought me a sleeping bag and gave me some cash to tide me over. The length of "over" remained to be seen, but I knew what I had to do.

PART III

10

Media Frenzy

The article came out, and even though it did not disclose my work with Shin Bet, it had immediate consequences. It affected everyone with whom my life intersected: my father, my family, members of the church, Matt's parents, the FBI, the media, Christian communities. It was a bombshell in the Middle East. If I'd just been one more anonymous Arab or even a Palestinian terrorist, it wouldn't have caused a ripple. But here was the eldest son of not only a leading Muslim religious leader but one of the founders of Hamas and a leading politician well known on TV, so it caused a tsunami. The story was picked up all over the world, the basic line embodied in the lead from the UK newspaper *The Telegraph:* "The son of one of the most revered leaders of the Palestinian Islamist group Hamas has renounced his religion to move to America and become an evangelical Christian."[5] Well, sort of.

My main concern was how my family would take it. A few months after arriving in the States, I had spoken directly to my father, telling him of my study of the life of Jesus and his appeal compared to dogmatic Islam. He took it as a heavy blow. Now I tried to call him to warn him that it was going to go public in *Haaretz*, but he was in solitary and couldn't be reached. Even my family couldn't reach him.

I had stayed in a relationship with my family. They thought I had some "situation" that was forcing me to say what I did. They were supportive and encouraged me to come back home. My mother spoke to me as though nothing had happened, but I learned later she was crying all day. I think this was their tactic rather than losing me forever. Of course, they didn't know the other half of my story, which, as a result of the article, was now being discussed as a book.

The heartbreaking part was that I knew all along I had lost my family, as I was never going to go back, and they were in a big prison, unable to ever leave to come and see me. At this point, they did not disown me. It was my sister Tasneem who distinguished herself by being the first family member to claim that honor, no doubt with the good doctor's assistance. I received a brief email from her: "If you don't come back to Islam, you're not my brother and I don't know you."

For the church members, and for Matt and his parents, this meant an abrupt change from what had been a mini-excommunication. I came under the spotlight in this small world, as all of a sudden there were cameras everywhere and national media. The church faithful were excited—it beat graffiti expeditions. A few weeks before this, they had worried that the FBI was going to come and shut down their church for harboring a terrorist. Then the FBI did show up, but they didn't arrest me or kill me. They said they had no charges against me, that I was already applying for asylum, and that they had never heard of me until they saw the story on the news. They were at the church to advise on security—mine and the church's. Everybody started to calm down. For Matt, this was so cool. And the media was hot on the story, a story even bigger than Matt had ever thought, and his church was the hub of this breaking story. Matt approached me and said he had been doing some heavy praying and the result was, he thought I should come back to his church.

It was evident that one of the benefits of going public was being provided with public protection, though perhaps the more immediate benefit was that Matt's parents now offered to let me stay on their boat—the cleansing salt air was a definite step up from the bloodied carpet. Two weeks later a very generous and supportive member of the church, Denise Holmberg, offered to let me stay at a house of hers in La Mesa. She was living in Chicago, and her brother and her son were living in the La Mesa house. I stayed there for two months.

AL HAYAT AND FOX NEWS

The church phones were ringing with calls from TV stations, newspapers, literary agents, and organizations offering me speaking engagements. The two television outlets that would be the most significant for me as I moved forward would be Al Hayat Ministries (Middle Eastern Christian broadcasting) and FOX News. I gave my first interview in Arabic to Al Hayat, which beams to all the Middle East. I used to watch their broadcasts on satellite TV back in Ramallah. They were critical of Islam but raised important questions, making us think. Since satellite TV couldn't be blocked back then, anybody who wanted to could watch, and many had been influenced by it. Of course, they were promoting their beliefs, but they did deal with profound questions of life and faith. They had been one source making me question my inherited belief system, though I had no idea that this station was coming from up the freeway in Orange County at a secret broadcast studio. Everyone assumed it was beamed from Cyprus. Since the original article in *Haaretz* was in Hebrew, many assumed it was Israeli propaganda. But when people heard my voice in Arabic on the Christian Al Hayat, it went viral.

The founder and CEO of Al Hayat, Harun Ibrahim, came down to San Diego to interview me. Quickly we discovered we had much in common. He was a Palestinian and we came from villages that were only five minutes apart. He was brought up a Muslim, though his family was certainly more secular than ours. He converted to Christianity and the family disowned him; his brother swore that he would kill him for such dishonor. It was time for Harun to get out of Dodge.

When it came time to get out, an accident of history made our stories wholly different. After the 1967 war, the border between Israel and the territories was drawn right between our two villages. His village, Abu Ghosh, became part of Israel, so the family became citizens of Israel, which meant he had an Israeli passport and could travel. My village was designated outside of Israel in the West Bank. He made it to Europe and went to Finland, married a Finnish woman, and became a Finnish citizen. He got a green card for the United States through a lottery. Good luck would follow Harun.

Meeting him and feeling that immediate connection, it was clear this was an exceptional human being. He spoke seven languages fluently; he was a poet and a talented musician. He had a wonderful family. He was also very funny. Harun founded Al Hayat, and it grew to be a significant Christian voice in the Middle East and to the Arabic-speaking audience in the diaspora. No small accomplishment for a village boy. I was grateful this was the first voice I heard that brought a bit of fresh air in the fetid atmosphere. Over the next year, I would broadcast over this channel several times.

Back in Ramallah, I'd had extensive experience with the media. As a spokesperson for my father, I had a good sense of how the system worked and the biases of the players on the field. As far as American media in the US were concerned, I was a babe in the woods in their heavily politicized game. Once again, I would have labels slapped on me which weren't me at all. Still, the label *evangelical Christian* would provide me some protection from predators in the media and in government.

My association with the conservative FOX News began when they heard about me from the *Haaretz* article. Their first take was that this could be a news item with which to poke President Barack Obama in the eye. Here was the son of a top Hamas terrorist, living the high life in Southern California, having a good ol' time surfing and partying. How the hell did he ever get into our country? Never mind that I entered the country under the Bush administration; according to Fox, I showed that Obama was asleep at the wheel. One more chance for FOX to nail the "Muslim" president.

So a crew appeared, led by the British journalist Jonathan Hunt. After a few days of trying to film me surfing, which I was terrible at (I don't think they ever managed to get a shot of me standing up on the board), I realized what story they were seeking to tell. I took Jonathan aside and opened my heart: I told him this was life or death for me, not a lark. He listened and said he, too, was a Christian and that the evangelical Christian angle was a lot more interesting than the son of a Hamas terrorist riding the waves in sunny San Diego. *This courageous convert is supported by his church, which is connected to the Southern Baptist Church, and he's willing to criticize Islam and Hamas from the inside.*

He thought this could be gold for FOX. Southern Baptists are an important segment of their viewership, and a critical and fearful view of Islam resonates big-time with their audience. I had certainly learned that everyone and every organization has its own agenda. And I knew their agenda, though here they were offering a priceless platform for me to express myself. Under the dark shadow of deportation, with the stakes literally life and death, this was an unexpected blessing. Our separate agendas, with a dose of compromise, had sufficient overlap to serve both of us.

So FOX pivoted to the storyline of the terrorist who finds Jesus, becomes a Christian, and renounces Islam and Islamic-generated terrorism. Consequently, what was to be a single news item was now planned to become a forty-five-minute special. This meant doing numerous interviews with me over the months of production, and, yes, they had a shot of me in a wet suit carrying a surfboard. I knew enough about the media to know that it's not you telling your story; instead, they've decided what your story should be. For some reason, I never sensed I was being set up. I had my say in the interviews, and they were edited fairly. I never mentioned the ten years of intelligence I did. That would be for later. And that would prove to be a bigger story, for which I would pay a bigger price.

The result of that months-long investigation was *Escape from Hamas*, which was described as

A FOX News Special Report on Mosab Hassan Yousef, the son of Hamas founder Sheikh Hassan Yousef, and his decision to abandon his Muslim faith, denounce his father's organization, move to America and become a Christian. How a chance meeting with a Christian tourist was to change his life forever. Now, despite an Al Qaeda death sentence hanging over him, he speaks out for the first time about Hamas, an organization he says betrays the Palestinian cause, tortures its own members and will never honor any ceasefire with Israel."[6]

It aired on January 3, 2009, just at the time of intense fighting over Gaza between the Israelis and Hamas. This presented an opportunity to peg the special as providing an inside look to explain the endless enmity between Palestinians and Israelis. The show would prove of great benefit to me, enlisting high-profile Christian support when the battle over deportation became its most intense.

In our extensive interviews, the journalist pushed me on whether I had "blood on my hands" and whether or not my conversion to

Christianity was sincere or just a commonly used ruse to obtain asylum. The journalist visited Jerusalem, Ramallah, and Megiddo Prison and interviewed a bearded imam who said that I was "100 percent lying," especially about torture and murder by Hamas in prison. Also interviewed was an expert who gave credence to my assertions. And he interviewed Avi, the *Haaretz* journalist who had broken the story of my Christian connection.

THE BIRTH OF A BOOK

The idea of publishing a book that could produce income was completely foreign to me. Matt was impressed with my stories and asked what I was planning to do with them, as it was a heavy responsibility. I knew that if I didn't record my experiences in some fashion, that piece of history would be buried with me. Encouraged by Matt, I began to write down bullet points with the help of a young woman in the church. My English at this point was not what it would become.

The idea of writing a book evolved through several steps. The first notion Matt and I discussed was that he would write the book and take 50 percent of any royalties. Matt's perspective, of course, was a Christian one, and to move the project forward, he contacted literary agents from the Christian world. The agents came, and they were blown away by my story and its potential. They thought the story could have a broader market than just Christians. But before they could pitch it, and sworn to secrecy about the project, they had to have a signed contract that we were hiring them to represent us.

Sitting down with the contract was entering another minefield for me, where one false move could mean that in my ignorance I'd be taken advantage of. I didn't have the wherewithal to hire an experienced attorney to review the contract. I was basically homeless, depending on friends. I had never signed a contract with anyone before. It was written in a technical legal language I didn't understand, with some terms that even the agents couldn't clearly explain. Whenever I saw something that looked suspicious, I noted it down. For example, I marked parts giving rights to TV series, documentaries, and a movie based on the book and giving rights to any future book based on my life that I might write. My basic position was only to give them the right to find a publisher for this one book. *Done.* I didn't want to be enslaved to anyone.

There remained, however, the original idea of Matt and I writing the book together. It was soon evident that this formula was not realistic. I'd known Matt for only a few months and had seen firsthand how busy he was. I understood from the agents that it was common for a publisher to hire a professional writer. For my story, that writer should be very knowledgeable about the Middle East, terrorism, Islam, and the Israel-Palestine conflict. I did not want Matt to feel betrayed, and so I offered to write him a check for his introduction to these agents.

I signed with the agency for only that book. They sent our proposal and reportedly were turned down by more than forty publishers, even though it was known that FOX TV was interested. However, a Christian publisher out of Chicago was interested and ready to commit. While a Christian publishing house was not my preference, this was the opportunity at hand to have my story told. The publisher came out to California, and we hammered out a deal that seemed fair to me. I signed a book contract with an advance on royalties that allowed me to clear my debts and rent a studio apartment in San Diego. I finally had my own bed, off the floor, and change jingling in my pocket.

Now I could get to work with the writer of the book. Ron Brackin was an investigative journalist with broad experience in the Middle East. He had been in Ramallah and Jerusalem during the Second Intifada. I was warned there would be a lot of work involved, and indeed, it proved to be true.

WORKING WITH THE FBI

One of my boyhood heroes was the great martial artist Bruce Lee. My friends and I would flock to wherever we could see one of The Dragon's films. There he was, alone in the middle of a circle of ugly thugs. There was always that moment of tension when the audience was anticipating who would make the first move, until the action on the screen changed to a dazzling flurry of kicks, blows, leaps as we cheered the outnumbered underdog. I could relate to that. I felt surrounded by my adversaries poised to strike: Shin Bet, Homeland Security, the FBI, the evangelicals, Hamas, the liberal media, the racists. Despite now having some financial security, emotionally I felt under constant tension, not knowing from which direction the next blow would come. I did not have The Dragon's prowess to block the blows and counterattack effectively.

Next up to make their move would be the vaunted Federal Bureau of Investigation. Like all the other adversaries surrounding me, they wanted to exploit me for whatever value they could extract to meet their immediate needs. The FBI saw me as a potential asset in a long-standing criminal case they had against a Muslim charitable organization, the Holy Land Foundation (HLF).

I first directly encountered the FBI in San Diego at the time the *Haaretz* article appeared. An agent named Mike showed up at Matt's church to deal with the real security concerns in this fraught climate of paranoia and potential terrorism. I spent some time with Mike and later with another agent, Sonny. They had not heard anything from Homeland Security or anything about my status as deportee on the grounds of aiding terrorism. The two agencies are, like toddlers, loathe to share their treasures. I had already told Daniel and Matt some of my Shin Bet exploits, and so I told some to the agents so they'd know where I was coming from. Quite understandably, Mike didn't believe me.

"Even if only half of what you're saying is true, how in the world would Shin Bet ever have let you out of the region?"

"Good question."

"How can you prove it?"

"Ask Shin Bet. They're your brothers-in-arms."

"We did."

"What did they say?"

"All they said was, 'He is the son of a Hamas leader.'"

"That's all?"

"That's all."

It was very hard for them to understand. So I gave them details about an operation involving a cell out of Hebrew University that had killed a handful of Americans. I had brought those guys to justice. It was Ibrahim Hamid, Salih Talahmeh, Abdullah al Barghouti, and a bunch of other terrorists. The US government hadn't asked me to go after those people, and I hadn't cared if the victims were Americans or not. This is what I was doing. How could I be a terrorist threat? I'd met with them several times and given them a better understanding of Hamas, its structures, and its leaders. Whether I was credible to them, I don't know, but it must have been clear I knew a lot about Hamas from firsthand knowledge.

The year before, the US government had suffered a humiliating defeat in their case against the Holy Land Foundation in a federal trial in Dallas against five defendants, with a partial acquittal and a hung jury on all other charges. The Holy Land Foundation was the largest Islamic charity in the United States, founded in 1989 and run by Palestinian Americans with offices and representatives scattered throughout the US. The organization's stated mission was to "find and implement practical solutions for human suffering through humanitarian programs that impact the lives of the disadvantaged, disinherited, and displaced peoples suffering from man-made and natural disasters."[7]

Sounds good, right? But the fact was, HLF was a fundraising conduit for Hamas, and the monies went through their local charities, or *zakats,* in the territories to fund the whole spectrum of Hamas activities, from genuine charity to terrorist operations. It was only after September 11 that the Bush administration really woke up. In December 2001, the US government designated it a terrorist organization, seized its assets, and closed down Hamas's Holy Land Foundation. This then began the long process through the courts with a grand jury and then the first failed trial in 2007.

It was considered a hard case to win, especially as the accused were American citizens. In the United States, it is easy to open a nonprofit organization, whether as a Christian funding end-time zealots striving to ignite the terror of Armageddon or as a Muslim funding Islamic fanatics engaged in terrorism. The American Constitution protects their ostensibly charitable missions—up to a point. It would take the US government nearly twenty years to sentence the Holy Land Foundation defendants in American courts. (In Israel, "the only democracy in the Middle East," one secret report from an informant would have locked up the five for eternity.)

The amount of money HLF raised for Hamas was staggering. According to the US Department of the Treasury, HLF raised $13 million from 1995 until 2000.[8] But that was a joke; there were tens of millions more. The $13 million were funds directly wired to legitimate charity work, medical clinics, hospitals, doctors, schools, etc. But only a small portion was done by open bank transfer. How, then, was the money transferred? Cash carried in suitcases. A courier would take it from the US to the territories through the Ben Gurion Airport, the Queen Alia International Airport, or the Allenby Bridge. It was almost impossible to detect because the money was carried by American citizens. I met one of these transporters, Mohammed Saleh, in prison. He was caught with hundreds of thousands of dollars in cash in his suitcase. He was working for the Holy Land Foundation regularly delivering to Hamas. When an astonished customs agent opened his bag, he said he was bringing it for charity. "Why, then, are you smuggling it?" That was the first time the Israeli government and the Americans made the connection between the Holy Land Foundation and funding Hamas in cash. He was caught back in 1991, which shows how long it took to shut down this cash cow for Hamas.

The US government was under pressure, as a trial was imminent, which meant they were under a deadline. I was starting to look like the perfect witness, as I had direct personal experience about where and to whom the money was going and for what purposes. In the first failed trial, they did not have such an eyewitness, which could have helped convinced the jury. I was willing to be a witness, as this unholy foundation was responsible for untold misery and death. I found it despicable that Americans were being conned into contributing money for widows, orphans, and the homeless, or "the disadvantaged, disinherited, and displaced," thinking they were easing the suffering of an oppressed population when it was really going to an organization financing suffering.

The FBI approached me, asking me to help them with this court case. *Hold on*, I thought. *They're telling me that the might of the FBI, CIA, and Israeli intelligence is not enough to condemn five guilty individuals for funding terrorism? They need me?*

I'd been in America long enough to know that if you ever have dealings with the government, you better lawyer up. So I did. The truth was, I was alone. The only one in my corner would be my immigration attorney, Steve Seick, from San Diego. I was flown to Dallas on the government's dime. We met. They wanted me as an eyewitness to provide the final piece to solve the Holy Land Foundation puzzle. On the other hand, the same government was threatening me with deportation.

I asked them why I should do this. Outside the door were two thousand angry protestors. If I, the traitor, helped them win the case, the crowd would become my enemies.

"If I testify, will you give me American citizenship?"

"That is something to discuss."

"Let me talk to my attorney."

I went outside and called my lawyer. What did "something to discuss" mean? It turns out, nothing. He said, "Ask them about a witness protection program. They do that in a case where you feel there is a real danger to yourself. However, I don't think you're going to like it. You can be set up anywhere, but it could be shittier than what you had with your family and what you have now."

Kerri Calcador, a Homeland Security attorney, had earlier set me straight when she said, "We can give you any other program, but you can never become an American citizen. You were affiliated with a terrorist organization, and thus American law bars you from becoming an American citizen. We will fight you for twenty-five years in the courts, for eternity, even if we believe you. Nobody is above the law in this country."

"What about an exception based on the fact that I spent ten years in anti-terrorism?"

"No exceptions. You'll be wasting your time and our time."

"What about a special bill out of Congress?"

Later I did later pursue this in the halls of Congress, briefing members of Congress, committees, Congressional staffers, and the media on critical issues like the structure of terrorist organizations and how to best combat them. But that did not result in a special bill granting me citizenship.

When I came back from talking to my attorney, I reported that he had suggested asking about a witness protection program.

"Yes, we can give you a program where you can live and work in the country, but you can't become a citizen."

"How can I travel, then?"

"You can't leave the country, but it is a big country."

That would mean I'd be a prisoner in the US for the rest of my life. I'd had that experience once before and was lucky to escape. I went back out and phoned the lawyer and told them what they were proposing. I said there was no way I could accept it. "What do I do now?"

"Ask them whatever they wanted to pay you for that program that they give it to you up front, and then you can manage on your own so you can create your own life."

"What are we talking here?"

"A million, two, five million—whatever the government's budget will give you."

Okay, now we were talking business. For the first time I was getting advice from the American mindset. Money. Money talks.

I went back into the meeting and told them, "If you want me as an expert on the case, I have a proposal. I will give you the information for free. I've already given you enough. But I'll give you the names, all those people I knew in prison, how the money was going to finance terrorist operations, how all the money was only going to Hamas, not the Palestinian people—"

They interrupted me. "We know all this information. We have the intelligence. If we say it, it won't make a difference. Only you as an eyewitness testifying to this before the judge and jury in an American court will nail the case."

"Great, but let's not forget that my deportation is pending."

My state of mind and my morale were really at rock bottom. I was just so tired of this bullshit. I wanted $5 million and citizenship.

"Okay, what about I pass on the witness program, but you give me the money in the budget for what the government would be paying for that program, and I'll make it on my own?"

Our blonde FBI agent then basically said, "How about we make you testify?"

They knew that was a dead end with me. I was willing to testify, but there had to be a decent quid pro quo. I was trying hard to find a middle ground, but apparently there was none. The FBI could make promises; they offered to write me a letter of recommendation. Bottom line: I was a willing witness, but I wanted citizenship in return. However, there simply was no way around US terrorism law. If I testified, our blonde agent would be enjoying her new promotion and I'd be back on the street with a target on my back, fucked six ways to Sunday.

So it all fell apart, and it was goodbye Dallas, as they put me on an economy flight back to California. No resolution. I never heard from them again.

The trial went on without me, and the government obtained guilty verdicts on all counts against the Holy Land Foundation and the five individual defendants in the retrial. They each got between fifteen to sixty-five years. The HLF was found guilty of giving Hamas, a terrorist organization, more than $12 million. I was glad they won their case but even happier that I did not have to testify and end up back in the streets with nothing to show for it.

11

Talking to America

Just as I had no idea you could make money publishing a book, I had no idea you could be paid for public speaking. After the *Haaretz* article appeared, offers for me to talk at churches began to come in. To my surprise, my public speaking and the book were in effect trading my painful experience for a livable income. Though I had the deportation sword of Damocles still hanging over my head, the prospects in this refugee's life were looking up.

Matt, who was a strong speaker with a touch of charisma, sought speaking engagements as he was building his business. He jumped at every opportunity. The offers for me to speak came into the church, and Matt took some of those for himself without telling me. However, when the Christian agents for the book came into the picture, my literary agent, Wes Yoder, handled my speaking engagements directly. For me, this was a great opportunity to speak to a closed-minded group of people about a higher understanding. I was not shy about asking for a decent speaking fee, and, yes, I did get paid a lot of money. America prides itself on being a capitalist market economy ruled by supply and demand, and there was a high demand to hear me speak. Requests to speak came from churches, organizations, and a few synagogues that were interested in terrorism and the Middle East from my unique perspective.

Speaking to audiences was not a new experience for me, and, happily, I don't experience stage fright, which seems to afflict many. When I was fifteen, I would speak in the mosque before a couple of hundred worshippers. I had two great mentors, my father and my uncle. Both were charismatic, well-spoken individuals who built their careers on their ability to use the right language to move a crowd. Muslims would come from far away just to hear my father speak. Whether speaking to a small group in the mosque or fifty thousand in the public square, he always held his audience captive. When he was out public speaking and not in prison, I was with him, absorbing all his paternal oratorical skills.

Out of the hundreds of talks I have given, the most challenging was one I gave at my school in the West Bank when I was a teen. This was at a time when Yasir Arafat had just returned from exile and rival armed factions were fighting to control the Palestinian streets. The violence reached the schools. Followers of Hamas were a minority group at my school and were bullied by the bigger factions. They didn't allow us to publish any material or express any opinion. When we did, they beat us up. I was fed up with the situation and pleaded with my father to intervene, but he wouldn't. The Fatah students were young but brutal; they had knives, axes, and guns. And they had the police and the militia on their side. I couldn't accept being silenced by a student gang, nor a rival political party in power. The only weapon I had was my voice. One morning, in a loud, unruly classroom where it was impossible to make oneself heard, I leaped up on a desk and made my voice louder than the bullshit of the crowd. Suddenly, the room went silent—not because of what I said but because everyone in that room knew that it took guts to jump up on a desk and express yourself freely without a gun. Somehow I held that entire room captive for fifteen minutes with my voice. I still don't know how I managed to put my words together to convey an appropriate and effective message.

Yet here in America, speaking very imperfect English, the challenge was to find the correct pronunciation, and not confuse *hummus* with *Hamas*, especially before an audience! I was about to become a Christian celebrity for a brief time. I had one great advantage as a public speaker: I was speaking directly from my personal experience and only that. I did not need to research secondhand sources. I was not citing scripture or promoting a particular denomination or cult. My message was nonreligious, and I would be criticized for not sprinkling my talks with biblical verses. Throughout my journey, through the lows and the highs, my steadfast effort was to stay in my truth.

At the beginning, I would sometimes write down a few points to open the speech and a few to end it, but pretty quickly I started getting up on the stage without any notes. I think this always conveys authenticity. A read-aloud speech can lack a sense of spontaneity. Speaking directly to the audience but focusing on individuals gives you a sense of the audience, and you're able to respond in the moment. Also, humor is essential, and being in the moment can help you produce a spontaneous joke.

IS HE TELLING THE TRUTH?

To this very day, my credibility has always been questioned. Was I telling the truth? This has been a leitmotif of my journey. Back on the West Bank, it became a matter of life and death that varied hostile factions believed me. Landing in America gave me the chance to begin with a clean slate. No lies. With the threat of deportation always hanging over me, I was tempted to lie to the authorities who held my fate in their hands, but I still stuck to the truth.

In my first meeting with Homeland Security, I told the truth. When the *Haaretz* article appeared, the media questioned my truthfulness. And on the speaking circuit, there would be doubts. *Is he pretending to be a Christian in order to get asylum? If he's telling the truth, why hasn't he been killed?* This last one, which became more prevalent after my book was published, put me in the position that the only proof of my veracity was my demise. I wasn't anxious to satisfy that standard of proof. All I could do was to stay in my truth. The truth will set you free. And ultimately it did. But again, I'm getting ahead of myself.

It's always challenging having a group in front of you; they come with expectations. The Young Presidents' Organization expected something different than a Christian audience did, and even an evangelical Christian audience in California was a different experience from a megachurch in the Bible Belt. I enjoyed the opportunity to travel through this great land: New York, Minnesota, Michigan, Texas, Arizona, Oklahoma, Tennessee, Colorado.

The Christian audiences saw me as a terrorist who had seen the light and found Jesus. *I was a bad person, and now I'm a good person. Hallelujah.* They celebrated the fact that someone was coming from the other camp to criticize it, challenge it, and say the things they were afraid to say. I was publicly criticizing Islam and Islamic dogma and saying that I would like to see Islam emerge out of the seventh century into the twenty-first. I also explained why I definitely preferred the Christian religion in a constitutional democracy rather than Islam in a theocracy. I was labeled by liberals as an Islamophobe and a right-wing, evangelical Zionist. I told them that if they were to grow up in Gaza, they could well become Hamas members, terrorists. We are all human beings who are subject to the conditioning of our upbringings. My early speeches to churches were 99 percent "Love your enemy." The last thing I wanted to do was encourage hatred and fear or create a state of panic. Quite the opposite.

I explained to people that Muslims are wonderful people just like them. Yet when I looked out into the eyes of the worshippers as I spoke, I saw anger, hatred, and fear. My anger was a response to the ugly reality I had lived; it was not based on racism, self-righteousness, or a sense of superiority. Most of my audiences were not willing to listen to the other side I was trying to represent; they wanted me to be a religious propagandist for them. In the beginning, I was naive. They were expecting me to confirm the fundamentalist message of Christianity being the one inerrant truth and Islam being Satan's religion.

This only motivated me more. I was always on the offense, challenging their assumptions, getting them out of their comfort zones rather than telling them what they wanted to hear. Every once in a while, I gave them what they wanted to hear, which they loved, and then, *boom*, right after that I hit them with something that made them think in an unaccustomed way. I tried to be spontaneous, in that moment, speaking free from fear.

It turned out that the pastors did not always feel comfortable with my approach. I think it's fair to say that priests and teachers of the law in all religions have twisted and bent scripture to give them the authority to do what they want to do. For better or worse, I'm not judging them; that's how it is. However, from my perspective, what they value often has little to do with the one who was crucified.

These leaders are building empires using his name. And the larger their empire becomes, the more they are caught in the trap of having to raise money to feed the beast. That is why they're not pleased when a speaker comes along and contradicts their ideas about Christ. From the beginning, Christ did not meet the expectations of those awaiting the messiah. While tension with religious leaders was awkward as times, in general the reaction of the parishioners was very positive. A few times I would feel someone behind me putting their hand on my head or placing their hands on my forehead and asking if I minded if they prayed for me. I wasn't going to push them away.

UNWELCOME PROPHECY

The gap between Christian ideology and my message grew too wide to be sustained. Nowhere was the chasm wider than over the fate of the inhabitants of the Middle East, the fate of Palestinians and Israelis. Here, after all, we're talking about my people, the land I was born in, went through hell in. That experience was not an illusion; it was only too real.

But sitting half a world away in the pews of megachurches, I saw a deep longing for the fulfillment of biblical prophecies around the Second Coming of Christ, when Israel becomes Eretz Israel, or "Greater Israel." Christian Zionists encouraged putting the chosen people in the middle of Arab states as a step in fulfilling the prophecy. There have been over seventy years of war and Israel's territorial expansion toward Eretz Israel. Once Greater Israel is restored, they believe Jesus will return. The Christ of Love and the Prince of Peace himself will lead a heavenly army in the battle of Armageddon, the final battle between good and evil. Christ will head the victory over enemies who oppose God's authority and who treat God with contempt. This would not be simply in the Valley of Megiddo, referred to in Revelations, but would encompass the whole earth. Given today's realities and the fact that all but this category of believers are said to die at this future time, we're talking nuclear war. The next step is the rapture, where the true believers will escape by being lifted off their couches into heaven. Ironically, the Israelis, who have nurtured these evangelical Zionists for their powerful financial and political support, will all be incinerated in the lake of fire.

Now, I consider all of this total human delusion. But when such a delusion becomes political policy by a powerful government, it can result in the end of our species, or at least leave the meek little to inherit of the earth. The notion of a nuclear Armageddon held by these believers is beyond our imagination, and really beyond theirs, or else they would draw on the biblical Jesus Christ who preached, "Forgive your enemy and practice love." That is certainly the message I convey when they allow me to speak. However, questioning their scenario of the end of times does not go down well with those looking forward to those divine accommodations.

Mainly as a result of the FOX television broadcast, money began pouring in for me. America is the most generous country in the world. It's part of the American spirit, people sharing out of their grace and gratitude toward life. It went from simple donations to people writing checks for thousands of dollars. If I accepted their money, I would have to meet their expectations. I didn't want to be that person. So I had to reject the donations and put them into the offering plate of the church. The church takes money from the public and meets that public's expectations. I wanted to get out of the Christian community and not be responsible in any way to it. I only took money if I performed some type of work.

Plunging into the unknown where there were no security and no possessions was part of my journey. The moment you get possessions and money and security, that is your imprisonment. You become a slave to those things. You have to manage them. You have to maintain them, take responsibility for them. It takes away your freedom and your ability to perform fearlessly.

Work on the book continued apace. I traveled to Texas to meet with the writer, Ron Brackin. For a week I told him my story, and he recorded it. Then he went to work setting it down on paper. He would send me a draft. I would give my comments, and we would go back and forth over the year, draft after draft. The creative process still seemed rather miraculous to me.

A NEAR-DEATH EXPERIENCE

During the year of book writing and traveling to speak, now and then I would drop by Matt's church, staying somewhat connected. My life was hardly all work and no play, especially once I had my studio apartment. I was dating Maggie, a beautiful blonde model from Colorado. We smoked pot together. One evening she suggested doing LSD. That was tempting; why not? I took a dose, and nothing happened. I asked for another. Maggie questioned whether that was a good idea. But I was confident. I took the second dose just as the first one kicked in. I suffered horrific flashbacks. I struggled to gain some control. I was freaking out. My apartment was on the fourth floor with a balcony. I went out on the balcony, poised to jump, my hands on the railing. I didn't, but the margin between jumping and not jumping was razor-thin. I was really frightened. At four in the morning in my panic, I called Pastor Matt.

Mistake.

The good pastor didn't use it against me until a few weeks later. In my panic, I did confide in him. *Confide* is the right word; just as what is said between a lawyer and a client, or a patient and a therapist, is privileged, confidential, so it should be between a parishioner and a pastor. He began by telling this, my private business, to others of his more zealous flock, saying that he feared I was suicidal: "We have to pray for Mosab, text him our support." I was mightily pissed off. This was not support; this was judgment, violating a confidence and harassing me with concern through an avalanche of texts. I didn't respond. He then showed up downstairs with a group of eight of his zealous cohort. I let him have it. They were not respecting my space; they didn't understand the hell I was going through. I told him good-bye and that I wasn't going to their church anymore. I was really angry. Matt was also very angry. He told me God was not going to use me anymore. *Okay.*

A gentleman who was the head of the Southern California Evangelical Baptists later appeared, I suppose as a kind of intervention for the wayward. He was a very sweet guy and a man of sincere faith. But I was on my own journey, and Matt's church had been only one stop. However, this was not the end. Matt indicated in a text to me that he was going to warn people that I was a junkie. *Good grief.* Back when we had been having long, friendly conversations, he'd confided in me about something only too human that he was doing that he was having trouble controlling. If it became known, that something could put him at risk of losing his church. I didn't respond to him. I was not going to betray his confidence.

In our last conversation he was very upset and basically wished me luck and reiterated that God was not going to use me from now on. His friends told me that Matt felt he had failed—failed managing me, helping me. Though I loved San Diego, it was a small town in the circle that I had moved in, and I was continually running into parishioners. It was time to move on.

DARK NIGHT OF THE SOUL

You could call Santa Barbara the ideal town. This wealthy community of some 90,000 on the Pacific Coast boasts beautiful beaches, the Santa Ynez Mountains in the background, Spanish-style architecture, a lively cultural and café life, and a Mediterranean climate. It's a quiet, laid-back town where I had been once before. I felt good about the decision to leave San Diego and leave that chapter of my unanchored immigrant life behind. Good things were happening: the book was being written; the publisher was keen to hurry its publication; I no longer had to worry about where I'd sleep or where my next meal was coming from. The evangelical church gentleman called his friend, the Santa Barbara chief of police, to tell him that I was coming to his town. We should meet, he said, as he explained to the chief that there were some people who were pretty pissed off with me. If I needed anything, the chief would help me. Connections are always good, but beyond this, I was walking into a new situation, starting over completely alone.

When I'd arrived in the States, my friends had welcomed me with a place to stay, and life was able to move on from there. The church now was not an option: been there, done that—or been done by that. The problem was my ghosts; my demons came along with me as baggage. Stuffed in my trunk were rape, torture, images of death, mothers' tears, so much pain, layer upon layer of toxic memories jostling in my mind, the traumas embedded in every cell of my sick body.

You can be in the most beautiful of places, but if you're broken, it doesn't matter where you are if you see reality in gray scale. Santa Barbara would prove to be my "dark night of the soul." Some nights I felt I literally did not exist. Moving didn't change the reality of losing my family, nor did it stop the clock ticking down on my deportation. Put clinically, I was fucking depressed. The problem was, I didn't know what depression was or what was happening to me. Suicide was not an option. I didn't know how to get out of it on my own. There was no one to call, no one with whom to share my anxieties. I had found some ways to escape reality, from gambling to drinking alcohol to smoking cigarettes to doing all kinds of drugs. It was not in the form of addiction as much as an escape. I was fighting slowly to find a way out.

I see no point in revisiting the monotony of those darkest of nights, just to note it as a signpost on the journey, an inevitable one as a human: the signpost labeled "suffering." I was working on the book and having some speaking gigs. I had some fun and made some new friends. I would go to the gym, then go out at night to the cafés and overeat, putting on weight. I rode my motorcycle; Santa Barbara was great riding country. It had it all, from the mountains to the sea to great weather. Route 33 out of Ojai, with its climbs and sharp switchbacks, is known worldwide and attracts riders from all over. My bike was a crotch rocket, a Kawasaki 600. When you're hitting those turns at ninety miles an hour and you're laid so far out to hold the turn, bike metal is scraping the road's macadam. *Hooray. On to the next turn, lay on the other side, that little edge of tire holding hundreds of pounds of bike and rider according to some rule of physics.* The thrill is there to jolt the depression; the expression "holding on for dear life" makes you realize life is dear.

Speaking of thrill-seeking as my home remedy for depression, that could explain what had attracted me to an ad for skydiving. I sped down the 101 freeway at ninety miles per hour to the Camarillo Airport in Ventura County. First, the paperwork: I signed my life away. Then a half hour of preflight instruction with my class of four. We got our gear and boarded a small aircraft. The plane took off and climbed in ever-higher circles to two miles up as we, in effect, zoomed out from the living map below, showing the Pacific, the Channel Islands, the mountains, the cities. *Time to get up and stand in the open doorway, the wind rushing by.* You do the first couple of jumps with the instructor holding on to you. I was nervous but not afraid, as you wouldn't choose to do it if you were really afraid. "Ready, set, go!" You and your instructor leap into space for the 120-mile-per-hour, forty-second free fall. You feel the jolt of the parachute opening at about five thousand feet; the wind stops, and you peacefully float down to earth for a ride of about seven minutes. I went on to dive solo (yes, pretty thrilling) and jumped maybe ten more times. But that was enough; it was a bit of a hassle, and the thrill was wearing thin.

Those two activities showed an aspect of my character that now seems obvious: I have a penchant for risk.

A NEW RELATIONSHIP WITH TIME

From the moment of my arrival in the States, I had a different relation to time; a clock was always measuring the time before an awaited event. After I set foot in California, I had six months to wait before I could apply for asylum. Then I waited for my appointment with Homeland Security. Then I was waiting for the *Haaretz* article to appear or not. Waiting for the FOX documentary was one that was oft delayed. My time in Santa Barbara was simply marking time before the book was published. I had no idea what to expect when that time finally came. But first, there was something I absolutely had to do, and that was tell my father what was in the book before the world found out.

With a rare opportunity to get through to my father in prison on a smuggled phone, I told him a book was coming out and that I would be revealing that I worked for Israel for ten years: all the operations, everything we did, including protecting him. While he knew I was fed up with everything—I couldn't hide my disgust nor my anger at the other Hamas leaders—he did not think that I was an Israeli collaborator going against the plans of his movement. I told him the naked truth. Feeling that it was the only way for him to protect my other brothers, I encouraged him to go ahead and disown me.

"No," he told me. "It's not an option. You will always be my son, no matter what happens."

Later on, he had to do what I knew he had to do to protect our family. It was Wes Yoder, my agent, who tearfully told me the news. He had just read that Sheik Hassan Yousef had disowned his oldest son.

12

My Testimony

On March 2, 2010, after over a year of effort, *Son of Hamas* was published. From only a handful of Shin Bet members and others knowing the true story, now literally millions could read it, and I could go to my grave knowing that it was on the record—though there was always the risk that making it known to millions might inspire someone to send me to that grave. As far as I was concerned, there was a lot more to do before that fate which befalls us all.

The Christian publishers were very experienced in promoting their books in the Christian market. *Son of Hamas* offered the opportunity to target a broader audience. Fortunately for the book, a botched Mossad assassination in Dubai of Mahmoud al-Mabhouh, a cofounder of Hamas's military wing, made world news. He was drugged, electrocuted, and suffocated in his hotel room bed. The Dubai police chief posted the pictures of twenty-six suspects who'd been using passports fraudulently from dual-national Israelis. Surveillance cameras had caught them entering the country and had captured the hit team's movements in the hotel. Interpol put the twenty-six on their most wanted list, with their names and aliases. The Dubai prosecutor asked for international arrest warrants for Meir Dagan, then head of Mossad, and Benjamin Netanyahu, then head of the Israeli government. *Good luck with that one.* This real-life international spy story involving the Israeli-Palestinian war lasted a few news cycles and laid the table nicely for releasing the book.

An opportunity to broaden the potential market came up when CNN made an offer for two of their stars, Christiane Amanpour and Anderson Cooper, to interview me. Their offer required it to be exclusive, making sure they would be the first to break the story on TV. That would set the tone for the book launch, showing the book was of interest to a wide audience. Then there would be the usual tour booking me with the media in major American cities. It appeared a solid strategy, but what did I know? My role was to be effective on screen and interesting in interviews. The bottom line for the publishers and my agent was to sell the maximum number of books. It was a business, after all, and they had already invested in it.

ATTACKED!

So I was off to New York to start the whirlwind tour. First stop, CNN. As it turned out, I walked into a trap. Unbeknownst to me, Christiane Amanpour wanted to discredit me. I have thought about it a lot since that day and have come up with four factors that worked against me as I stepped naively into the CNN studio.

First, there was the CNN-FOX rivalry, the liberal/conservative political divide. To Amanpour, I was a favorite on FOX News, and so she assumed I was a right-wing Christian Zionist, Israel propagandist, and Islamophobe—i.e., the enemy.

Second, Amanpour had not read my book, nor had her "experts" on Hamas and Shin Bet, who she also had on. Their a priori position was "Too good to be true." Maybe they were relying on the press packet to understand the book, but one would think someone there should have read it. Yes, I had made statements bashing Islam and the Koran that could be considered inflammatory. However, these statements were based on my direct experience of terrorists justifying their heinous deeds with Koranic ideology, not because I was biased or prejudiced.

Third, my earlier sound bites turned off important Jewish support, notably from the American Israel Public Affairs Committee (AIPAC), one of the most powerful Zionist lobbies, that did not want to be affiliated with me. Also, Muslims in America were a minority suffering discrimination, especially after September 11. They were not the monsters I had in mind, but my diatribes, no matter how factually correct, were seen to be harming a religious minority.

Fourth, my story, if you hadn't read the detailed narrative in the book, sounded too amazing to be true. They say truth is stranger than fiction, which was true in my case, but that adage didn't help me with Amanpour. She prejudged my story as "not possible."

These were factors beyond my control. All I had was my truth and the ability to keep repeating what I knew to be true through my own experience. Right from her intro, I knew it was going to be a bumpy ride. It was full of "he says" and "he claims," her words dripping with doubt. A journalist should be professionally skeptical and ask difficult questions to get to the truth. However, we all operate out of a belief system; we all have our biases. Her belief system meant she was hostile to me from the get-go. I tried to stick with my truth, defending the book and my story, but at the end of the interview, depending on her "leading experts on the Middle East," she acknowledged that my efforts to save my father could be true, but my stories of involvement with high-profile cases were probably "gross exaggerations."

I got up from the hot seat shaken, feeling I'd been ambushed. The interviews with FOX had been fair. All my interviews with pastors at churches had been civil, even when I'd criticized their end-times doctrines. But what I had to say did not fit with CNN's secular political agenda. We all know what it is like not to be believed about something we experienced, especially by an authority figure like a parent. This was worse. It was televised.

Maybe I could make it up with the Anderson Cooper interview in the evening. The publisher's PR man went up to Anderson's office to confirm the details and was met on the stairs by Anderson's assistant. Anderson had canceled the interview.

This was a disaster—not because it would hurt book sales, but because my life was on the line. Avoiding deportation depended on my credibility. Credibility is not a renewable resource. Here I was being discredited on global television by a trusted celebrity journalist. Given the very nature of intelligence work, no one would confirm that what the book recounted was the truth.

The attacks against me kept coming. What ticked me off was that these people were comfortably sitting in their chairs judging me while enjoying liberties that others paid the price for. How many of them would risk their lives to be in a kitchen with five prospective suicide bombers cooking up their bomb? With no support or understanding coming from those free-thinking, liberal circles, it meant any support I had was coming from the FOX tribe, evangelical Christians, and pro-Israeli right-wing organizations. What was I to do, battling for my life, drowning in the ocean, and being thrown a life preserver? Was I to say, "No thanks, I'd prefer another one"—even though there was no other boat in view? That is what we call a rhetorical question. Of course, their life preserver came with expectations and an agenda.

Remembering that CNN interview still triggers hurt feelings. I wanted and expected someone to express appreciation for what I felt was the right action. Still, I had no excuse to feel sorry for myself. *Son of Hamas* was a success by any measure, making the *New York Times*

Bestseller List, being translated into Arabic and Hebrew, and being made recommended reading for IDF recruits. Audiences were willing to listen to my story. The royalties were generous.

My motive for writing it was to put on the record what I had done in those ten years back on the West Bank, as the handful of people who knew about it certainly wouldn't write about it, much less verify it. I was writing to defend myself, to make a case for myself. As I've recounted, I had no idea writing a book could make money. It turns out, it could. It totally changed my life, both in financial terms and in the pitfalls and opportunities it offered.

All of a sudden, my life took on a very different rhythm. I was still based in Santa Barbara, but I was rarely at home, as I seemed constantly on planes traveling around America.

While CNN had been a fiasco, a favorable review appeared in the *Wall Street Journal*. After *Son of Hamas* made the *New York Times* Bestseller List, the snowball effect kicked in with numerous requests for interviews. On my book tour, I went to major American cities like Chicago, St. Louis, New York, San Francisco, and other "smaller market" cities. Maybe practice didn't make perfect, but I had my talking points down, like a performer's routine. I'd learned from my speaking gigs that a good introduction by the interviewer is important so you get off to a good start with the audience and don't have to explain who you are and why you're worth listening to. Also, it helps to be briefed on who is interviewing you and to know something about the station or the newspaper and their audience.

The experience of promoting the book around the country would be a crash course in the American media. It's not the pretty face of an anchor on screen who decides what stories will be covered with what slant; it's the producer. Behind the producers are the owners, who are among the most powerful players on the planet. One could argue Rupert Murdoch was one of the most powerful people in the world pushing his agenda. Many have had the experience of being involved in an event and then seeing the media account and knowing that wasn't how it happened. The job of a journalist is not easy, having to produce a story in a couple of hours on the news of the day, framed within a given agenda. My agenda at this point was to survive.

Of course, there was a big reaction in the Middle East. It is hard to imagine anything worse than the son of an imam converting to Christianity and slandering Islam. Well, hold on, there is something worse! Being a spy for Israel. So it made a few news cycles in the Middle East. It was a first-page headline story in *Haaretz*. That had the fortunate result of reconnecting me with my former Shin Bet handler, Gonen (which I will share more about later). Gonen told me that when he saw his morning paper, it was a shock—and troubling. The Green Prince was one of Shin Bet's most closely guarded secrets.

The news did not go down well with my friends on the West Bank; then again, it didn't go down well with Shin Bet either. It also presented a problem for my Orange County Arab Christian friends. Becoming a Christian was to be applauded and supported; to betray the Palestinian cause was not to be applauded.

As to my father, this was potentially a major blow. My powerless father waited to be mercilessly torn apart. And yet what happened? The level of shame that I brought was so deafening and so blinding, his rivals felt compassion. They forgot for the moment about their political dispute and gave interviews and wrote posts supporting Sheik Hassan Yousef. I suppose this was a testament to the respect he enjoyed.

Back in the States, I heard from Matt, Tawfik, and Daniel. They knew some of my story already and were applauding me. We celebrated the book becoming a bestseller. I sent the book to Yvonne. Tawfik told me she'd called him after reading the book and she couldn't stop crying. I did see her once again when I was visiting La Jolla, but she didn't see me.

HOMELAND SECURITY AND A ROAD TRIP

I had a scheduled appointment with Homeland Security in the five-story federal courthouse building in downtown San Diego. I met my lawyer, Steve Seick, who had walked over from his office. The judge was not happy, as suddenly a whole new factor other than religious persecution had been thrown into the case. That is, my book claimed I was working with Israeli intelligence to combat terrorism, and yet the US government claimed I was supporting terrorism. That did not deter Homeland Security attorney Kerri Calcador, as she had their desk jockeys bravely scrutinizing every word in the text of *Son of Hamas*. They found some allegedly troubling sentences that they felt strengthened their case. My father had asked me to take the car and go pick up five Hamas members who had just been sprung from Palestinian Authority detention. That was like the story of filling my father's car with gas as a *prima facie* case of supporting terrorism. Forget ten years of fighting terrorism undercover.

The bottom line from that meeting was that a new hearing was set for less than two months away, on June 30, 2010, for both sides to present their cases with new evidence. I felt the judge's patience was running thin and there was a vibe of "Let's resolve this sucker." *Ticktock*. My time was running down.

In the effort to build my case and promote the book as widely as possible, my publishers and my agent urged me to write a blog. The publishers were getting letters and emails from readers. The publisher would pass them on, but with a popular book, a busy writer can't possibly respond to everything. Writing a blog offered a nice solution, especially since I was developing a fan base. Still, in my interviews and in my new blog, we had not made deportation an issue. The book described only my life on the West Bank. So we decided to go public with the threat of deportation. In my blog, I put in the name of the prosecutor, Kerri Calcador, plus her phone numbers and office address—just in case my fans wanted to weigh in with the person who said I would never become an American citizen.

The book, of course, resulted in more invitations to speak. There was some interest from Jewish groups, but again not from the major lobbying groups. Since *Son of Hamas* was published by a Christian publisher, most of the requests were from the Christian community, notably Baptist evangelicals. Again, this gave me the wonderful opportunity to get to know not only parts of America that were off the beaten track but to be welcomed by and to get to know these local communities. I spoke at some megachurches in Texas, to audiences as large as fifteen thousand people. They'd line up to get me to sign their copy of my book. When they didn't have one, they'd thrust their Bibles forward to have me sign the holy book. Who would have thought?

My agent, Wes, arranged a gig for me at a megachurch, the Highlands Fellowship Church, in Abingdon, Virginia, which was in the west corner of the state near the Tennessee border. At the same time, I got a call from Harun Ibrahim of Al Hayat TV. We had remained close friends, and every month or so when he would come to the States, we tried to get together. He logged some 500,000 miles a year visiting Arab refugees around the globe from Australia and New Zealand to Europe and the UK. Harun said he was coming to Washington. I told him I had this engagement in Virginia, so we agreed to meet up in DC, and he'd join me in driving out to Abingdon. He also said there was a high-level person in the State Department, a Christian, who had read my book and wanted to meet me. Harun had an extensive network and had access to so many people through his Christian connections.

I had given him a heads-up that the book was coming out. I had been appearing on his show, celebrated as a Christian. I told him, "You know the problems that rejecting Islam caused; well, this is a much bigger problem." He was one of the first to know about the revelation in the book about my work with Shin Bet, so we could speculate on what the impact could be in our particular universe. He told me not to tell anyone else, just keep it between him and me.

We met in DC, rented a car, and hit the road. There was a lot to catch up on, not all of it good. As I've recounted, the book was a bombshell in Middle Eastern, Muslim, and Christian circles. In the Al Hayat world, Father Zakaria Botros, who had welcomed me with open arms and attributed my embrace of Christianity to his broadcasts, went ballistic. In no way did he want to be affiliated with this "traitor, this lowest of the low, this scum," which is the way the people of my town perceived anyone who collaborated with Israel against the Palestinian cause. It appeared the Palestinian Christians who had celebrated my conversion hated me as much as Hamas. They felt my actions tarnished all Palestinian Christians with the brush of collaboration with Israel. They saw me as an opportunist who was using Christianity to cover my ass, not a sincere believer at all.

This meant that Harun took a lot of heat wherever he went on his travels, whether in Egypt, Lebanon, Syria, or out in the diaspora. It was a big problem for him to explain his relationship with me. Harun was not shackled by the constraints of nationalism and was much more open-minded, someone you at least could reason with. He didn't hate Israel; he loved Israel and was an Israeli citizen, even though in his DNA, he was an Arab. He didn't own the title of *traitor* as I did. Harun understood my position and did his best to defend me. He took the position that at the end of the day, I hadn't done anything wrong. I had saved lives. I wasn't lying. I was being honest and had written a book about it. It wasn't the case that others had discovered my perfidy and brought it to light, exposing me. At the same time, Harun was running a major enterprise and raising millions of dollars to support it. Any association with me was a negative one.

So it was a bit of a heavy trip on our way to Abingdon, though our time there would do much to restore some joy and hope. My best experiences while touring were at churches around the nation. Harun and I drove from DC across the state of Virginia to the different world of Abingdon. As in so many other towns in the Bible Belt, the church was the center of communal life, the most important institution in the community that brought people together, fulfilling that human need we all have to belong. I can be quite harsh about religious dogma, but the church or the mosque does perform an important function.

I have wonderful memories of that particular visit. It was spring, the trees and flowers were in full blossom, and it was so green. For someone who grew up in a desert climate and lived in Southern California, this green along with the fragrance in the air was a pleasant sensory overload. They proposed we go horseback riding. They were very careful with me at first, afraid I might hurt myself, but when they saw I could ride, we flew across those green pastures at full gallop. The pastor had two lovely daughters, and it was such a pleasure talking to them with their melodious Southern accents. We also hiked in the forest. During the church services, it wasn't as though I stood in the pulpit and gave a sermon; no, I sat with the pastor, who interviewed me, and we had a dialogue. Those in the pews seemed to feel an ideological connection with me even though I was someone quite different from those they were accustomed to hearing. Talking to them, it was evident they welcomed hearing from this ex-Muslim, now Christian, who understood their concern about the threat of terrorism and Islam. They were fearful despite the fact that they were tucked away in distant, bucolic surroundings. They told me it was a great honor to have me there, which was very flattering. After church, there was a barbecue in my honor with some hundred people attending. I remember one man came up to me and said, "Son, I have a lot of land here. I'd like to give you an acre or two. You can build your house, get married, have the family you wanted, be part of the church." Despite such generosity, it was not the type of life I envisaged for myself.

Another reflection of this generous spirit in these megachurches was their humanitarian efforts in third-world countries, serving, in effect, as technological missionaries. That was how I had met Tawfik and Yvonne, which so changed the trajectory of my life. In this church, they were taking pumping systems that had been thrown out but were perfectly serviceable and taking them to Africa, installing them, and providing clean water. Also, in this country where people feel they need the latest cell phone every year, they were collecting thousands of old phones and distributing them to Africans who couldn't afford the latest technology. They did the same with computers. I was impressed with the dedication and sincerity of these Christians.

Harun and I were there for just a few days, but they certainly were full days. It was so different than California or New York. Somehow I felt I was in the real America, back in a movie from the 1950s.

My agent, Wes, always made clear to those who invited me that I was a target for assassination from terrorists and they should provide security for me. So I always had a security detail charged with protecting me. I tried not to get carried away with it. Here I was, a stateless person without any status in this country, hardly a recognizable public figure, surrounded by gun-carrying friendlies. Among the parishioners, especially in a megachurch of thousands, there were many happy to protect a brother Christian who came from a war zone they knew only too well. I'd known the rifle pointing at me; now it was defending me. Over my many trips, I had in my security detail veterans of Iraq and Afghanistan as well as Army, Navy, Navy SEAL, Marine, FBI, National Guard, local police, and Secret Service agents. They'd drive right up to the plane at the nearby airports and escort me to the pastor's house or wherever I was being lodged. They must have had some kind of identity badges to pull that off. I suppose my fellow passengers wondered who the hell I was, especially with my Middle Eastern looks, debating whether I was being arrested or being escorted as a VIP.

As it turned out, our drive back to Washington would be the last time I'd see Harun. The pressure kept mounting on him to distance himself from me. I think he just got tired of it, and we lost contact. He certainly is one of the most extraordinary people I've ever met, and I treasured our friendship. After many years, he was able to reconcile with his family. Now, he is able to go back to his village, enjoy his mother's food, and share that part of his life with his Finnish wife and children, like nothing ever happened. All because a line was drawn on a map placing his village formally in Israel. What would his life have been like if he had been born on my side of the line?

TEACHERS OF RELIGIOUS LAW

While most of my visits with churches were wonderful, like in Abingdon, some were not. I was usually still warmly welcomed as one of theirs, and even when I disagreed with the pastor on stage, I was treated graciously. And I cannot judge how positive their extensive missionary work was in the third world. But I would often grow uncomfortable with the gap between my vision of Jesus Christ (what he stood for in his life) and the vision that I encountered preached in some of these evangelical churches. A friend of mine once remarked that Christianity in Europe became a dogma, and in the States it became a business. That certainly is the case with what I experienced in my visits to churches that preached the "prosperity gospel." The promise was that with strong faith and generous donations to the church, one's material and financial wealth would increase manyfold.

At the time, two of the major figures in this movement were the famous televangelists Benny Hinn and Paul Crouch. Benny Hinn was born in Jaffa in 1952 to parents born in Palestine with Greek-Egyptian, Palestinian, and Armenian-Lebanese heritage. There was a lot of history of exile in that heritage. After the 1967 Arab–Israeli War, the family migrated to Toronto, part of the exodus of Christians from Palestine. Somehow, I kept meeting people born not far from my home who had made their mark in the broader world. As a teenager, Hinn converted from Greek Orthodoxy to Pentecostalism. The rest, as they say, is history, as he created a vast evangelical empire preaching to multitudes outdoors with his miracle healing services and building a television audience of millions. All of this was supported by tax-free donations from the followers to his nonprofit charity. "The Gospel is free to all, but taking it to the nations is very expensive. Stand with Pastor Benny Hinn to take the life-saving and miracle-working power of Jesus Christ to lost and hurting souls around the world. Because of your support, no matter the amount, someone will hear about Jesus Christ for the very first time today. Will you give your most generous gift right now?"[9] Good pitch, as they say in the fundraising biz.

He and Paul Crouch and others preached that wealth was a sign of God's favor, and it must be said that their considerable wealth— Rolls-Royces, Gulfstream jets, his-and-her mansions in gated communities—could be considered evidence of what they preached.

Both Benny Hinn and Paul Crouch thought big, and early on they realized the extraordinary potential of global television. Crouch and his wife started the Trinity Broadcasting Network (TBN), which became the largest Christian television network in the world and was the third-largest group owner of broadcast TV stations in the US, ahead of CBS, FOX, and NBC. TBN was viewed globally on dozens of satellites and over tens of thousands of television stations and cable affiliates. Crouch mentored Hinn, whose ministries had a similarly impressive global reach, pitching support for orphanages and programs for children. These are big enterprises with millions spent on fundraising campaigns alone.

One example perfectly illustrates the gap between us when it comes to how we see Jesus Christ and how we apply his teachings to our own lives. Crouch, along with his handsome Arab-convert assistant, and I went out to dinner in Newport Beach, California. We were escorted to the corner table always reserved for Crouch. I don't remember what we discussed nor what we ate, but I do remember the lunch bill came to over $1,000. They raise and spend millions. Who are they accountable to? I did not want to become involved with them.

And what seems to accompany extreme wealth regularly shows up in their Christian counterparts as well: scandals, lawsuits alleging sexual affairs, divorces, plagiarism, wrongful terminations, allegations of fraud, inheritance squabbles, out-of-court settlements. And, in this particular niche market, tearful public pleas for forgiveness. These churches become playgrounds for the politicians; the pastors and politicians are friends, and they push each other's interests and their common political agendas.

I must say from my perspective, I never met a pastor—and I met many dozens—who really impressed me. Don't get me wrong, I did meet many warm, caring, and friendly pastors. It's not an easy role to assume—whether you're a pastor, a priest, a mullah, or a rabbi—if you're a teacher of the law. Too many pastors are comfortable putting their followers into a state of shame and guilt if they don't follow the law, which entails that the pastors, too, have to restrict their freedom and follow the law. If they, the representatives of the law, break the law, then they are riven with shame and guilt. If you preach *Turn the other cheek,* you better take the slaps. If you preach *Drinking alcohol is a sin,* you better not imbibe.

For some reason, perhaps since I was an outsider, in my one-on-one conversations with pastors, they would often confess their transgressions that were keeping them up at night. This would range from one confessing he would sneak off into the woods to enjoy his cigar to another pastor who cried when he confessed he was addicted to porn. And they have to hide it. Come on, guys. Light up and lighten up. The appeal Jesus had for me was that he was someone who rejected the religious establishment and hung out with society's rejects, those labeled as sinners.

"When the Pharisees saw this, they asked his disciples, 'Why does your teacher eat with tax collectors and sinners?' On hearing this, Jesus said, 'It is not the healthy who need a doctor, but the sick. But go and learn what this means: "I desire mercy, not sacrifice." For I have not come to call the righteous, but sinners'" (Matthew 9:11–13 NIV).

His approach was nonjudgmental, based on grace and love. He paid for it with his life, as would others throughout history who challenged the prevailing dogma. Muhammad is a prime example who was ahead of his time when he challenged slavery and female infanticide. At least he escaped the many assassination attempts. On a personal level, those who have assumed the mantle of priest are just humans doing the best within their abilities. I can certainly identify with their struggles. But it can be a hell to repress your desires rather than to understand them as a mechanism for survival and part of the human experience.

I'm speaking only from my own experience while on my journey. There are over 350,000 congregations in the US,[10] and certainly many do good works and are feeding the poor rather than taking others' last dollar. I'm not denying the important role religion plays in setting ethical limits on the worst of human instincts, helping to maintain a certain social order, keeping the animal in check. For me, the true journey for the human is to integrate into a higher potential, a higher level of consciousness.

As I've mentioned, my father is a very powerful public speaker; people would come from miles around to hear him speak, and he attracted large crowds. He's a short man, maybe five feet four. His voice is so strong; mine comes from like halfway up my throat, but his comes from the gut. He's very eloquent, very emotional, and very angry. He ignites a fire in the crowd, which makes him so dangerous.

My model for a religious leader was my father. When he preached, the crowds were transfixed, unable to even move their heads. He got them addicted to the stress, the hatred, the anger, the promises of revenge, and the blame he sows in every field but Hamas's. You can see that powerful vibration in his veins, as though his face is about to explode. His religion gives him a sense of superiority and a confident self-justification that enables him to be a terrorist leader. It was this public speaking ability that gave him his standing and his power, nothing else. This is a man who was very peaceful around the house. He did not interfere with house business unless he could help. It was my mother who was the aggressive one and did the screaming. My father would be very aggressive only if the public image he established as Sheik Hassan Yousef was threatened. Personally, he did not exist; it's his public image that exists out in the world, and his greatest fear is losing that image if something negative is said about him. Anything can be sacrificed to maintain that image.

I sought a different voice: the voice of love, not hatred. This was, or should have been, a familiar message in Christian churches, though I spoke in a post–September 11 world. As I was billed as a Muslim terrorist who had found Christ and escaped and someone who had spoken strongly against Islamic ideology, congregations expected me to confirm their beliefs not only that Islam was evil but so were Muslims. Many anticipated I'd feed them red meat, and here I was, if not a vegan, a vegetarian. I was not going to follow my father's example, even though when I looked out at the faces in the church audiences, they looked the same as the those in the mosques, receptive to an emotional, negative harangue. I was different from my father in that I was not trying to create an empire for myself, and when I spoke to people, I spoke with a sense of responsibility. I represented only myself; I didn't need validation from the crowd, from anyone.

13

My Trials

Since my arrival in the States and my disastrous meeting with Homeland Security, the specter of deportation hung over my head. The one group that appeared to be supporting me was the evangelical community. In my position, I could only welcome their support from such a politically powerful bloc, as they could lobby with the authorities in Washington to grant me asylum. However, perceptions of me from Christian leaders often went from good guy to bad guy back to a good guy to the point of causing whiplash. I could certainly relate to Jesus, who was cheered one week and then crucified the next. Christian fundamentalists tried hard to contain and direct me. When I didn't give in, they attacked and slandered me. Their praise turned quickly into blame. A brief honeymoon indeed.

Two people played an important role for me in the early months after the book came out: Walid Shoebat and Joel Rosenberg. Both sought to control me. If there has been a theme to my journey, it's that attempts to control me have not succeeded. My freedom has always outweighed the comfort and security of belonging to a community, be it religious or secular.

In a world where terrorism—and specifically, Islamic terrorism—became public enemy number one, it is not surprising that a cottage industry grew up with people claiming to be former Palestinian Muslim terrorists who converted to Christianity and who strongly support the State of Israel. This gave them a source of income mainly from fundamentalist Christian groups, as well as some visibility through media and speaking gigs. As propagandists, their message of anti-Islam and pro-Israel, despite being extremist, found an audience eager to have their hatred stoked by a seemingly authentic source.

THE CROWDED SPACE FOR DONOR DOLLARS

Walid Shoebat is a Palestinian American born in Bethlehem who in 1993 converted to Christianity from Islam. He claimed that he had been a PLO (Palestine Liberation Organization) terrorist and had firebombed an Israeli bank in 1979. He confessed to being a very bad Arab who hated Christians and Jews and wanted to kill Israelis, but suddenly he saw the light, which made him hate the Arabs instead of the Jews. Living in the States, he set up the Walid Shoebat Foundation, an organization that claims to fight for the Jewish people and solicits donations.

As a self-proclaimed expert on terrorism, he was introduced as such on outlets like CNN and received paid speaking gigs on terrorism and the grave dangers of Islam. Riding the current trend, he became a prophet of the end-times "Stone Age" ideology. When my book came out with considerable attention, he saw me as another Palestinian, billed as an ex-terrorist and a convert to Christianity, who was on the speaking and media circuit expounding on the same subjects. *Uh oh.* This was a limited, niche market, and like any business, you could either merge with or discredit your competitor.

He approached me several times wanting us to work together. I would join his nonprofit organization, become part of his team, and he would be my mentor. He was getting hundreds of speaking engagement offers. He figured he could contain me under the umbrella of his nonprofit. If he were my mentor, I would be accountable to him. That would increase his credibility and the credibility of his nonprofit foundation.

I turned him down. This pissed him off. He saw my independent existence as a threat to his insecure kingdom. He then launched the familiar calumnies to discredit me. I was a double agent, part of a Hamas conspiracy. Or I was part of a plot by the Muslim Brotherhood to infiltrate American churches to make Christians hate Israel. I didn't bother to answer these stupidities. No way I was going to stoop that low.

Yet many evangelicals believed him! Just as they had immediately believed me, they now immediately believed his slander. His public attacks turned fans into enemies. My church speaking engagements dried up. Walid won the fight, though at this point I had not fired a shot in self-defense.

Subsequent investigations by the *Wall Street Journal* and CNN on Walid and some of the other clowns showed their claims were based on lies. Walid had no proof he was ever a member of the PLO; no bank had been burned in 1979. And who would care if a PLO member had a sudden change of heart? The PLO was no immediate threat to America. He was desperately creating a problem that didn't exist so he could be the solution. As I mentioned earlier, when my book came out, the *Wall Street Journal* wrote a favorable review. And for a year they had an investigative reporter attending my talks, notebook in hand, but she found nothing that would establish me as another opportunistic fraud. Still, many evangelicals believed the discredited Walid rather than the secular press like the *Wall Street Journal*.

I was trying to communicate with my people, Arabs and Palestinians. When my story came out, they thought it was a Zionist conspiracy against the Palestinian cause. I told everyone that this was not a conspiracy; no one was telling me what to do, what to say. This was my conviction. I was speaking to them from my heart. I wanted to reach them.

Walid used a different strategy: either you like Palestinians and hate Israel, or you hate Palestinians and love Israel. There was no middle way. But I was not against a group. I didn't hate a group. I criticized systems, dogmas, and stupid beliefs that lead to terrorism. I was acting responsibly, not motivated by hatred. I am not against national interest or Palestinian national aspirations, but those aspirations have been hijacked by selfish people who are dragging everyone toward death. The "cause" is hiding a very ugly reality. It's not working for anybody. Children are paying the price.

Walid didn't like my position, especially my attitude toward my Muslim family. It was like he was running a cult that required one to renounce all those who did not embrace the cult leader. Why would I reject my family? I didn't want to lose them, regardless of whether they'd had to disown me to be able to live in their society. How could I be against my mother? Against my father? Against my siblings? I wrote the book for my family; it was dedicated to my father, to my mother, to my people, right there on the first page. It was not dedicated to evangelical Christians. The book was written with tears, with blood, and with a lot of pain. It was not written with ink. For me, I could never support Walid and his organization.

THE CEO OF THE END TIMES

Joel Rosenberg is a very successful and prolific Christian Zionist author, well known as a propagator of the end-times teaching seeing the violence in the Middle East as a signal of the coming of the apocalypse and the fulfillment of biblical prophecy. His agnostic parents became born-again Christians, as did he when he was seventeen.

Working as a research assistant to Rush Limbaugh, he later opened a political consultancy business where among those he said he consulted was former prime minister Netanyahu. When Netanyahu lost the 1999 election, Rosenberg turned to writing and launched his best-selling career as a novelist. His conservative connections and evangelical credentials provided him with a sizable audience base. His first of many end-times books dealt with terrorism. The fact that he lived in Israel meant, unlike the Christians I met on my speaking gigs, he was well versed on the subject. Joel Rosenberg was and is a major figure in the evangelical Christian movement.

He supported my book when it first came out. This was significant, as he has a following counting in the millions and I can only assume his endorsement helped sales. I didn't ask him to endorse it. A very friendly Joel came to me assuming that his self-declared role as my mentor to guide me through the complex world of Christian Zionism and Washington politics would be welcomed. He had important connections in Washington through the Jewish lobbies, the evangelical lobbies, and members of Congress. In sum, he was a player. He made it very clear that I should be accountable to him. Here we went again—my independence versus support from a powerful person who could help with my deportation case.

For example, he was on my case about my not quoting biblical verses in my talks, anchoring them in scripture for the audience: "Memorize a few key verses and sprinkle them in your speeches. You have to give your talks the Christian religious dimension"—shades of Pastor Matt. I did not quote the Bible. I always spoke from my own life, which, after all, was why I had been invited to speak. I was speaking on my own authority. I hadn't lived the lives of David or Isaiah, much less the life of Jesus. But Joel's mentoring began to require certain conditions being met to continue his support.

"What church have you been attending?"

"I haven't been attending any particular church in the last year."

"Why is that?"

"I've been in a lot of churches as I've been on the road, but . . ."

"I mean, what church do you belong to?"

"I know that's what you mean, but the honest truth is, I don't feel that I need to go to a church for anybody, you know."

"Look, that's not good. This is not how it works. You have to be accountable to be part of the Christian fellowship."

Really? I didn't answer. Wasn't being accountable to God enough? Why did there always have to be the pastor, the mullah, the priest, the middleman between the believer and whatever divinity they were propagating?

Joel went on to bolster his case. "Otherwise, you are vulnerable to all kinds of attacks and you could be swayed by their ideas. Ideas that are far from the mainstream of our faith."

Where do you even start with a statement like that? This had been a constant battle on my journey to maintain my freedom to think for myself and to pursue my truth. What is it about those in power who demand that their followers stick to the party line? Any deviation, any attempt to freely inquire, to disagree, can be met with excommunication, expulsion from the party. Again, I was grateful I was living in a society with a constitution that established freedom of speech. Where would human progress be without the dissenters, those thinking outside the dogma? In other societies without such guarantees, deviation, whether real or fabricated, could be fatal. That pretty much ended that conversation.

However, Walid's attacks against me troubled Joel. Joel had endorsed my book, and it was proving to be an embarrassment to him. His followers were asking who they were to believe, Mosab or Walid? Joel said I had to respond. "If you don't call him out for these lies, it makes you appear guilty. And I look like an idiot who's been duped. You have to defend yourself publicly."

No way I was getting into this ugly, stupid fight. For what? Walid wanted recognition and the Christian honeypot. Was I going to fight him over that? I didn't need recognition; I knew who I was; I knew why I'd done what I'd done; my motive had been humanitarian, not monetary. I pointed out to Joel that we both knew that Walid had been discredited. The idea of two former "terrorists" slugging it out in the mud over money was anathema to me.

I already have a lot of evangelicals against me when I tell them they are complicit in the bloodshed in the Middle East. So be it; I'm speaking my truth as fearlessly as I can, which isn't that difficult when you have nothing to lose! Even though I might say something silly and stupid or something that could be misunderstood, it really doesn't matter as long as I'm speaking my truth to the best of my ability and my understanding keeps on growing.

But Walid's attacks were taking away what little support I might have. The truth was, evangelical Christians were the only group that was supporting me—not liberals or the liberal media, not Shin Bet or the FBI. These Christians were the ones who enabled me to take a breath, get some needed oxygen. And they gave me a platform to speak, which I absolutely needed to tell my story. Otherwise, I would be stuck with these false identities through eternity. Walid didn't have the facts; he took things out of context and slandered me. Only his greed mattered to him.

The idea of engaging in this ugly, meaningless fight set me off. I had been in the field for ten years risking my life daily. I had authority. I'd walked the walk before I came to this country. I'd saved American lives. I'd helped bring to justice those who had killed Americans. My credibility was based on action; his was based solely on words. Talk is cheap, though apparently it can generate donor income. Mine was not a "born-again" moment transforming a bad guy into a good guy, like with Walid and the others. It was not a road-to-Damascus moment, but I was on the road to America, fighting for my very life.

Okay, take a deep breath. Two big breaths. This whole Walid attack was, to say the least, emotionally upsetting and depressing. No one was there backing me up or holding my hand. I could not validate my claims at that time. It was all underground. His attacks making me a bad guy with his constituency led to others piling on. Some Palestinians chimed in, "I listen to him in Arabic, and he says things differently than what he says in English." "He's a Muslim Brotherhood fighter here to turn Christians against the Jews." *What?*

Three deep breaths. I relented to Joel's forceful demands and agreed that I would respond. But how could I do it and keep some self-respect, some dignity? I went full-out *Christian love, turn the other cheek* so that hopefully this approach would prevent an already ugly fight from becoming even uglier.

THE LAND OF LAWYERS

It turned out that Walid's attacks were not my only problem. My days of being an object of desire for the American legal profession were not over and had been triggered by my book. At times it seemed like every other person I met was either a lawyer or striving to become one, so it seemed inevitable that they would become part of my American experience. I didn't appreciate being subpoenaed by lawyers and government officials over political and financial lawsuits.

I was at a book signing event at a Jewish organization in New Jersey when an obese gentleman approached me. He handed me a paper. He was a Jewish attorney who had driven down from New York, having seen an announcement for the signing. The paper was a subpoena. At the time, I did not know what those were. It appeared that I was being ordered by a government agency, this time a New York court, to be a witness in a trial. It said that if I failed to appear and testify, I would be "penalized." This was unexpected. Outside of Shin Bet, this was one of the few times in my journey that my predator was Jewish. His pitch was to do the Jewish people (him) one more favor. His motive was not justice for the plaintiffs, victims of terrorist attacks—he was not working pro bono. He wanted his fee of 20 percent in a billion-dollar lawsuit against the PLO. Not a bad day at the office for his firm. When I looked up *subpoena*, I found the Latin means "under penalty." The lawsuit was asking for a billion dollars with hundreds of millions to be paid for a suicide bombing attack. The victims were the Israeli Jews who had been killed (though at least one of the victims was probably Palestinian, since they make up a large portion of the Israeli population), hence the lawsuit against the PLO.

This opportunist was able to take advantage of American law that allowed parasites like him to sue foreign organizations, banks, or governments if they had a connection or a presence in America. It happened that the US government had removed the PLO from the terrorist organization list once it publicly renounced violence. The PLO then opened an office in DC, and Congress funded the PLO and the Palestinian Authority with American taxpayer money. So our clever lawyer was coming after these funds, but he needed evidence to connect Yasir Arafat's PLO directly to the terror attacks involving his clients. The case had been languishing for years, and once again they were facing a deadline to bring it to trial. When my book came out, he thought he'd found his messiah to testify to that connection, and he was more than happy to crucify him.

The PLO now had a new base on American soil. They were not going to come after this fat cat, but they could come after me if I testified against them. It might endanger my family back in Ramallah, as well. The PLO had already interrogated at least one of my brothers who was secretly in touch with me at the time. The PLO had their lawyers in DC, and since I'd been subpoenaed to appear as a plaintiff witness, they had the right to depose me. I ended up in a windowless room in Washington, DC, across a table from the PLO's lawyers, who turned out to be the nastiest motherfuckers I've ever faced. Every time I'd open my mouth, they'd cut me off with an objection or some legal term. They saw me as a Zionist propagandist, which was the tune the liberal media was humming. I was allegedly a tool for the conservative media. They had subpoenaed my agent and publisher for all my communications, so they knew all my income from the book and how much I was paid for my speaking engagements. They tried to discredit the information in my book. They, like their Jewish brethren on the other side of the case, were also wanting their cut of congressionally mandated dollars. Here we had the Israeli–Palestinian conflict playing out in the United States, with big bucks at stake. As the Dylan song says it, I was only a pawn in their game.

I had no idea that my bestseller would make me so popular with readers in the legal profession. Being paid to travel around the country and speak is different from being ordered to run from court to court, trying to help them for free so the lawyers could make more money. *I can't afford it. Why am I supposed to help? Can't they see my grief? It's like they're dancing at my funeral.*

I told my lawyer about the subpoena.

"Oh shit."

"What do you mean?"

"There's a date on it, and you have to appear in front of the judge and the court on that date."

"Forget the judge and the court." I was fed up.

"What do you mean?"

"I'm not going to New York to be a witness in their stupid court. I'm not going anywhere. Let them come to California."

"You're kidding, right?"

"No, I'm not. Put it this way. How about everybody go fuck themselves, including the judge and the court?"

"You can't do that."

The plaintiff's lawyer, Counselor Obese, who had the most to lose, weighed in. It seemed for the first time he realized how much I was hurting. He said, "It's not so hard; you get on a plane; come in and testify; go straight back home."

When he realized I was dead serious, he called me again and said, "Listen, this is a very, very serious issue. You don't mess with the American judicial system. Nobody is above this. You don't want to go that route. They can deport you now."

I'll never know if that was real concern in his voice or his own self-interest. I told him, "I don't care. Send me back right now. Bring Yasir Arafat back from the dead to be your witness. Leave me alone. Enough is enough." He didn't know that I had a list of firms and government agencies also on a deadline waiting for me to do their fucking jobs.

So I didn't show up on the required date. I didn't obey the court. My publisher had a heart attack. My agent had a heart attack. They feared the authorities would come down hard on their client—maybe deport me as a felon.

What were the repercussions for flouting the law? None that I ever knew. Go figure. But it wasn't the end of being in demand.

Another law firm, representing the American victims of suicide bombings, was suing Arab Bank for knowingly providing material support and services to Hamas, in effect funding and encouraging terrorist activities. Arab Bank contended that it was not wittingly part of the terrorist financing. It acknowledged transferring close to $100 million to Palestinians for humanitarian aid but said it abhors terrorism and had no intention of subsidizing suicide bombers. The plaintiffs' attorneys asked for my help for the "sake of the victims." The same song and dance, but my dance card was full. I'd had it. As it happened, I did have solid information about Arab Bank.

An Arab Bank manager used to bring documents to my father's office; my father didn't have to go to the bank. He was an important client, as the bank was making major profits off of these international transactions. The money was going for Hamas's purposes, like suicide bombers, their families, prisoners, "martyrs," etc. The documents had thousands of names on them. And all of those names were on the payroll.

One day, as I was driving my father around, he put some bank documents in the glove compartment of the car and forgot about them. The next time I looked in the compartment, I found a treasure trove. Thousands of names. I made photocopies and gave them to Shin Bet. No, I did not bring copies out with me when I left. I left everything behind: documents, house, mother—everything and everyone. Those documents would definitely help the plaintiffs' case. Me just claiming they existed, compared to the actual material evidence, could be cast in doubt by the defense. And how credible was this Ramallah boy with his tall tales, whom the American government had on its list to be deported? They should have asked Shin Bet for the documents, and they probably did. As it turned out, the plaintiffs did win their case in 2014 after ten years of battling to get a court's judgment.

MY SISTER SABEELA

I still had one thread left from the family who had disowned me. That was my sister Sabeela, the oldest sister of the three. She, too, had suffered her share of trials. She'd finished high school and was going to college. A father with his son, who lived in the US, came from their nearby village to see my father to explore arranging a marriage. Like many males who emigrated abroad, they would return home to find a wife. In this case, the son was presented as a well-educated, practicing Muslim who worked in a bank in San Francisco and had built a house in their village. This looked promising for Sabeela's long-term security, especially as the house was an asset that was visible wealth. So it was arranged that the future husband would return to the States for a year, Sabeela would finish college, and then they would get married.

A year later he returned and they had a fine wedding, which we all attended. They moved into the new house in the village some twenty minutes away. It turned out that her husband's parents were living there too. The groom stayed for two weeks with Sabeela as a married couple, and then he went back to San Francisco. The plan was that he would return in a year and take her to the States. They were in touch, and he would send her some money. But she ended up like Cinderella, taking care of the parents: feeding them, bathing them, clipping their nails, maintaining the home, shopping—a full-time job. And the parents were healthy and perfectly able to manage on their own.

The husband did not come back after the first year. My sister was not looking well. Then he didn't return after the second year. What was going on? My father was in prison; I was deeply concerned and responsible for my sister. There was something fishy. Did he have another woman? Was he gay? I talked to him on the phone: "Did you want a maid to take care of your parents?"

The third year he still didn't come back. He was not telling the truth; he was a liar. My sister had been enslaved for three years in a new house in a village where she knew no one. This wasn't a marriage. I counseled that he had to give her her freedom back and divorce her. He agreed but only gave excuses to explain why the papers weren't arriving. In the meantime, my sister moved back home. The deserter's brother, a reasonable man, saw the injustice and took Sabeela's side, pressuring his brother to give my sister her freedom back.

In this culture, once divorced, a woman's market value would go down like a used car. Divorced men in the area felt they could now afford my sister. Anyone could come and propose. The mothers checked her out and made proposals. She was pressured by people saying that if she did not comply, it would cause damage and destroy relationships. No Prince Charming appeared for Sabeela.

After four and a half years, the divorce papers came. She went to the Open University of Israel, where you can study at home and then go sit for the exams. My mother, who had completed two years of college back in the 1970s, also went back to college.

By this time, I'd left for the States. And now there was an unexpected entry onto this marriage scene: Amer Abu Sarhan. Amer had been born in Bethlehem. At age nineteen he took a kitchen knife and went out and stabbed to death three Israelis and wounded twenty others. This was revenge for the Al-Aqsa Massacre (October 8, 1990), where around twenty Palestinians were killed and 150 injured. Celebrated as a "hero," Amer was sentenced to three life terms plus 100 years.

My father, who was often transferred from prison to prison, spent time with Amer, who saw my father as a mentor and guide. Amer did what he could to help my father with such things as washing his socks or arranging food, but my father was very self-reliant and never wanted others to bother on his behalf. Other prisoners admired my father for his modesty, his truthfulness, and his ability to endure the pain of isolation, which showed a different kind of strength. Even his enemies respected him.

So Amer, serving three life sentences plus one hundred years, proposed to marry his mentor's daughter. My father said yes! This was not a prison situation where there could be a marriage and then conjugal visits to produce babies. The Palestinian leadership turned down any such proposal; it was either marriage in freedom or not at all.

Prisoners facing the rest of their lives in prison hope for a prisoner exchange in cases where an Israeli is held hostage. The Israeli soldier Gilad Shalit, captured on the border of Gaza, was held by Hamas for more than five years. Finally, in 2011 a deal was struck in which he was exchanged for 1,027 prisoners. Two hundred and eighty of those were serving life sentences for attacks against Israeli targets. One calculation was they were responsible collectively for the killing of 569

Israelis.[11] Amer was included in this swap and was released to Gaza, where he was welcomed as a hero.

So Sabeela would find another husband after all. Since my arrival in the States, she would call me from time to time, as we had each other's numbers. Always compassionate, she said she felt I was lonely and wanted to know how I was doing. When the news of my story broke and my heartbroken father disowned me, Sabeela was the first to call me and say, "No matter what, you will always be my brother."

Where would the marriage take place? Due to enforced security requirements, Amer couldn't leave Gaza, and Sabeela was not allowed to go to Gaza, where she'd never been. In other times when there were no borders, no walls, no fences, no checkpoints, it was a two-and-a-half-hour drive. A plan was devised where my mother and sister, neither of whom had a security file, would make the ten-hour trip to Amman in Jordan. They then would fly to Cairo and from there travel through the Sinai Peninsula to the Egyptian border with Gaza and manage either through a tunnel or at a border crossing to enter Gaza, a territory that might as well be called a prison. After a circuitous trip of four days, my sister met her future husband for the first time.

In Hamas terms, this was a royal wedding: the oldest daughter of one of Hamas's founders united with a hero of the resistance. This marriage would also help to restore some of my father's standing damaged by my treason. The wedding was broadcast on Hamas's satellite TV with all the top leaders present, either gathered in one room in Gaza or with my father and others in Ramallah. My father could not be there to give his daughter away, but with the miracle of the internet, he was asked for his approval, which he gave. They then all drank coffee and ate sweets.

The last conversation I had with my sister was after her marriage.

She called me and asked, "How come you haven't talked to me this past year?"

"You're married; you have a new life. I don't want to be part of it."

"What do you mean?"

"You may see Amer as a hero, but he's a killer, a butcher. I don't know how your destiny brought you there."

Amer then grabbed the phone. "You know, I thought you were forced to say the things that you said to the media. I've been following you, and you broke your father's heart. You really hurt your family, and we all felt compassionate toward you as a victim of this whole thing. Until this moment I didn't realize that you actually mean what you say. I thought you were just being told to say the things that you say, or were forced to, or lost your mind. The way you talk about me to my wife shows you have no limits. Allah, blessed be his name, is sending you to burn in Hell."

"You know we can shed blood in the name of the nation, or God, or religion, but at least I don't have blood on my hands, and you do."

And that was it. He hung up. That was my last conversation with my sister and my first and last with that monster.

I became friends with an Israeli actor, Lior Raz, who had the lead role in the popular Israeli series *Fauda*. His girlfriend was one of those whom Amer stabbed to death. It's a deep loss when someone is so brutally taken from your life and your planned future. He would chastise me for my "brother-in-law." Apparently, there are some advantages to being disowned.

14

Going Before Congress

Since the book had come out, I'd been in frequent contact with my agent, Wes, and with the publisher. Though the book was still on the *New York Times* Bestseller List, the early demand for interviews and appearances had diminished. Wes called me and said I'd been invited to receive an award as a "Speaker of Truth" at the *Rays of Light in the Darkness* awards dinner in Washington.

Why would I want to travel all the way across the country, probably have to get dressed up in a suit, and give some little speech? I was not interested in awards. Wes was insistent: "This is a prestigious event in the nation's capital, and they'll cover your expenses. The lady behind it, Sarah Stern, is a real power player on Capitol Hill. She read your book and was very moved by it, and the award is for people like you who speak the truth at great personal risk. You need all the people in your corner you can get."

I couldn't disagree with that, but Judge Richard Bartolomei was getting ready to preside over my asylum case. The hearings were only a few days away in California, not on the other side of the country. I just needed to stay in my situation there and figure things out. Still, Wes urged me not to miss this opportunity: "You never know where it will lead or who you will meet. Come on; fly in, spend two nights, fly back, and you're home." I told him I would consider it.

I googled "Sarah Stern"; there were many, but Sarah N. Stern had to be the right one. "Sarah Stern is the founder and president of the Endowment for Middle East Truth (EMET), an unabashedly pro-American and pro-Israel think tank and policy institute in Washington, D.C."[12] Middle East truth? We all have our truths; I certainly do. She looked like a hard-core Israeli propagandist. And yes, there was an awards dinner. "The *Rays of Light in the Darkness* awards Dinner is the nation's premier event that strengthens leaders who speak the truth about Israel and the Middle East, despite the political cost they face every day. [. . .] EMET is the first organization of its kind to honor these speakers of truth who stand up in the face of deception and violence, sometimes at great political or physical risk to themselves and their loved ones."[13] Everyone has their agenda. I certainly have mine, and at the time that was to avoid deportation. I told my agent I'd think about it, but right then I was thinking about what could help me with the deportation case. This might. But I also discovered unexpected help from someone I knew back home.

GONEN'S DILEMMA

Back when I was in San Diego, after the original *Haaretz* article appeared, I received an email from Gonen, my former handler. This was totally unexpected. I had known him as Loai and also by other names, not his real name, and, though he was the one Shin Bet person with whom I felt a certain human connection, he still was part of that insentient machine. I didn't know anything about him, about his personal life, and he knew everything about me back then in Ramallah.

For him to contact me was to violate all agency protocols, unless this was one more of their games.

It turned out that he had been dismissed from the agency, and so he was putting himself at risk by reaching out to me. I knew those people; they were ruthless in enforcing their *omertà*, just like other criminal bands like the Mafia or Hamas. After a month and a half or so of exchanges by phone and email, he came to visit me in San Diego. For the first time since those days, we sat down together in the same room. I had the chance to get to know him as a real person, as Gonen. I felt that this was not some agency gambit to draw me back—or worse. He would visit me a couple more times when I was in Santa Barbara. His decision to reach out to me, sparked by that article, would end up radically changing both our lives.

Because of our shared background, he was someone I could talk to about whatever I was going through. He understood my struggle and where I was mentally and emotionally. Having that anchor often saved my ass big time; he truly was and is my protector. He knew I had risked my life for many years and understood how dangerous the job I did was, and he knew what it took for me, a Palestinian, to defy my culture. My problem since *Son of Hamas* had appeared was whether or not people believed the book was telling the truth, whether it should be shelved as nonfiction or fiction. The hearing date was set, and my fate could depend on my truth being confirmed by a credible third party. I had been naive enough to think that the book would prove my case. But Homeland Security killed that hope. After finding the passage where I described picking up five prisoners being released, they discovered that these same men later committed terrorist acts.

I called Gonen and said, "Brother, I've got the US government against me now. They're using the book to deport me."

I had continued to update him, but now he knew I was in trouble. In terms of confirming my service in Shin Bet and my "supporting terrorism" being a necessary part of my cover, Gonen was the only person who could possibly vouch for me. He knew that. Shin Bet was not going to publicly say that The Green Prince had done what was described in the book.

Even though my life was at stake, I knew there was no way I could ask him to testify on my behalf, because I knew such a decision could put his life at risk. There are certain things you don't ask even your best friend or brother, certain lines you do not cross. No, his testifying could destroy the life he had built. Despite all that, he said he was considering coming to help.

It is not possible to exaggerate the pressure an Israeli in this situation would be under if he even considered supporting an Arab whose father was a leading terrorist. It's not as though a court or agency had ordered him to testify and confront a moral choice publicly. His identity was still secret. If he chose to openly defend his friend, that was a voluntary decision. If he said nothing, who would ever know?

It turned out that after being unfairly dismissed from Shin Bet, he sank into a deep depression, not leaving the house for a year and a half. His wife told me he was completely crushed. Gonen was terrified of Shin Bet, and every protocol they followed emphasized never going public with their operations. If he testified, he would be violating the two most sacred and abused words of the militarized state: *national security*. He was about to graduate from law school, and if criminal charges were made, he would never be able to practice law. More importantly, Gonen's family was against him taking such a needless risk. His father had been a general in the army, serving in the Six-Day War and the First Intifada. After fifty years of service and well-deserved prestige, he didn't want his son to do something stupid and embarrass him, and for what? Gonen's wife was against risking the family's reputation, so there were two pillars of Israeli society, army and family, ranged against this lone individual.

These are the moments in life when you discover how real a person is, how they respond to a moral choice that their conscience has laid before them. To whose truth do they respond? Gonen made the decision to obey his own truth. He told me over the phone he would come to America to witness on my behalf at the asylum hearing. This could save my life. But for me it felt just as significant to find another individual doing something for the sake of their truth.

I wanted him to feel free and told him, "If you decide not to witness, I'll understand, and it will always be the same between us. I know you're sincere and want to do it, but we don't know what you're going to face."

Both of us expected the worst-case scenario. If he went back to Israel after testifying, he would certainly be arrested. It was hard to imagine what the best-case scenario would be. I'd already started planning how he could stay in the States after witnessing, and also how he could bring his family here.

Gonen gave an interview to *Haaretz* with our veteran journalist friend, Avi Issacharoff, about my situation, but the article did not reveal his identity. The interview referred to him as "G" or "Captain G," a common practice in Israeli media for attributing information to intelligence sources. Gonen was still in the safe zone.

His flight booked, he asked for a meeting with Shin Bet in the evening. They met around 9:00 p.m. in one of their secret locations. He pled my case that they should intervene on my behalf, as I was in real trouble. The book had not only given the American government more ammunition to deport me as a "terrorism supporter," but now the book had exposed me as a traitor working with Shin Bet. "We owe him," he told his former colleagues.

Their answer was very clear. "Fuck you and fuck him. We don't owe him. And you stay out of it. It's not your job. You are forbidden to confirm your identity or confirm his account or help him in any way."

Their threats were only too real. Gonen risked eight years in an Israeli prison if he went ahead and helped me in any way.

Gonen said that his internal response to their threat was, *Okay. If that's how they want it, fuck them.*

Before he flew to America, he appeared on one of Israel's major radio shows, the IDF station *Galatz*, and spoke openly as Gonen Ben Itzhak about his commitment to witness in an American court for Mosab Hassan. He said he believed he was doing what was right. He'd crossed the Rubicon and burned his bridges behind him, to mix two clichés, now that he'd revealed his identity. He'd also protected himself. If he faced imprisonment, media attention could cause public pushback against those gangsters.

As he waited in the Ben Gurion Airport for his flight, his family called him. They gave him their blessings so he could be at peace. "You have our support whatever you do, whatever the consequences." This led them to discuss whether or not they should bring the children to the airport on his return if Shin Bet was to arrest him on the spot. They decided not to bring the children to the airport.

Gonen's crowded Tel Aviv flight arrived on time at LAX. We spotted each other as he emerged from customs. We embraced and, I don't know why, we just started laughing and laughing for what seemed the longest time. I drove us up the Pacific Coast Highway north toward Santa Barbara with the sparkling Pacific to our left, a good opportunity to catch up.

Gonen had been right in the middle of taking his final exams to become a lawyer and had two more to take, but they conflicted with the hearing date, which he considered more important. What days these had been for him to decide to jump. He told me he'd never believed in demons, but he did now. He saw them at work in all the overwhelming drama surrounding him. Again, I wanted to assure him that, if he had second thoughts, which would be only natural after a jump, I'd understand. But his resolve was evident in everything we discussed. He conveyed the warm fraternal greetings from our friends at Shin Bet from his meeting only a few hours before.

We reminisced about a botched "7UP operation" where the head of Shin Bet interpreted a terrorist leader's text requesting 7UP as code for seven imminent terrorist strikes. The Shin Bet leader ordered them to go in and arrest everyone even though they could miss their real target, the head of the snake, Ibrahim Hamid. They ended up in a firefight that demolished an eight-story building, and all they found in the rubble was a case of 7UP soda. Gonen had been against going in prematurely and ended up being the scapegoat on a bogus charge.

Gonen had gone from being a successful handler with the power of armies and weapons at his command—which is how I'd known him—to being ostracized, totally broken, and stripped of his civil rights, employee rights, and pension. He finally sued to get his pension, but the judge told him, "Forget about it; go home." The judges were all afraid of Shin Bet, as were the politicians; everyone was.

Gonen said he was jealous of my freedom. I had lost everything and was in the middle of the storm, but I was free. My example encouraged him to break the chain of fear that the demon Shin Bet still had wrapped tightly around his mind. He was taking back his freedom from those bastards whom he'd served and who'd treated him like a dog.

When we settled into my modest digs in Santa Barbara, I told him about this invitation to go to Washington for an award ceremony. Would he be interested in going? He said, "Let's go."

I called the number I was given, and Sarah N. Stern answered, which was my first contact with this woman. She had a warm but strong voice. No one had been offering me any awards, and the way she described what the award was for, I must confess, made me feel good. I looked forward to meeting her, as she sounded like someone who understood what I was about, who honored *why* I'd done what

I'd done, not just *what* I'd done. Her voice for the moment drowned out the voice of my harridan prosecutor, Ms. Calcador, playing on a loop in my mind and saying that she, representing the full might of the US government, would fight me for eternity.

MEETING SARAH STERN

I had arrived in the US during the Republican Bush years, but a different Washington met us now. The Republicans had not only lost the White House but Congress as well. Those who had been defending me at that time—FOX News, the evangelical community, and some Jewish groups—were not happy with Barack Hussein Obama. That much I understood. But I had no idea how the political system in Washington actually worked or how to maneuver in it. Again, my lodestar in an alien and unfamiliar situation, if not in every situation, was to stick to my truth.

Gonen and I went to a café near Capitol Hill to meet with Sarah Stern. It's very hard for me to trust people, but I felt a connection with Sarah right away. She came across as a caring and loving person. It was mutual; as she would always say, she was my Jewish mother. After we sat down, it was immediately clear how fortuitous it was that Gonen had come. Gonen not only gave my story credibility, but he himself was credible, the son of an Israeli general, not someone off the street. Right away he and Sarah spoke Hebrew, since they had similar backgrounds.

She'd read my book, believed my story, and was very touched by it. She recognized that I was following my moral compass, pursuing human interest over tribal interest. I was challenging the collective consciousness of a nation that praised suicide bombers. In my experience, the West Bank was a nation sinking and drowning in hatred, the most negative and self-defeating of human emotions. For this Orthodox Jewish woman, she followed the Jewish proverb that whoever saves one life saves an entire world.

As I mentioned earlier, the title of the dinner was *Rays of Light in the Darkness*. She saw me as coming out of that darkness and telling an honest truth. For Sarah, the question became, *How could I not give the award to this Palestinian who perfectly matches the award criteria?* Generally, the awards went to congressional members, political figures, philanthropists, those leaders who shared the belief in a strong United States and a self-sufficient Israel. Some had already been chosen, and she hastened to add me as a last-minute award winner.

The more I became aware of all the forces at play, especially in Jewish circles, the more I realized how courageous her decision was to give this award to me, such a controversial figure. There were Jewish organizations, most notably the all-powerful AIPAC, which at that point didn't want anything to do with me, as I've mentioned. Some misgivings could be attributed to not believing me, but most were a result of political correctness.

The issue was my criticism of Islam. I was saying on CNN and FOX News that Allah and Muhammad were terrorists, and that the religion was fostering terrorism. Everyone was fine pointing to modern terrorists and the devil bin Laden, but Muhammad himself carried a sword. Why be afraid to criticize the Prophet or the religion itself? I had the authority to question it, as I had come out of the mosque. I was naming things for what they were. I was not a white supremacist or a right-wing Zionist. I was just a Palestinian Muslim who had sacrificed a lot for the Muslim project. If they wanted to fight terrorism, that wouldn't stop honor killing or rape or using women as slaves. Why not attack the dogma, the seventh-century beliefs imprisoning Muslims that produced bin Ladens?

When I spoke this truth, I was made to sound like a madman. That was Amanpour's message. AIPAC did not like my extreme approach, thinking I was promoting Islamophobia. In America, Muslims were a religious minority, as were Jews, for that matter, and you did not full-out attack a religion—especially at this time, after

September 11, when the Muslim community was being harassed and discriminated against.

Ironically, some years later I changed my views on Muhammad, taking a deep dive into his life and then writing a novel portraying the many-faceted Prophet as a man of peace forced to take up arms by the Meccan establishment threatened by his enlightened views—such as abolishing slavery and female infanticide.

We were halfway through our tea and conversation when I mentioned how grateful I was that Gonen had come all the way from Israel to testify at my deportation hearing in San Diego.

"Your what?" Sarah asked.

"Deportation. I'm a deportee. The government wants to send me back to Palestine, as I supported terrorism."

For a moment Sarah was speechless. She saw that this would be a death sentence for me. I could see her mind racing, fueled by outrage. "You're condemned by your own people, disowned by your family, and now Obama's deporting you!"

From that moment on, Sarah's priority become fighting my deportation, not the awards event. Never mind that the effort to deport me had started in the Bush administration; Sarah saw herself stepping into my corner facing the representatives of the Obama government. The narrative to save this hero's life from a grave injustice was set. And a receptive and influential audience for this story was gathering in the Capitol tomorrow.

The dinner was held in the impressive rotunda of the neoclassical Capitol building, the epicenter of legislative power in the country. Inspired by the Pantheon in Rome, high above was a golden dome and on the walls large paintings of events from early American history. Our event occupied one side of this rather awesome space, with chairs, tables, and a speaker's rostrum imported for the occasion. When Gonen and I arrived, a crowd of invitees had already gathered, drinks in hand, their chatter echoing off the walls of this cavernous space. I didn't recognize anybody. Certainly, I figured no one knew me, though my name as an honoree must have made people curious. Scattered among the suits were some Africans and Asians in more colorful and imaginative garb. This assemblage was right-wing conservative Republicans and Democrats strongly supportive of Israel—mostly members of Congress, staffers, ambassadors, high-level government officials, think-tank types, lobbyists, and selected sympathetic media.

We were warmly greeted by Sarah. She took me around to introduce me, being quite selective to home in on those who could help my cause—now *our* cause. As the consummate lobbyist, she stayed on message, as they say. The message was, "This hero who fought against terrorism is seeking asylum in our free country but is being deported back to certain death by Barack Hussein Obama because of his political beliefs." She adjusted her message depending on the listener, but it elicited the desired responses, which were along the lines of "That's terrible!" and "We have to do something about that!"

I was surprised to learn that among this group, the current party talking points were that Obama was secretly Muslim and, with the help of the Council on American–Islamic Relations (CAIR), was recommending Muslim ideologues for top positions in Homeland Security under then-secretary Janet Napolitano. To those with these beliefs, it made sense that I was being punished for my beliefs and actions. Several people had heard of me and the book, and many who were either Christian or keeping up to date on the Middle East invited me to come to their offices in the Capitol to share my views on the Middle East. Sarah introduced me to the bald James Woolsey, whom she called Jim, former head of the CIA and an honoree from last year.

The time came for the awards. The honorees for 2010 included two or three members of Congress, author Amil Imani, and me, not only a foreigner but a deportee. Sarah introduced me both in a heartfelt way but also with a very accurate account of what I'd done, why

I'd done it, and the price I'd paid. And of course, she stayed on message. There was no reason for me to get up and say anything after that; the audience was totally with me. Still, they all were expecting me to say something. My English was not nearly as good as it is now, but I had by then considerable public speaking experience in this country. If the mantra for the political lobbyist is to stay on message, mine was to always stick to my truth. I don't particularly remember what I said, but I do remember I got a standing ovation, though that could be attributed to Sarah's priming the pump with my résumé.

One important result of the evening was that Sarah's friend Jim Woolsey wrote an op-ed in *The Washington Post* that sent to a broader audience the message of the evening. He even went so far as to call Napolitano's decision in my case idiotic. Which it was, but it wasn't her decision, as I'm sure the former governor of Arizona had never heard of me. The decision was made from the lowest echelons of Homeland Security back in Anaheim during the Bush administration. The piece did raise the question of whether the decision was simply a bureaucratic one that could be easily remedied or whether this was a Barack Hussein Obama policy.

Anaheim was when the bureaucratic train had left the station with Judge Bartolomei and Prosecutor Calcador coming onboard. But now the Sarah Express was picking up speed on the same track, barreling toward the same destination. This being Washington, everyone reads the liberal *Post*, even the far right. So there was no way this was going to escape Madame Napolitano's attention. For better or worse remained to be seen, as this opinion piece could produce the opposite result. "Idiotic" is not a term of endearment. As it turned out, Sarah wrote the op-ed and Jim signed it. The next stop for the Sarah Express was Congress the next day.

Gonen and I met with Sarah early in the morning in the same rotunda to start our rounds from office to office, rushing down the long Capitol corridors to be on time for the next meeting. The

Sarah-Gonen-Mosab dog and pony show was out of the gate early. She seemed to know everyone, and most on a first-name basis. Every time we got in an elevator, it was "Hi Sarah" with a smile and maybe a bit of quick gossip or business talk. This was her beat, after all; she was a professional lobbyist, a pro, and her organization was well funded and had some clout, as we had witnessed the evening before. Gonen was an expert in intelligence and Israeli domestic politics, and of course he gave me the all-important bona fides. I was the protagonist in the drama of whether my head would be chopped off or not.

Here I was being swept along toward the showdown in San Diego. Luckily in the partisan, divided legislature, I had two cards playing in my favor. Because of what I'd done and what I professed, two groups supported me: pro-Israel circles and Christians. In the partisan landscape of American politics, these two issues enjoyed mostly bipartisan support. Israel was a third rail of American politics; at that time, if you wanted to get elected and not electrocuted, you did not criticize Israeli policy. And what politician would pass up the opportunity to toss out a few "God bless Americas"? So whatever office we went into, whether Democrat or Republican, I received a warm welcome with either of my two labels, *Muslim converted Christian* or *Israeli hero*, or both.

We made a formidable trio. Mother Sarah was the one who knew everyone and made them feel comfortable. Gonen had come from the war zone of Israel and was a veteran of well-respected Israeli intelligence. I was the one who made people uncomfortable, the wild one. It was not as though we went hat in hand pleading my case; no, as three experts on the complexities of the conflict-riven Middle East, we had a lot to offer. We met with staffers on the Senate Committee on Foreign Relations and the House Permanent Select Committee on Intelligence, and we even ventured into the Homeland Security committee offices to visit the Subcommittee on Counterterrorism, Law Enforcement, and Intelligence. The staffers tended to be better informed on

specific issues, more so than their bosses, the representatives, who had
to cover so much, especially given half their time was spent dialing for
dollars in the money-driven American electoral system. The staffers
asked good questions, and discussion was productive.

When I say I made people across the table uncomfortable, it was
when the issue of my pending deportation would come up. I took the
tack of, "You want to deport me? Go ahead, but my blood will be on
your hands."

I was aggressive, because my head was on the block, and that went
beyond good manners. Sarah and Gonen would sharply jab me in the
ribs to shut me up or at least tamp the fire down. This set our listeners
back on their heels, as most had not heard I was being deported. My
passionate behavior, however, did not derail the Sarah Express. The
staffers promised to convey the message to their boss. We did have a
chance to speak to some representatives; a few were at the event the
night before. One Democrat from California presented me with an
American flag that had once flown over the Capitol. Back in Ramallah, it would have been hard to imagine such a scene taking place.

One idea was to pass a special resolution from Congress granting me citizenship. This would have to be inserted as a rider to a
larger bill, usually on a totally different subject. A few in Congress
seemed to be on board with it, but the right to do it was controversial
enough without jumping through all the legislative hoops. Making
noise in Washington to drop my deportation case was an easier sell as
we made the rounds.

So what did this unexpected whirlwind effort accomplish? The
departments of the federal government, like Homeland Security
or Energy or Defense, are theoretically accountable to the legislative branch and their committees, which exercise oversight over the
bureaucracy. Twenty-two members of Congress, from both major
parties, signed a letter to Janet Napolitano supporting my asylum
case. The op-ed piece in *The Washington Post* also certainly meant

that my plight had come to the attention of the secretary. So the issue was on her desk.

Still, for Homeland Security bureaucracy, it was clear by my own admission that I had broken the law. In this country the rule of law trumps (almost) all. Having supported a terrorist organization seemed to override any claim to refugee status because of religious persecution. After all, the "bleeding-heart liberal" President Obama became the "deporter in chief," with more than 2.5 million "illegal alien" scalps on his belt. *Would I be one of them?*

What has stayed with me years after all this drama was the support of Mother Sarah. Sarah belonged to the ultra-orthodox conservative persuasion of Judaism and was part of a very religious family. When she said, "You're like one of my family," she meant it, as she later invited me to her daughter's wedding. It was an Orthodox wedding, with men and women separate, just like a traditional Muslim wedding, which was quite familiar to me. It could not have been easy for Sarah to invite me, as I was controversial, to say the least, and not from this Orthodox tribe, nor even from a Jewish background. Once she came to visit me after Walid had slandered me publicly and said, "I don't know if he's telling the truth. I don't understand Arabic. I don't care what you said. You will always be my son and part of my family." She was always there for me.

MY FATE: ASYLUM OR DEPORTATION?

Back in Santa Barbara, Gonen and I managed to catch our breath after that whirlwind visit to the nation's capital. The climax of all these efforts was to play out in a couple of days in that courthouse in San Diego. I was mentally prepared for being deported, though the results from the DC trip were encouraging. Also buoyed by faith in the innate justice of the American constitutional system, I nurtured the hope that it would be a happy ending. Naive? Maybe.

Friends called to say that they would come to San Diego to support me on the day of the hearing. That was nice to hear, but I didn't encourage them, as it certainly wouldn't affect the result. This wouldn't be decided by a head count. I was keeping my blog up to date, so that was how those interested followed the situation. I had a fan base! There was a petition being circulated in my favor. Again, this was not something I had orchestrated or even suggested; it just was happening.

The next development was when my attorney, Steve, called and said the venue had been changed. It was now down by the Mexican border at the Otay Mesa Detention Center for federal immigration. That didn't sound good. They said it was for my own security. As an open critic of Islam and a former spy for Israel, I could be a target for assassination. The authorities worried there could be a large, hostile crowd outside the courtroom in San Diego, which could lead to violence. I had put up on my blog the phone number of the prosecutor, Kerri Calcador, and other relevant Homeland Security numbers along with my asylum case code number. They'd been deluged with calls both from the States and abroad and were taken aback by the public reaction. The authorities believed they could better control an angry crowd and shield me at this high-security Otay Mesa location. Better to be safe than sorry.

This struck me as rather paradoxical. The government was arguing I was a threat to American security, but they were taking exceptional measures to protect my security so a hearing could be properly held and they could deport a live body. It was like someone terminally ill on death row being kept alive by the doctors so he could be executed on the scheduled date.

The day before we were to head south to Otay Mesa, the story was on the local TV evening news. And it was on FOX nationally, a David and Goliath story with mighty Goliath saying David had threatened his security, which in the Bible story turned out to be fatally true. A FOX commentator also mentioned how unheard of it was for an intelligent agent like Gonen to go public, compromising their identity, to testify on behalf of a former asset. Given this media buzz, it was not a complete surprise, driving into Otay Mesa after passing the obligatory check- point, that I saw a crowd and five or six remote TV broadcasting trucks. At least the familiar bright logos of the FOX and NBC local channels gave some color to this desolate desert landscape and the forbidding detention center, crouching behind chain-link fence and razor wire.

We got out to face the day. Gonen and I were properly attired in dark blue suits; Gonen wore a tie. I was clean-shaven, no ter- rorist black beard. Walking with Steve, my lawyer, we headed for the entrance, accompanied by cameras and microphones and jour- nalists' questions. It wasn't so long ago on my journey that the boy from Ramallah had been alone without an attorney confronting a disbelieving Homeland Security officer in Anaheim. In the crowd I spotted friends: Denise, who came all the way from Chicago; and Ron Brackin, who had worked with me on the book. Matt Smith waved, and I recognized some faces from the church. There were a lot of people I didn't recognize, but right away I got the sense they all were in my corner, some shouting encouragement. No hostile shouts or insults. While the vibes from the crowd were positive, facing the chain-link entrance festooned with intimidating red warning signs, I had the sense this was the anus of the immigration system. The only reassuring sign read "Weapons Free Area." The sole weapon I had was my voice. This time I would speak, unlike some other perfunctory hearings when I hadn't been allowed to speak. Still, I could imagine Dante's famous inscription over the Gate of Hell: "Abandon all hope, ye who enter here."

The three of us were checked through past the metal detectors by uniformed guards. For my specific case, the only people allowed into the center were those who were directly involved in the proceedings. They didn't want to risk chaos in the courtroom. That meant the media and my friends, some who had traveled long distances, couldn't attend the hearing, which they could have if it had been in San Diego. It was going to be a long day. I felt for them, waiting out there in the brutal desert sun.

We moved through a warren of corridors. Gonen was peeled off and escorted to a witness holding room to wait for the judge to call him. They did not want the proceedings to shape his testimony. We exchanged encouraging glances.

My lawyer and I were shown into a small hearing room. The colorless walls seemed to exude the dashed hopes of the thousands who once sat in the chair I headed for. There were police officers and immigration officers present, and a stenographer was busily typing. There, sitting at a small desk to the left of the judge's bench, was my nemesis, Prosecutor Kerri Calcador, chief counsel for Immigration and Customs Enforcement (ICE), ready to fight me through eternity. The Honorable Judge Bartolomei sat in an elevated position and appeared to be consulting papers. I, the security threat, sat down to face the stalwart defenders of the homeland. This time I had my lawyer. I readied myself for battle, cultivating my arguments, though knowing I depended on Gonen and my lawyer, who could communicate in legalese.

The judge looked up from his papers and nodded to the prosecutor to begin. *Here we go.* Calcador stood and began to talk, but I didn't understand what she was saying, perhaps due to my limited English. She then handed a paper up to the judge, who looked surprised and glanced at my attorney. Steve was looking at me in a very strange way, like he was completely shocked. I didn't know why he was shocked; I wanted to ask what was going on, but I couldn't interrupt the judge. There was a moment of confusion. I heard the judge saying "subject to a normal background check." The judge banged the gavel down. *Is my worst-case scenario being played out?* The judge stood up. Kerri Calcador stepped toward me with her hand outstretched and said one word, "Congratulations." *What? Why? I still don't understand.*

Steve said the government was dropping its case. "You are granted asylum subject to a normal background check."

Another day at the office for them; a new life for me.

All of this happened in less than two minutes, and I had no idea what was happening. I could hardly believe it, nor could my lawyer. It took a while for the smiles to break through. For it to end this way was so unexpected, it took time to register as real.

Gonen appeared in the room, having no clue what had just happened. Somebody went to call for him and he figured his big moment to testify had arrived. I told him what had just happened, and he was as surprised as everyone else and as happy. The irony, of course, is after all his soul-searching in Israel, burning his bridges behind him, he never got the chance to testify. But his presence in Washington with Sarah and in Congress definitely made a difference. And the point never was about whether he testified or not; it was about who he was.

We stepped out of the detention center into the bright Southern Californian sunlight, me with a new label, *asylee*. Taken by surprise as much as we were, the relaxing media snapped to it, cameras out, as we were surrounded by our well-wishers, hugs all around, amazed laughter, me thanking everyone. Celebration. Gonen and I embraced for the cameras. Everyone was happy; the media had a good story, and now we all had an unexpected free day in front of us. For me, the expression *free day* had a lot more meaning. That sword constantly hovering above my head had been withdrawn. I called Sarah to give her the good news, which was due in large part to her efforts.

My story made the evening news and the printed media the next day.

A NEW NORMAL

Gonen and I, relieved and happy, returned to Santa Barbara for a couple of days before he was to fly back to Tel Aviv. He called his wife with the news. We had already informed some of the Israeli media. I was prepared to launch a campaign if anything happened to him on his return.

Of course, we were in touch with our go-to journalist, Avi Issacharoff from *Haaretz*. Before he became a journalist, he was in Israeli special forces operating in the Palestinian territories, and his job included a skill set ranging from arrests to assassinations. Most people didn't know his background. He moved freely back and forth to Ramallah, dealing with militias like Hamas and Fatah and with officials. He'd attend every demonstration walking among the crowds, trusting that the big letters "PRESS" across his back would protect him. I used to caution him to be careful, and he was, as he was justifiably scared. Later, in 2014, at a violent protest demonstration at Beitunia, a Palestinian demonstrator accused him and his cameraman of being Israeli intelligence agents. They were attacked and beaten by an angry mob of masked rioters. He told me he had been terrified. He saw death in the chaos of the mob. He was lucky that the Palestinian Authority police were there and intervened, saving his life.

Gonen, bless him, is the sweetest person you can imagine. He witnessed and lived the brutality of that dark world. Shin Bet disposed of him, not because of a bogus charge of financial wrongdoing; they thought he was too soft. Later, Gonen became active in Africa, fighting for the wildlife like elephants and gorillas against AK-47–toting poachers. He trains game park rangers in this bush war, not unlike the war on terrorism targeting the innocent. Recently, carrying an Israeli flag, he threw himself in front of the prime minister's limousine to protest Netanyahu's corruption. He was hit by a Shin Bet officer and slammed to the ground. He is still fighting the good fight, no matter how the media frames it.

I drove Gonen down to LAX to catch the plane back to his fate in his homeland. As it turned out, nothing happened. He went through passport control and customs, like any returning Israeli citizen, and embraced his wife. I think he believed that Shin Bet basically said, "Okay, we'll let them have this one." I'm not so sure. The media, including Avi, was waiting there, after all, and if he'd been detained, there would have been a brouhaha.

I could rest easy. The dread I had been feeling before the hearing dissolved. Now I could go about my life in Santa Barbara. I was not a citizen, but I was no longer under the authority of that Homeland Security officer in Anaheim.

15

Life in La-La Land

The book was still generating income, and invitations to speak continued to come in. I also received inquiries about the "property," to use a Hollywood term. A production company from Hollywood, Sixth Sense, expressed interest in making the book into a major motion picture. My lawyer Doug Stone, who had been fielding inquiries, said they were a company that had a track record and were willing to drive up to Santa Barbara to meet me. *Why not? Let's see who pays for lunch.*

Coming with the two producers was an assistant, Sam Feuer, an American Israeli who had been born in Connecticut and served three years in a combat unit of the Israeli Air Force. He had a busy career as an actor, had been in Spielberg's *Munich,* and, enamored of the movie business, aspired to a career behind the camera as a producer. Sam was a fan of the book. I didn't give it much thought, and Doug was always letting me know that even with a bestselling thriller spy story, a popular movie genre, the odds of ever seeing it made were long indeed. That's show biz.

As money initially started to roll into my bank account, I went out and bought a Ford Mustang. After all the drama of the asylum hearing, I was happily driving along one day and passed a Porsche dealer. As someone who has always enjoyed a good car, I thought, *Why not take advantage of these dealers and take a test drive?* Well, the Cayman drove like no other car I'd ever driven. When I said to the beautiful lady behind the desk that I wanted to buy it, she saw a third-world type with an accent, definitely not born in Montecito.

"What about your credit?"

"I'm paying cash."

"Cash?"

The bank was nearby, so I walked there, came back with a cashier's check, traded in my new Mustang, and within half an hour drove away in my new Porsche.

My motive for buying the car was how much fun it was to drive. People assumed I bought it for the prestige. That was the last thing on my mind. I could afford it. I bought it. No problem.

My friends, though, saw a problem. They thought I was crazy, since I was supposed to be hiding out, being inconspicuous. *Shoot, I never considered that.* It must be stated that despite the risky downside, the Porsche also had a rewarding upside: women loved it.

I had some friends who lived in Scottsdale, Arizona. I had met Ruth Lefebvre in San Diego, her husband being a famous figure in Major League Baseball. We'd stayed in touch, and Ruth had come up to Otay Mesa to support me. Now she called me and invited me down to visit them. So, revving up the Porsche, I hit the highways and byways to Arizona. When I drove up to their splendid mansion in my Porsche, Ruth didn't know how to respond: "When I knew you in San Diego, you were homeless. How do you always manage to do the unexpected?" They were a down-to-earth American family, Christian and conservative Republicans, wealthy but humble. They opened their hearts and their home to me.

Scottsdale turned out to be magic, one of the best times of my life. The beauty of the desert was magnificent, the dryness similar to summers in Ramallah. Prices were much cheaper than they were in Santa Barbara. Ruth asked me to stay at their place, but within a few days I found a perfect contemporary studio nearby and settled in, leaving Santa Barbara behind. I felt very safe in this part of America. Feeling safe was not a feeling I'd enjoyed often in my life.

I got into cycling for the first time, and ran, hiked, and did some yoga. I bought a good bike, and two to three times a week I'd head out into the desert for a thirty-five- to fifty-mile ride. Rising above Scottsdale and the Phoenix area was Camelback Mountain, which had two steep hiking trails, Cholla and Echo Canyon. The rocks were desert-red, some of the narrow steeper portions had handrails, and the rocky trail could be tricky. And you had to keep an eye out for rattlesnakes. I would run it; up and back was only a mile and a half, but the last part was a challenging scramble over large boulders. The view from the top was worth it, as the urban sprawl of Phoenix spread out forever across the flat desert land below. I even did a couple more skydives so I could see the view from 10,000 feet. With all these workouts I was as healthy as I'd ever been—and I think perhaps the happiest: I was free from so many worries that had dogged me in San Diego and Santa Barbara—not to mention Ramallah!

At the same time, this proved to be a period of unavoidable introspection. I realized that true knowledge is self-knowledge and that my expression was not enough. No matter how articulate my language was, I was unable fully to convey my truth. What was my mission? Was it all nonsense? This was the first time that I really wanted to study philosophy, which I started reading.

In the meantime, I was diving inside, traveling into my inner self trying to understand the structure of my mind and how it had come about. I wanted some experiences to be real, and others I wanted to forget. I discovered that I had something to say. I had witnessed everything for a reason. I wanted to learn the truth of human nature and share the beauty in it. Somehow I had confronted the truth of death, realizing we were all in denial. Yet I also knew there was no place to hide from it.

After nearly a year in Arizona, Doug Stone called and said we had a movie deal to make *Son of Hamas* with Sixth Sense. I decided I needed to move to LA to be close to the filmmakers and learn what it was like to make a movie. I wanted to be available for any writer, though they wouldn't cover my expenses to be there all the time. The truth was, I was very excited. For a Muslim, going on *hadj*, traveling once in a lifetime to Mecca, is a prescribed religious duty. For anyone with aspirations to become part of the glamorous world of making movies, Hollywood was the mecca.

GOING HOLLYWOOD

Like everyone in the world who watches movies, growing up in Palestine we had our fantasy about Hollywood. My fellow Palestinians thought America was whatever Hollywood showed us. Now I was driving into this reality. I was not a starstruck, pretty girl from the Midwest getting off a bus in downtown LA, nor even an ambitious film school graduate driving across the country in his VW bus. I was driving into LA in my Porsche with money in my pocket and an option payment from a production company, ready to make a major motion picture from my book. That had to be an auspicious start. I had learned something in my short years in America: money rules, appearances matter, and have a good lawyer! That was certainly true for Hollywood.

I settled in at the Hollywood Tower luxury apartments, which promised "French Norman architectural details . . . to those with a taste for glamour, romance, mystery, and fine craftsmanship. Stepping through an enchanting doorway that once welcomed Monroe, Bogart,

and Chaplin, you'll discover timeless Hollywood style reborn."[14] I
went for the more modern Sunset and Vine Tower in this complex
that had floor-to-ceiling glass windows with magnificent views of
downtown LA and the Hollywood sign in the Hollywood Hills.

From my vantage point, down on the street there was always some
film being shot with the production trucks and the crew scurrying
about. I settled into my magnificent digs, shopped at the most expensive clothing stores, and had my dry cleaning delivered to my door. I
was "going Hollywood," adding a new label to be affixed to me.

I called Sam Feuer, wondering if I should drop in at the Sixth
Sense production offices in Beverly Hills. Sam would be my guide
and intelligence source throughout my Hollywood adventure. He
remains a close friend to this day. He said they were still looking for
a screenwriter, so there wasn't anything for me to do until they found
the right person. He said that he and I should meet, but not at the
office. Sixth Sense's office and website address were in prestigious Beverly Hills. That address, however, was a tiny shop in Beverly Hills that
advertised, "[If] you are looking to project a professional image for
your business, . . . we offer mailbox rentals with a Beverly Hills street
address. No PO Box!" In Hollywood, appearances count.

In reality, they worked out of their apartments and took meetings
in upscale coffeehouses or trendy Hollywood watering holes. For me
they proved to be a good entry point into the Hollywood working
world, as I had the opportunity to meet directors and writers who
would invite me to screenings and receptions where I'd meet other
people, which would lead to more invitations. That's how the Hollywood snowball rolls.

Once a movie is given the green light, the first step in the lengthy
process of producing a movie is devoting attention to the script. Alfred
Hitchcock once said, "To make a great film, you need three things—
the script, the script, and the script." After my arrival, Sixth Sense
took two months interviewing potential writers. I took that time to

learn more about the film business. In 2010, of the roughly 50,000 screenplays that are registered with the Writers Guild of America each year, not to mention the thousands more not registered, Hollywood studios released about 150 movies. This meant that the chance of having your screenplay made into a feature film released by a studio was less than 1 percent—0.3 percent, actually, or one in three hundred.[15] To beat the odds, it made sense to hire a writer with a successful track record. The producers finally hired David Aaron Cohen, who had written the successful movie *Friday Night Lights* about a heroic high school football team in a depressed Texas town. *Friday Night Lights*, which went on to become a hit TV series, was adapted from a book, as would be the case now with *Son of Hamas*.

David was a beautiful man, a nice guy with a wonderful family. I was to spend a year working on the script with him, which, just like the writing of my memoir, entailed endless rewriting! I learned that once a script is approved, the next step is to set a budget. The budget will give the best estimate of what producing the movie will cost.

Movie budgets have two parts: one part is termed *above the line* and the other part is termed *below the line*. Above the line includes the costs of the story rights (where I came in) and the costs of the high-end talent, like the main cast, the director, the producers, the writers (David), and maybe the composer and the director of photography if they're "names." People's fees are subject to negotiation (enter agents, managers, attorneys). So much of the talk at company meetings and over coffee was about the talent. *What would be the ideal casting for this project we're working on? Okay, who could we get realistically?*

Let's say we wanted Star One. *Is he available? Do we have a way of getting around Star One's agent, who won't even read the script? Isn't that makeup girl on his last flick still fucking him, and doesn't Charlie know her well? Yes, but the director we have in mind swore he'd never work with him again. Yeah, but I hear his marriage is going south and he's going to need money, big money.* And so on. Gossip, okay, but there are similarities with the intelligence game: know everything and have good sources, and that gossip can result in putting together a blockbuster or, in the intelligence game, preventing a block busted.

All this talent has to be contractually locked in before principal photography begins, as that's when your below-the-line money's flying out the door and you can't afford a dispute derailing production. The market system determines a hierarchy of values to these players. The average moviegoer's first question is "Who's in it?" not "Who wrote it?" Hence, A-list actors are the most expensive, writers the least. For those who see themselves playing a role behind the camera, the constant refrain I heard was, "I'm in props, but eventually I want to direct" or "I'm a camera assistant, but eventually I want to direct." The director carries the prestigious, main creative position, the one of control. Writers and actors often aspire to be directors. And everyone seems to be writing a script. Such is the Hollywood merry-go-round.

The below-the-line budget is pretty much everyone and everything else to cover production and postproduction. If you've stayed in your theater seat (or on your couch) long enough to watch the credits endlessly roll by, you can't help but be impressed by the number of people and jobs and technology that it takes to make a motion picture. From the budget perspective, below-the-line elements like the crew, editors, extras, bit players, locations, wardrobe, art department, and so on generally command known rates, as most are unionized. These are your fixed costs, while above-the-line items require the producer's negotiating skills and connections.

Hovering over all of this is the question of finance. Once a budget is set with some "players" attached, the producers need to find someone to supply the money. Movie studios are not all that profitable, despite box office numbers being hyped on the daily news. Moviemaking is both an art and a business, and many are drawn to it because of their love of movies, not because of monetary profit.

Once the script is written, the budget signed off on, and finances assured, the project is no longer what's technically termed "in development" (sometimes called "development hell"). Early one morning on a hushed set come the voices, "Sound rolling. Camera rolling." The director calls out the first "Action," and the marathon of production begins. My hope, after this quick educational interlude, was that all that effort by so many people working together would manifest itself on the big screen, that it would mirror our reality, project who we were. Film is such a powerful tool, perhaps more powerful than religion—though combining religion and movies has proved a winning box office bet.

Working with David on the script, getting guidance from Sam, and being invited into the circuit of screenings and receptions filled in part of the Hollywood coloring book for me. I never lacked for something to do. I was busy during the days and many of the nights.

MY PATH TO YOGA

As someone who always sought to be physically active, I kept up the bike riding that I had enjoyed in Scottsdale and continued to pursue yoga. Bikram yoga, or hot yoga, taught by an Indian named Bikram Choudhury, had taken Hollywood by storm, and the classes were crowded with celebrities. His trademark was teaching his students in an overheated classroom, up to 105 degrees Fahrenheit. He fit right into the California culture, with a sharp business sense for self-promotion and branding for his hot yoga. He drove around Los Angeles in a Rolls-Royce convertible with the top down and vanity license plates that read "BIKRAM." Living the American Dream, I guess. He franchised yoga studios all over the United States. When I first arrived in the States, Yvonne took me to a class, and I had continued the practice off and on since then. The LA classes with Bikram himself teaching became a staple of my Hollywood life. I enjoyed it; it relaxed me and kept me healthy, sweating, and stretching along with all these gorgeous half-naked students, many of whom I recognized from the screen. I attended classes consistently for three years.

A class was ninety minutes, and sometimes Bikram gave us a break and then we'd go right into the next class. Toward the end of my three years in LA, I felt the limits of his very physical style of yoga, almost militaristic in the same postures, or *asanas*, repeated daily. He tried unsuccessfully through the courts to patent the series of asanas in his routine in his name. Had he succeeded, an earthquake in India could well be attributed to the yogis of some five millennia stirring in protest in their graves. As I write this, my daily regimen is three hours of Ashtanga yoga every morning, and so I have come a long way from the hot yoga of Bikram. But he had introduced me to the practice of yoga, and I'm grateful for that.

ADVENTURES ON TWO WHEELS

I got pretty serious about bike riding while in LA, which seems to reflect my penchant for discipline when I take up a new activity. Throughout my life, I've been physically active, often quite intensely. It doesn't guarantee good health, but it's better than being lazy. After exercising every day for many years, I have become accustomed to a certain level of energy I don't want to compromise. Also, it boosts confidence. But there is also the risk of getting so attached to intense physical activities that they become an addiction. Balance, always balance.

I had one of those superlight carbon fiber bicycles that weigh just over ten pounds. You hardly feel it; it gives you the advantage of speed, and you can travel long distances on it. I had all the gear, looked the part, and it kept me in good shape, burning up the calories of all those finger foods I ate at receptions. I got in the habit of cycling thirty-five to fifty miles a few times a week, sometimes doing one-hundred-mile rides up and down the Pacific Coast, inhaling that ocean air. Also, biking is often a faster way to move around a city like LA with its congested traffic. I could go from Hollywood to the ocean in twenty minutes compared to the trip taking up to forty-five minutes by car.

Ever since I lived in San Diego, I've owned a motorcycle, sometimes even two. In Hollywood I had a Ducati Scrambler and a Harley Breakout. I've had broken bones and my share of nasty road rash to remind me that I do have skin in the game to lose. It's risky for sure, but the spirit of adventure will not be denied. The thrill is there, partly I suppose because it is risky. I did go back up to the Ojai Valley from time to time with all those great mountain roads I raced around on my Kawasaki when I lived in Santa Barbara.

My motorcycles, like my bicycles, proved useful in traffic-challenged LA for getting from place to place and finding a parking place. They had it all over my pedal bikes when it came to climbing grades in the hilly City of Angels. Also, the motorcycles were a great opportunity to get further out of smoggy LA, hit the open road, and feel that fresh California air stream by my helmet. I was still flying quite a bit around the country. I could leave my house and be at the departure gate in less than half an hour. How was that possible? Less than twenty minutes on my Ducati to LAX, which by car can take thirty-five minutes to an hour. If you have a motorcycle, you don't pay for parking, and so you park close to the terminal. Then security. We're in the post–September 11 era where fear still reigns; a handful of Saudis led by Osama bin Laden had utterly changed the experience of travel for millions upon millions of citizens, who now had to be searched and sometimes humiliated. Rarely have so few affected the lives of so many. But here I was stateless, the son of a terrorist, accused of being one, and fitting the terrorist profile, and I was breezing straight through security, no taking off my shoes or my jacket, no taking off my belt, no showing my carry-on or my laptop. *Hello?* The government wanted to speed up the process and give priority to those who traveled a lot. I passed a security clearance test to be fast-tracked. So I always went into the fast-track lane, and across from me in another lane was a long line of passengers, standing, waiting, a testament to how much of its freedom America has had to give up.

THE GREEN PRINCE

Early in my Hollywood sojourn, Doug Stone called and said, "Out of the flood of inquiries I've been fielding, there is a new one of possible interest. They want to make a documentary based on the book. The producers are Oscar-winning producers John Battsek and Simon Chinn, out of London, extraordinarily prolific and definitely at the top of their game, connected to everybody. They produced *Searching for Sugar Man, Man on Wire,* and *One Day in September,* all winning the Oscar for Best Documentary." And they knew the subject matter. As to the director, Nadav Schirman, a German-Israeli, he didn't have much of a track record, so Doug couldn't give an opinion on him. However, if Battsek and Chinn were backing him, he thought, that certainly was a recommendation. I told Doug I was definitely interested.

However, when Nadav looked into the story, he was not interested. But someone told him, "Put the book aside; at least meet with the guy." Nadav called from London to say he'd like to meet with me in New York. I was at the country music Stagecoach Festival in Indio, California, with a friend, and we were drinking our asses off. I caught a flight out of Palm Springs to the Big Apple to meet the director about a possible film. It was May 2, 2011. I didn't know it when I was on the flight, but the news had just broken that Osama bin Laden had been killed. When I landed in New York, that's all anybody was talking about. I met with Nadav in Manhattan, and somehow the most natural thing to do was to head down to Ground Zero, the site of the former World Trade Center. Nadav said, "Let's go."

It seemed all New York was gathered at Ground Zero, everyone yelling "U.S.A., U.S.A., U.S.A.!" I stood with everyone and could not help shouting out loud in that unified voice. I had seen on television the towers going down ten years before. It was when I was deep in the battle against terrorism, against people like bin Laden; I had met them in prison; I knew their true nature and the chaos this billionaire AK-47–toting Saudi wrought in his cave by inspiring tens of thousands of terrorists and fanatics around the world to kill innocents. And here I was, alive when I thought I'd never survive the Middle East.

It was a fucking great moment.

Unforgettable.

"U.S.A., U.S.A., U.S.A." I'm not pro-nationalist at all. Until recently, I've never even been a citizen of any country. It was not a matter of celebrating America or celebrating a man's death. Shouting that for me was actually saying, "Freedom, freedom, freedom," as that is what America means to me. As strange as it might sound, I always considered myself an American, admiring the freedom, the vastness, the greatness of the country. Everywhere I lived—San Diego, Santa Barbara, Scottsdale, Hollywood—I saw the contradictions, the dark side to my idealized version of badass America. But despite that, I have always felt super connected to the essence, the great ethics, the Constitution that sets America apart. What makes America the greatest for me is not the politics, not the right or left, not Hollywood, not the money-making, not Wall Street, but all of that, and beyond—way beyond.

Nadav couldn't believe it. He was blown away. At that moment I forgot that he was even there. But he saw me there, and I think it was right then that he decided to make the movie.

THE HIGH LIFE

There I was, a young, very single man with a Porsche, a Ducati, a Harley, and a six-figure bank account, living in Hollywood Tower with my celebrity neighbors, no mortgage, no family, no debts, no obligations. An objective observer would call me not only a free man but a fortunate free man with infinite possibilities before him. "Will this recently homeless hostel-hopper be able to remain a free man in this world of beautiful women, material possessions, and the pleasurable symbols of wealth?" That sounded like the pitch for a daytime soap opera. I hadn't been born into this; I hadn't gone to Hollywood High or followed in Dad's or Mom's footsteps into the industry. Being an outsider I hoped meant I wouldn't get carried away and could still laugh at the whole thing as well as at myself. Still, when in Babylon, do as the Babylonians do. And, yes, I have to acknowledge I did party a little bit.

Sex, drugs, rock 'n' roll—check, check, check. Going to a party could mean a night of all three. There were constant parties, up in the hills, down in the valleys, out in the canyons: pool parties, mansion parties, beach parties. Some lawyer or some investor or somebody who thought he owned the industry would invite a bunch of people over and throw a party. Most of the invitees and gate-crashers were on the make: *Who can I meet to move my goals forward, become a star, finance my project?* They circulated and dug for gold. This wasn't a dating or marriage market; it was a career market. The first thing someone would ask you was, "What do you do?"—which is a very American question. Your answer would place you in the industry's hierarchy, on your rung on the ladder. Should you continue the fishing expedition with this dark Arab or move on, prospecting for a more promising vein of gold?

Sometimes the party would have an ostensible reason, like New Year's, Halloween, Yom Kippur, closing a movie deal, or just plain old Saturday night. As my birthday loomed, I decided to throw my own Hollywood birthday party. I hired a sushi chef who really killed it. I hired security guards. There was my spectacular apartment, and we had this amazing swimming pool. I figured a hundred people might show up, but a hundred and fifty did. Word had gotten out. All these actresses, Playboy bunnies, wannabes, girls like nineteen, twenty, twenty-one years old, showing off their perfect bodies, with plenty of fake boobs. Everyone was asking, "Who the hell is this guy?"

I looked around and realized I didn't know any of these people. None of them were my people. And they wanted to have their picture taken with me. Just in case. Like Jay Gatsby, a certain mystery enshrouded me. *Where did he come from? How did he get so rich living the bigger life? He's someone to get to know.*

Drugs were freely available at parties, all kinds, which I took advantage of. But there was one drug I was offered several times, often by the most gorgeous of ladies, and I said no. I was scared of it. Cocaine or coke. If I had tried it then, I would have been done; I wouldn't be writing this book.

I'm glad I had the chance to fully live this phase of my journey. If I hadn't, it would continue to be a fantasy that I hadn't lived. It was fun; it was great. But everything has its end, and it was as empty as you can imagine.

Working with David and getting to know him, his wife, and family was a real privilege. For me, they represented the best of Hollywood. We certainly got to know each other, since David had delved deeply into my story and was touched by it. We connected. He knew the difficult times I had lived in when I arrived in the States and how I had lived under the threat of deportation. David cared about me, which was proven when he became responsible for the most remarkable and moving experience I had during my Hollywood journey.

David invited me to his house in North Hollywood one night, telling me that very special people were coming for a special ceremony. They wanted to meet me. It didn't sound like an industry networking event. When I walked into his large house, the place was full. There were some fifty people, including a handful of Native Americans there, all waiting for me. David explained that these people wanted to do a special ceremony to officially welcome me. "After all you've been through, the actual people of the land want to welcome you their way."

David was from Chicago but had lived a long time in the West, and he had made friends with Native Americans here. I sat in the middle of the circle they formed around me, many sitting with their drums. They started fanning smoke. I was already transported to another space. The thumping drums began. Dum, dum, dum—a mesmerizing beat, more smoke, and then the Native Americans began singing in their native language, screaming their guts out to the gods. There was nothing for me to do but surrender as they went through the customs of the ceremony. Smoke and ashes were part of it. It gives me goosebumps as I remember it, it was so powerful.

In a town where you never know who or what is real, this was real, straight to the soul. That was the moment I knew I was welcome in America. I was not afraid of the government anymore, nor afraid of all the politics surrounding my case. It was not as though these people gave this special ceremony for every arrival in the country. They declared me welcome: "The land welcomes you. The tribe welcomes you. We give you, our brother, protection from all enemies, predators, and opposing forces." That was the peak of my Hollywood experience.

Finally, after nearly a year of working on the script, the time had come to deliver the final draft to the production company. Unfortunately, they expressed disappointment; it was not what they had hoped for. They dropped the project.

Wow. After a year's work, that script joined the tens of thousands of others on dusty shelves. David received his $200,000 writing fee minus his agent's cuts. My contract, which was typical, made a smaller initial option payment but promised the big bucks only upon the first day of principal photography—the wisdom of which was only proven by our situation. At the same time, I'd had a wonderful experience, learned a lot about screenplay writing, and made good friends—not only David but Sam. Did this somehow discredit the story which had excited them? Not in the least. My story was the same. Hey, this was Hollywood.

JEWISH CONSPIRACIES?

When I was in prison serving my last sentence, I tried to spend as much time as possible reading. Aside from the Bible, the dictionary, and as many English language books as I could find, I read books written by Hamas leaders and Hamas intellectuals. In fact, I had to fight to get books approved by Hamas, and of course those were riddled with conspiracies, foremost being the Jewish conspiracies and how the Jews, with their global reach, conspired to influence and control Muslim populations and promote Hamas's enemies—notably Israel, but also the United States. The Jewish conspiracy had three dimensions: banking, Hollywood, and fashion. The irony was that after my Hollywood stint, I could say I had direct experience with all three dimensions. I had the great advantage of being able to travel, an advantage denied to that Hamas intellectual who likely never left the territories. Like most conspiracy theories, there is some truth in it, since Jews play a prominent role in all three dimensions and generally support Israel. However, my direct experience with these three areas was that it was not true that these three institutions were designed culturally, politically, or financially to destroy Islam.

My practical and personal experience with Jewish bankers and the banking system I can only report as positive. I could travel the world with little cash and use my credit cards. Better than putting one's wealth into gold or paper money to be eaten by worms, storing it in a bank gave the bank the possibility to offer loans to borrowers to launch a business or buy a house. This was sorely lacking on the West Bank, which made my remodeling a penthouse costly and frustrating. Of course, this credit system demands a sense of responsibility, and when greed rules on both ends, consumers can end up debt slaves to the banks and credit card companies. But that is human nature at work, not a Jewish conspiracy.

The fashion conspiracy idea was quite bizarre, as if fashion had been designed to become an addiction. The conspiracy idea was that Jewish companies make women look sexy so they can control politicians and the economy, while also controlling people's minds through lust and illusion. Poisoned by commercials, seductive dress, and makeup, the populace is driven to go after material items and forget God. I think a better explanation is that clothing companies will do whatever it takes to sell their products—no conspiracy needed.

Hollywood indeed has enormous global influence, and Jews have always played an outsized role in the industry. So what? On the issue of whether those in Hollywood are propagandists for Israel, making pro-Israel movies, my experience was the contrary. A wealthy Jewish friend and a big fan of my story had his well-connected attorney try to persuade his friend, a top executive at Universal, to do my story: "It's a great story; a spy story, after all." The executive could not be convinced, firmly believing that movies about Israel were box office poison.

Of course, hypocrisy reigns. Hamas leaders and their intellectuals dress in fashionable suits, have large bank accounts, and in most cases are watching porn, probably Hollywood produced. If two or three wives are not enough, they can always add a fourth. They're fighting their inner monsters, but on the outside, they're blaming someone else rather than looking within themselves and being honest with themselves. When the mind lives in hatred and darkness and has never traveled out into the diverse world we live in, has never been in a church or synagogue or Buddhist temple, then it settles on conspiracy theories to explain the problems of the world.

It seems a bit nuts to think that there are super evil masterminds who control everything with the intention of enslaving humanity, and the only way to emancipate ourselves is to go kill these masterminds.

But that is how some Palestinians and other Muslims are conditioned to think. On my journey in this search for what was true, I encountered fashion, Hollywood, banking, and those individuals who made it all run, and I discovered that it's impossible to declare everything either evil or good.

A GREEN LIGHT

The Green Prince was finally green lit, meaning it was a go. The production team hit the road. I found myself flying to Munich first class in a Lufthansa double-decker Airbus A380. This whole documentary experience would be first class all the way. I remember the airfare was like $12,000, and the film's budget some $2 million, a figure most documentary filmmakers could only dream about.

Our film set had been built in Munich. Gonen was there, as we were the two main characters in the story. Of course, we stayed in a five-star hotel. The producers, Simon Chinn and John Battsek, proved to be wonderful human beings and true artists. *How could I be so fortunate?* Being on the set gave me the direct experience of what it was really like to create a film. I was in effect an actor playing myself. This was not a documentary where I was being followed around by a cameraperson amid a real-life situation; I was in a studio speaking, not to another actor, but directly to the cold glass lens of a camera.

I would start a line and suddenly hear, "Cut!" The lighting wasn't right. *Okay.* "Action!" I'd get out a few words, then, "Cut!" Sound issue, getting some static. "Please repeat that last bit a little louder." The lighting was making my face a bit shiny, as I was sweating. The lights were hot, and I was under pressure to get it right. So a makeup assistant would come in and powder the shiny spot. Or maybe the director wasn't that pleased with how I'd spoken that line. "Can you repeat that again one more time, please?" Then, again, "Just one more time."

Playing yourself is strange; it's hard to be spontaneous and be your real self. My real self was saying, *Fuck this*. But I knew enough by then to know that this was normal filmmaking; perfection comes, after all, in the troublesome details. With live audiences, if you screw up, you screw up. With film, they somehow edit it, and they make it look real, though it's not real. I was recreating something that I had lived to meet with the expectations of another creative mind. I developed a practice that helped me do this. For some crazy reason, first thing in the morning I jumped into Munich's Isar River, which flows out of the glaciers of the Tyrolean Alps. Ice-cold. Everyone thought I was crazy. Day two I swam alone. Day three the director joined me. And by day five the whole crew jumped in. At night we had long dinners with rich conversations. And it was all good.

And yet.

Something wasn't right within me. Even Gonen noticed that I was a bit off. The pressure of the shoot to get it right? No, the filming only lasted a week. The dredging up of that past? Maybe. I stayed in Munich for a few days and did countless interviews that were both emotionally draining and triggered repressed traumas. The darkness was starting to close in again.

I flew back to LA, my second time in first class, not yet spoiled. I had one more day of shooting in LA and that would be it for me. It had been a very professional and efficient production with a great crew. They needed to shoot more in Israel and in the Palestinian territories, which of course was one place I would not be going. So we went our separate ways. I tried to immerse myself in the Hollywood culture, or the lack of it, and they had all the editing and the post-production to complete before launching *The Green Prince*.

But I was losing it. I decided to get away, get out of Hollywood, take a trip to Scottsdale, where I'd been happy and where I felt I could restore some balance to my troubled soul.

So I drove south to Arizona to visit my friends and maybe have a new restorative experience. As it turned out, I did have a new experience. My journey has been full of experiences that I can honestly say have changed my life. Shopping at Whole Foods with my friend Denise unexpectedly turned out to be one of them.

At the checkout counter, I collapsed and passed out. Whole Foods is a very expensive, upscale store, but it wasn't seeing the total cost of my bill at the register that caused me to pass out. The report later said my heart stopped for possibly thirty seconds. It wasn't like everything went black and the next thing I knew I was waking up in a hospital. No, I was there on the floor, and I was still conscious. But I didn't feel anything. I didn't feel my body. I didn't feel gravity or air pressure. I could still hear, though I couldn't speak. I was very entertained by Denise's comments. When the paramedics arrived and swung into action with all their equipment, one of them pulled out a pair of scissors to cut off my jacket.

Denise protested, "Don't do it!"

"Why not?"

"Because when he wakes up, he'll kill you!"

That was Denise. She meant it, as she knows I'm crazy. I thought that was hilarious, and I was laughing in my silent state of consciousness. I wanted to tell her not to cry, but I couldn't. I was there, and I was strangely happy. I was conscious but in a different way. Was it a near-death experience? Was it death? Was it somewhere in between? I didn't know.

I'm usually very sensitive to needles. If I just see a needle, I might pass out. The paramedics were sticking needles in me and using their medical gear to bring me back, but I didn't feel any of that. It didn't have any impact. They took all my clothes off, except for my pants, and I was aware they were moving me around. I have a vague memory of moving or being in an ambulance but not the sound of sirens.

I knew my friend was there. It was all very strange. I came back, as it were, in the hospital.

In an attempt to understand my experience, I looked up what happens in death. I read that consciousness is still there for a while; hearing lasts longer than seeing. The person can be conscious of the main things happening without their being able to communicate. Even when the doctor declares the patient dead, there can sometimes be some consciousness. What was most interesting was that I did not want to come back. Death is something we're supposed to be afraid of, but when it partially happened to me, it seemed great, without gravity, without feeling; it was fantastic. There was no anxiety. I was very calm and comfortable.

Maybe it was because of all the traumas I've had in my life that I didn't want to come back. I assume the experience can be different for every human being, but for me, when I was free from the body, it was very liberating. Free from the material, free from what I was striving to get and free from what I was trying to escape. I was rather indifferent about whether to go back or not. There was no regret.

I returned to Los Angeles, and I now saw Hollywood through a different lens. That life was no longer full of color, but black and white, with the white quickly draining out, leaving only black. I felt I was in a dark tunnel, a dark dead end. I was on the edge of an emotional or nervous breakdown. The desolate truth was that all these distractions and the material possessions on the outside were not enough to fill the void of my life, the void of a vanished family, nor to help me erase the traumas registered in my system, engraved deep on my bones. I knew in my very being how somebody can get to the point of killing themselves, because I was there. But it was not an option for me because I had not answered any of my fundamental questions. There was still a desire to know the truth, but many more questions than answers appeared. It all became chaotic. I felt powerless, lost.

Was it all worth it? The world I wanted to change and the peace I wanted to bring—I had failed horribly. *Was it worth my mother shedding one tear? For what? Freedom? What's that? Truth?* It was all overwhelming. I questioned everything, and it all seemed nonsense. *Why was there no way for me to just avoid causing suffering to people I love? Even if I wanted to be a Christian, why was that not accepted by my parents, by my people? Even if I wanted to be an Israeli, why did that have to be labeled as treason, as a betrayal, and lead to being sentenced to death? Why are people thinking this way? What motivates them? What motivates me? Who's wrong? Who's right? If I was wrong to save human lives, then is it worth living anymore for anybody? Is this life?*

I was in a smothering mental cul-de-sac. Like that time with Shin Bet and their lie detector, there was that moment of great clarity despite all my confusion. I was done. I'd had the chance to fully live the Hollywood station on my journey. What people came to Hollywood for—the attention, the recognition, the representation, the big checks—I'd experienced that, but there was no real satisfaction in it. Everything has its end, and Hollywood was as empty now for me as you can imagine. It was over.

I needed not just change but radical change. I wanted something different, different than Hollywood, the church, Islam, even if it meant hunger or homelessness or death. But what?

Given my condition, any doctor would have prescribed a great antidepressant, or there were street drugs, but drugs were no longer an option for me. I needed to escape, yes, but not into oblivion.

One night I spent the whole night crying. A very concerned Sam was with me, and he ended up crying along with me. I had clinical depression, but he had clinical compassion.

Gonen had been worried about me ever since Munich, and, knowing me so well, his worry had turned to fear that I would commit suicide. His reading of our communication was that dire. He figured he'd better drop everything in Israel and fly to LA. He'd rescued me once before from the jaws of Homeland Security, and he knew what depression was after being cast out of Shin Bet. He was in touch with Sam, and Sam said although he had never seen me in such a state, he thought Goen's fears were wrong, that I was not suicidal. He told Gonen, "You don't need to come. He's just hit a dead end, is looking for a change, but doesn't know what to do or where to go."

I canceled all my engagements and said goodbye to that world. I sold everything—the Porsche, the Ducati, the Harley, my furniture; I gave away my wardrobe, paid my last rent, left Hollywood Tower, and just walked away. I reduced my possessions and my life down to one backpack.

Now what? I don't know where to go. I had the idea to hit the road, start walking north toward San Francisco, or strike out east toward Arizona. I was considering Latin America or Europe too. But I was still stateless. How many countries could I go to? I even said goodbye to Gonen. I called my attorney in Hollywood and told him that if the movie ever came out, all the money would go to Gonen. To my family, I was dead. I had to find somewhere I could obtain a visa to visit as a stateless person with just a US travel document. I applied for a visa to a country in Southeast Asia and got it the next day. So that settled that. Gonen had told me about an island there that was popular with Israelis going on vacation after leaving their obligatory military service.

16

Meeting a True Yoga Master

On the flight over the Pacific, I read Paramahansa Yogananda's *Autobiography of a Yogi,* where he describes the life of yogis living without possessions, eating one meal a day, maintaining great physical and spiritual strength. My only experience with yoga had been with Bikram, which kept me fit and flexible, thank you, but it was really what we would call an exercise program well suited to Westerners. However, Bikram had been trained in hatha yoga from the age of four by Yogananda's brother Yogindra. That was interesting to me.

I arrived on the island by boat. The first impression for me, coming from the dry desert climate of Southern California, was the tropical assault on my senses: the warm, humid air; the fragrance of the lush vegetation; the visual variety of tropical colors; the sounds of unfamiliar birds and animals. The tourist brochure promised a picture-postcard beautiful island with soft, white sand beaches; clear, turquoise oceans; and a lush, green mountainous jungle interior complete with many waterfalls to explore and some great hikes to stunning viewpoints. They also said it was a spiritual island with amazing, world-class yoga and meditation retreats.

I rented a bungalow on the island. I was still in the Hollywood mindset, so it was a luxury bungalow, really unnecessary, though the rental was relatively inexpensive. As I walked around, it soon became apparent this was a thriving Tantra center. If you threw a stick, you could hit a yoga teacher, but the better odds were on hitting a sex guru. People descended on the island from a wide variety of backgrounds, countries, and cultures. Some kind of natural selection was in operation, as the women were gorgeous. Drugs were another recreational and mind-altering option. The temptations abounded. Having just read the Yogananda book and having some background with Bikram, I was searching for a yoga teacher.

On the third day, I walked into a yoga class at a local healing center and met the master who saved my life, a true master of Ashtanga yoga. Out of all the yoga classes in all the world, I had to walk into his. It could not have been a coincidence. There he was with his wife, teaching only three or four students. They were such a strikingly handsome couple, she a Japanese goddess, he a lean Englishman. Many students came there to be taught by him, but he only accepted those he felt were ready and committed. And he required that those he took on stay for at least a month. I don't know why he accepted me. Perhaps he saw me as a broken being, but I'm sure he also saw I was open to totally surrendering. I was willing to die, for my old self to die. Its expiration date had long passed, and change had to happen if I were to live.

It was refreshing that he was not interested in money or filling a studio. You could make a donation that went toward food for these teachers. Where he taught was only temporary, as the owner liked him and let him use the space. This was the opposite of Bikram, though bless the Rolls-Royce–driving teacher, as his ambition did bring better health to thousands. When I visited the master's very rudimentary bamboo bungalow in the jungle, it was clear the couple led the simplest of lives along with their young son. To qualify to be an Ashtanga teacher, you have to practice every day for ten years. He had been practicing daily for more than twenty years. When you decide to teach, you get up three or four hours before your first class and do your practice; you are always a student.

I fell into a routine: getting up at dawn, walking to class, often passing those just coming back from all-night partying. I cut myself off completely from my past life: no internet, no emails, no news, no social media. I'd warned Gonen I'd be incommunicado for a while. The luxury place I was in was not the right fit for me, as I sought to deflate my ego and go back to the basics. I moved to a very humble bungalow on a hill, where I still live today in a house I built myself. I was getting healthier and my sleep got better. The master never commented about food, but I found myself eating more and more a plant-based diet, with the tropical fruits being abundant. I had just come from a culture where you make a call, and on your doorstep arrive the tastes of the world—Chinese, Indian, Italian, French, Middle Eastern, Thai, Mexican, Greek, whatever. It was time to lose the luxury of living with so many options and restore a balance.

My life became about the practice. Ashtanga opened up my body, my nervous system, my mind. I'm grateful every day for such a genius, intelligent program that does not depend on ritual or theory or religion or nonexistent gods. Before I came to Ashtanga, I was just hoping for a stronger, leaner, sexier body; it was all about the body. Ashtanga was dealing with my body but also with the nervous system and the structure of my mind, which became for me the subject of intense study. It requires study, observation, and being honest with yourself as you let go of certain habits, addictions, ambitions, and your past and your traumas.

I had such love for my master and felt so connected to him, which made him feel uncomfortable, as he didn't want me to create delusions in my mind about him. He always tried to reduce himself in my eyes. He wouldn't take any credit, nor would he demonstrate a physical posture in front of me. People would rarely see him doing any asanas. People who knew him from Mysore, the Ashtanga center in India, saw him practicing at 1:00 or 2:00 a.m., doing the most advanced Ashtanga postures that only a handful of people in the world could perform. Ashtanga does produce masters, but he would not let us call him "master," nor even "teacher." What then could I call him? He said "brother"; that is what he called me. I did not feel comfortable with that. I felt I had fallen into the divine; yes, he was a man, not a god, but he was a divine inspiration to me. To this day, ten years later, I am still pursuing my daily Ashtanga practice.

The challenge in practicing is being able to do the primary series every day. No matter how you feel, no matter what's happening outside—cold, hot, windy, calm—if you're sore, tired, depressed, or injured—you're human; you're committed; you overcome it. You have to go to bed early so the body gets enough rest. You cannot eat all types of foods. You need to pursue moderation if you want to continue doing this every day. Otherwise, it's going to be a very painful experience. The beginning is very hard. You risk hurting yourself and being in lots of pain until you learn how to breathe and how to identify the mental limitations and transcend them. I thought I'd found my messiah, but he was not going to do it for me—that was my job. I had to do the work. My responsibility. Echoes of rising in the darkness to accompany my father to a mosque, the stamp of discipline indelibly printed on my DNA.

Though I was not doing what most people came to the island to do, I was pursuing a normal life, eating in restaurants, celebrating birthdays, and enjoying the natural beauty of the place. At the same time, there was something mystical about how I was making those connections. The boy from Ramallah brought up in a straitjacket of taboos was still fascinated to be in a place where people could be so openly broken; it was almost celebrated. Hollywood broke many of those taboos, and I'd had my experience with the partying and the women, but it paled in comparison to the island. America was still a relatively conservative society. Encounters here on the island were free, direct, and unencumbered. Here I experienced the love of a master who so inspired me and expected nothing in return, which is the definition of a master.

RETURNING TO AMERICA A DIFFERENT ME

After four months, the time had come for me to venture back to America, a different me than the one who had first landed in Los Angeles some three years before. I think our teacher was trying to help us understand there is no reason for anxiety; everything is going to be okay; you just need to find your own power. When you let go of relationships and possessions, you can clear space in the mind. The more possessions we have, the more insecure we become. The teacher was showing us you can live for a long time on one bag of rice; if you keep the practice, you can sleep in a hammock on the beach under the coconut trees and you will survive for a long period until things change, and they will change.

I landed back in Los Angeles four months later with just my carry-on backpack, two shirts, a pair of jeans, a toothbrush, and my one concession to technology—my laptop. There was no luxurious apartment, no Porsche, no Ducati waiting for me. But Sam was there to greet me at the airport, happy to see a different Mosab than the one he'd seen off who'd had him so concerned.

I now had a very different approach, as if I were seeing things through a different lens. And it seemed, as I moved about town, that I was now seen differently. I would find myself in Beverly Hills mansions, invited by billionaires. These were the ones who funded the film business and had dozens of movies under their belts. They were the ones who could make things happen. This was not where I'd been invited before. The Jewish community was now reaching out to me.

Sam told me that *The Green Prince* had been accepted into the Sundance Film Festival, America's premier film festival, and we'd be leaving in a few days for Park City, Utah. When Sam told me what the odds were for getting into that festival, I was impressed. They receive fourteen to sixteen thousand entries a year, accept about one hundred, and in the category of feature-length documentary, there are slots for some twelve films. Calculate those odds! Of course, Simon and John were well-known veterans of the festival, and *The Green Prince* being accepted was perhaps not such a surprise but at least an indication that it must be pretty good.

We headed off to the mountains of Utah and met up with our friends from the film. The night of the screening, which was the world premiere, I sat in the audience. This was my first time seeing *The Green Prince*. I enjoyed hearing all the applause. It was quite exciting being in that cold, snowy village in the middle of winter moving from event to screening to party. Our film was a hit and won the prestigious Sundance Audience Award. We had our moment: red carpet, photo shoots, lots of attention, invitations to all the high-profile parties. I was up there on the screen, thus recognizable, even greeted in the street, unlike a writer or a producer. Not that I recognized anyone. When Sam and I were in the queue to get into the HBO party, along with beautiful women all dressed up, Sam nudged me hard. He told me that Robert De Niro had just passed by me. I hadn't recognized him. But those were the kind of A-listers who were at the parties we went to. At that HBO party, we had our own table and people were super excited to come by, congratulate us, take a photo with us, kiss the asses of Oscar-winning producers. The whole experience was fascinating and overwhelming.

What did I think of the film? I was not in the same position as the audience, who on the night of the premiere, could go out and discuss it over a coffee and then move on to the next screening. First of all, it was based on my story (and Gonen's), and as a documentary, it was me, not an actor, up there on the big screen. The great lesson I've learned is that no movie, no book, no ten books, can convey the truth but only the shadow of truth. Also, at the time I viewed the movie, I had been an avid student of the filmmaking process, working with David Aaron Cohen on a screenplay, where you are constantly making choices about how to tell a story, what to include, what to leave out. When the filmmakers sat in the editing room with all that footage and all their ideas, they had to decide how to tell the story. I had learned from my media experience that when they say they're interviewing you to tell your story, they are actually interviewing you to tell their story of you. Speaking with the director, I understood his struggle to find that theme, that through line. It came to him pretty far along in the editing process, and the theme was friendship—friendship between the Palestinian Mosab and the Israeli Gonen. That certainly struck an emotional chord with me and clearly with the audience, as evidenced by their enthusiastic reviews. I was wonderfully treated and handsomely rewarded. More importantly, the film was one more convincing piece of evidence in my long struggle to build my case that I was telling the truth. It was the media—book, interviews, TV, and this film—that allowed me to reach out over the government's tall wall to people who cared about social justice, to the taxpayers to whom the government was ultimately accountable.

The Green Prince was not nominated for an Oscar by the Academy of Motion Picture Arts and Sciences, even though we had a special screening at the Academy with more than a hundred Academy members. We received lots of support. I was interviewed by the Academy members, and I spoke from the heart. It was a beautiful experience.

Somehow, since my return, the cards turning up on the table were winners.

Back in Los Angeles, I was finally a free man, beholden to no one. But it came with a price. Still, all the choices I've made have been mine. I look back and marvel at all the "could haves" and all the temptations on my journey. I could have been a significant figure in Hamas; I could have stayed with Shin Bet; I could have joined the church and had my own nonprofit, gotten married, made a baby, and eaten deep-fried chicken on Sundays; I could have signed up with FOX News as a Middle East pundit or become a Hollywood producer. Not to forget, I could have been killed; I could have spent a life in prison.

I have no regrets. My worldly possessions, my one pair of jeans, a hoodie, laptop, toothbrush, now all had to fit into my backpack. During this period without a place of my own, no car, no closet, I stayed mainly with friends like Sam in Los Angeles or Ruth in Arizona, though much of my time would be spent on the road.

THE BILLIONAIRE CLUB

On my return to Hollywood without the external trappings of success, for some reason I found myself visiting Jewish billionaires. I never quite fathomed why these mega-wealthy Jews invited me to visit them. I stayed at their palatial residences from London and Las Vegas to LA, New York, Toronto, Mexico City, and other cities. Certainly, the book and my talks led many Jews to see me as a hero. Also, I had the sense with some that the fact that I was a free man, carrying my worldly possessions on my back, intrigued those for whom great wealth had become their master. Though I like to think I was stimulating company, and my hosts were always interesting, another factor was that I was not asking them for anything, which is the bane of the wealthy. In fact, one billionaire who liked what I was saying and what I was doing offered me $500,000. He said I needed somebody to support me so I would be free to do whatever

I wanted. He said I would be "exponentially more effective in pursuing [my] goals. No strings attached." *Ah yes.*

When after the FOX TV broadcast I received an outpouring of donations, I gave all that money to a charity. Even a gift comes with expectations. Billionaires have their political agendas. Not wanting to appear controversial, they can push you to confront their adversaries, fight on their behalf. With money involved, the quid will always find its quo. I declined his generous offer of support, which did seem to surprise him. At times, turning down invitations could be rather awkward. Once an Israeli billionaire called and said, "I'm sending you a first-class ticket to Athens where you'll be picked up and taken to my yacht. We're going island-hopping in the Aegean, and there is going to be no shortage of beautiful young women. How do you say no to that?" I did find a way.

As we already covered, I was never a friend of AIPAC, the American Israel Public Affairs Committee. They describe themselves as "a bipartisan American organization that advocates for a strong US–Israel relationship."[16] One of Washington's most powerful lobbying groups, they are both feared and cheered. They have an annual budget of $100 million.[17] Everyone running for Congress has to pass their interview or deal with their opposition. They are the absolute *bête noire* for anti-Israel Palestinians, figuring prominently in their conspiracy theories.

Some years later I was on my first trip to Israel after all that had happened to me since leaving the Middle East. I was touring the country and was all over the news, giving interviews, even briefings in the Knesset. The leadership of AIPAC goes to Israel every year for a round of meetings with politicians, media, and opinion leaders. It happened that they were there at the same time I was. They expressed interest in meeting this Green Prince. I said I'd drop by to say hello. We met and they started asking me questions. They run a tight schedule, and we were scheduled for a twenty-minute interview, but it ran for more than an hour and a half. They were in shock; "Why in the world haven't we been already working together?" they asked. They were enthusiastic and took my phone number. But in these matters, with busy people, who knows if you'll ever hear from them?

When I returned from Israel to Los Angeles, Shane from the LA AIPAC chapter called me and invited me to have lunch with them at a vegan restaurant. The organization proposed sending me out on the road to speak at AIPAC events. AIPAC is such a powerful and well-funded organization that Israeli prime ministers and even American presidents welcome an invitation to address their Washington meetings. AIPAC is active across the country, holding events in synagogues and Jewish community centers. They always want to expand and increase their membership and look to enlist speakers with a fresh appeal. Now that they'd come around to viewing me as a positive, I hit the road and traveled around the country speaking at AIPAC events, staying in hotels. I didn't know what to expect, but it turned out the son of Hamas was an attractive draw. People were curious. *Is he a friend or an enemy?* Tickets sold out. Hundreds of extra chairs were needed at the last moment. Several of the chapters told me they'd never had such a large turnout. They were well funded, well organized, and knew how to put on a big show. Other Jewish organizations had asked me to tour for them, but AIPAC was the big dog. In the greenroom waiting to go, I often sat next to congress members and senators and got to know a number of them. When I went on, I didn't give a speech. I preferred the interview format, where I would be asked questions by a moderator and then by the audience. I did my best to answer them as honestly as possible, as though it were my father asking me the questions.

With this successful run in regional theaters, the powers that be decided I was ready for Broadway: AIPAC's annual meeting in DC. This was a massive event held at the Walter E. Washington Convention Center. The main stage was the venue for prime ministers and presidents and other notables. Other speakers and organizations held forth in smaller adjoining meeting rooms. To my surprise, I was listed as a featured speaker on the main stage. You can imagine the security for such an event, especially if a prime minister or a president were to appear. With my background, how could I even get within blocks of the event? I was given the top security, which was a kind of recognition and respect. My heavyset bodyguard was a former DC police officer who picked me up at the airport. Security at the event was orchestrated by Shin Bet and the Secret Service.

As my bodyguard and I approached the entrance, there was a long line to the right, and those ticket holders, including billionaire donors, were being thoroughly searched. I assumed I'd be searched. For some bizarre reason, I seem to have a gift for bypassing the normal lines and going through the VIP line. My bodyguard motioned me to go left. He exchanged looks with the control person in the left line, who gave a slight nod of her head for us to proceed. We just walked straight through. No metal detector, nada. I couldn't believe it.

Once inside, crowds were milling about, many people greeting each other, some familiar faces, even a congressman who signed the letter that helped with my asylum petition. My bodyguard led me to the greenroom to await my turn to speak. There I met a bunch of Israeli ministers. We shook hands, and they gave me their cards. "Whatever we can do for you, sir." That was encouraging as I readied myself for the main stage. I did feel a tremendous responsibility; I did not want to disappoint.

I walked out onto the stage of this vast auditorium and, before I even got a word out, 15,000 people stood up and applauded. *Is this really happening? For the boy from Ramallah, no less. The son of a Hamas leader.* It took my breath away. For me, yes, I have to say it was a magnificent moment. Like my whole journey, both strange and exhilarating. When they sat down, I gazed out at the sea of faces. Billionaires, two-thirds of the US Congress, ministers, celebrities, politicians, diplomats, religious leaders, members of the media. All fellow human beings. The amount of money and power in this one room would be enough for nuclear fission to reach critical mass. At this late stage of my speaking career, I hadn't prepared a speech. Instead, I would sense the audience and draw on the deep well of my experience. I don't remember at all what I said, and that's not what was important. What was important was the fact that I was there at all.

There was a long way for both sides to get to this point. For them, there were many issues to get through: *He's an Islamophobe. He's a deportee. Can he be trusted? Is he sincere? Why should we take a risk? Should we support someone who's a traitor to his own people?* There was certainly an internal debate over accepting me, as AIPAC is a very diverse organization, including those who are hard-core Zionists and religious fundamentalists. For me, this was the enemy I had been brought up to hate, and the evil AIPAC was a part of the conspiracy pressuring the United States to quash Palestinian aspirations. I had to overcome political and cultural barriers as well.

I also knew I couldn't screw up. My sincerity and my love had to come across. When I finished my talk, there was another standing ovation. This time mutual trust, admiration, and, yes, love were flowing between me and the crowd. There was a real connection. At this moment all the walls between me and the Jewish nation fell. They saw me for who I was. And I saw them for who they were. And maybe we all saw what was possible.

As I headed for the exit, one of the AIPAC leaders whispered to me, "You killed it!" I took it as a sign of approval! When I walked out of the auditorium, I was surrounded, literally mobbed—my brief rock star moment. People were very emotional—the young, the elderly; there was such admiration. Everyone wanted to shake my hand, have me sign their programs. Eventually, I migrated to the different meeting rooms, where I spoke to different groups. It got rather insane, as more people than the rooms could hold tried to get in. What was clear was that I was getting an emotional response. This was not a policy statement by a minister; this was a heartfelt declaration coming out of a Hamas household.

During this unexpected chapter of my journey, I met the young leadership of AIPAC. They did not appear to be the devil's spawn, have visible horns, or drink children's blood, as they had been depicted in that Hamas book that I'd read in prison. They were some of the most eloquent, knowledgeable, confident, and highly intelligent people I had ever met and were fully devoted to their cause. One of them, Eliot, was a scholar of Plato, and no matter the topic we were discussing, for him it always came back to Plato. I was invited into their homes, held their newborns. Experiencing their warm family atmosphere touched me. Shane invited me to his LA apartment to celebrate his child's birth and share that family moment with them. He told me, "It's not just political between you and us; you're one of us, family." When the shield of a powerful and protective organization like AIPAC drops even for a moment and we can connect at a human level, that is an accomplishment.

This experience at the meeting made me feel like I could close a chapter in my life. I had a sense of resolution. The truth for me was once again based on my direct experience, not secondhand. If I was able to overcome hatred and truly love them, the other, touch the hearts of the majority, and show that love was possible, peace was possible. For me, that was mission accomplished.

MY TRAVELS

When I was in that prison tent out in the Megiddo desert, I found a treasure: a world atlas. I studied each country, its capital, population, language, and currency. There was Hawaii, with a faded picture of surfers, tiny figures on towering waves. What wonders! Wonders I thought I would never see, much less surf. All that was beyond my imagination. I was just praying that I would get out alive, as I was a suspect and Hamas was torturing and even killing those they suspected of collaborating against them.

Yet against all odds, those atlas pages came alive across five continents as I circled the globe countless times, racking up millions of air miles. I even surfed the gentle waves of Waikiki Beach in Hawaii! I was able to travel so extensively because I accepted so many invitations to speak before groups. The two largest audiences were Christian and Jewish groups. I was even invited to countless Jewish film festivals. Also, I would speak on Middle East topics to various professional groups like CEOs, think tanks, and university students. Intellectuals were the best audience, as they read a lot and were more informed. I spoke to several parliaments, including those in Switzerland, Australia, Hungary, and Finland; the House of Lords; the Knesset; and the US Congress.

Back at the time I was stateless, and despite my deportee status, I had been granted a Refugee Travel Document, which allowed me to travel and reenter the United States. The first opportunity came with an invitation to do a keynote speech in Toronto to a high-level meeting of lawmakers, politicians, governors, mayors, and members of the media. But when I went to check in at the airport, I was told, "Sorry, sir, we cannot allow you to board. You have no visa for Canada."

"Visa?"

"Yes, with this document you need a visa."

"Even for Canada?"

"Yes, it's another country, sir."

I called my sponsor in Toronto. He panicked. The talk was the next day. "They're all coming to hear you speak," he said. It was the weekend, and even if it had been a weekday, no way could I get a visa in time. So what happened? My sponsor managed to get through to the interior minister who was responsible for immigration. He managed to issue a special visa electronically and called the airline to make an exception and allow me to board. I received a special reception at the Toronto airport and was escorted through the diplomatic line. I never saw an immigration officer, but when my document was handed back to me, I found the first stamp in my visa-free, virgin document. I was officially in Canada. The deportee had become a VIP.

Another opportunity came from my friend Harun in Finland. As I recounted earlier, he had grown up in a Muslim family in a nearby village that happened to fall within the new State of Israel, which gave him an Israeli passport. He became a prominent Christian and married a Finnish woman. He arranged to have me speak in Finland before 35,000 people at a summer conference camp at the time of the summer solstice. I flew off this time with a proper visa. The trip turned out to be one of the most beautiful experiences of my life. The landscape at this moment of spring changing to summer was all greens and blues, with the forests of pines and birches and flowering plants and endless blue lakes reflecting the blue skies. At 2:00 and 3:00 a.m. the sun was still in the sky casting its golden glow across the land. I spoke to these 35,000 in an enormous tent, the largest audience I'd ever addressed. Afterward I was surrounded by what seemed like hundreds of well-wishers who wanted autographs and signed posters but also just wanted to talk. What a beautiful people, the Finns.

Harun and his family had a summer cottage on a lake. We were in Scandinavia, the land of hot saunas and cold lakes. We would all strip down, be buck naked, work up a good detoxing sweat in the sauna, dash out and leap into the freezing lake water, gasp for breath, thrash around a bit, run back to the heat of the sauna, then run back into the lake again for a dip. Hey, that's the value of travel—joining in the local customs. The fresh homemade bread and cheeses couldn't have been tastier. Harun's in-laws and family were most welcoming and charming. It was so peaceful there, a welcome break from the fast-paced United States. This was really the first country I was able to travel to and enjoy for some days.

Harun said the minister of the interior was anxious to meet me, and I welcomed the opportunity. She was responsible for security at large events like the one I was speaking at, so she was well aware of me. She drove her own car, with her three children and her husband in it, to our meeting. We had a couple of hours together; the minister, her children, and her husband were full of questions. We spoke freely without the media and media agendas about the Islamic paradigm, jihadists, and motives behind terrorism. They were fascinated and didn't want to finish, and I was happy to answer what I could, always based on my firsthand experience. It was very productive, and we had a real human connection.

It was fortunate that English had become a kind of universal language. It also was fortunate that as a stateless person with the status of deportee, I was able to meet with these high-profile people. I felt it was my duty to convey what I knew living in the heart of the mosque and growing up in an Islamic household. No expert parachuting in can come close to that. If the policymakers of the West, like interior ministers, do not understand the problem on the ground in-depth, they won't find a sustainable solution.

When I arrived in the West, it was beset with fear and chaos, and there was no confidence that the asymmetrical War on Terror could be won. From my position, I had a certain authority to counter the fear and hatred, not only from the jihadists, but also from white extremists who sought to label all Muslims as terrorists. I knew what it took to create a terrorist, what motivated a suicide bomber; I personally knew them. I'd encountered too many dangerous individuals, even the masterminds, on my journey. What we had was an ideological and cultural problem. This is the reality we grew up in, the reality that conditioned us. I always told audiences that if they grew up with that same ideological conditioning, they, too, might well be terrorists. That message seemed to be understood: *These people are like you but with very different cultural and ideological conditioning.* I was, as usual, highly critical of most Islamic ideology, which in some quarters labelled me as an Islamophobe or a Zionist. No matter. I was not attacking Muslims or the Muslim people. My goal, though it might sound grand, was to build a bridge of understanding between East and West.

The next day I briefed the Finnish parliament. Some weeks before, I had been briefing the US Congress. I flew back to the States after a most enjoyable and stimulating time in Finland. I'd had so many challenges with governments, intelligence services, lawyers, and my Christian critics that whenever I had the opportunity to express myself and share my hard-earned knowledge, I took it.

VIP AND DEPORTEE

Another memorable trip I took that illustrated this crazy duality of VIP and deportee was when I was invited to speak in Hungary. I was barefoot and shirtless on my island when the Israeli ambassador contacted me to speak to a group consisting mainly of diplomats at his home in Budapest. Aware that I was stateless and controversial, he told me he would attempt to have me treated as a diplomat. So I hunted about for my shoes; put them both on, along with a clean shirt; packed a few items; and flew off.

Arriving in Central Europe for the first time, I was greeted upon landing at Budapest Ferenc Liszt International Airport by seven members of the Hungarian secret police responsible for diplomats. They took my document and stamped me out, and waiting outside were three Audi A8 armored vehicles. They would be with me the entire trip, treating me like the Israeli prime minister come to town. Accompanied by very visible security and staying in a five-star hotel, the question was always, *Who the hell is this guy?*

Actually, I would have armed security details at every one of my public events, often with dogs scanning the crowd for bombs. I didn't take it lightly, as ill-intentioned people could always show up where I was speaking next. The meeting at the Israeli ambassador's residence went well, and this led to me speaking at the Hungarian parliament. I looked forward to a relaxing flight back to bare feet and shorts on the island.

On my way home I had to transit through Shanghai. When I presented my document, the Chinese official looked at it skeptically.

"What's this?"

"It's a travel document."

"You cannot get into our country without a visa."

"I'm in transit, making a connection. I don't want to get into your country."

"You have to have a visa. This document is worthless without one."

We were in the computer age, so compounding the situation, it came up on the screen that I was stateless. More officials arrived, and I had no idea what they were chattering about. I was getting frustrated and started to yell at them that I was missing my flight. Scores of frustrated passengers were backing up behind me. All they saw was a Middle Eastern guy arguing with officials. These officials insisted I had to get into the country first. Finally, they came up with their only solution: "We let you in and then deport you." *Here we go again.*

"What? I don't even want to stay in the country."

"You better cooperate. We will take you directly to your flight."

My unimpressive document got stamped an impressive "Deported." I had two Chinese security officers following me through the airport. With all my mileage points, I had access to the five-star airline lounge, where we parked for a moment, waiting for the now-delayed flight. A Chinese officer sat on either side of me. Again, that turned heads. *Who is this important fellow?* They did not put me in handcuffs, as that would have conveyed criminal status. When it was finally time to board, we went through the boarding gate and onto the tarmac. They took me to the aircraft in a special vehicle. They boarded the flight with me and even buckled me in.

As I said, I spoke to Christian groups all over our planet. I seldom identified with any specific tradition or group anymore. I always challenged them in their church, just as I challenged a Jewish audience in their synagogue. I always stuck to my truth. I knew what they wanted to hear, but if my truth based on my experience was contrary to theirs, I said it. And they still asked me back!

I was invited to speak as an "honored guest" to a Christian group in Colombia. Sam joined me. It was to be one of those high-profile gatherings at a private home, and the president of Colombia had accepted their invitation. This is probably what merited the VIP treatment at the airport, where I was once more hustled through customs with armed security and picked up in an armored vehicle. My first view of the capital, Bogotá, was through the distorted bullet-proof glass of the passenger window. The poverty, the smog, and the clogged traffic were quite shocking to me. How most of the dilapidated little cars, especially the taxis, could qualify to be on the road and not in the junkyard, producing clouds of black pollution, was beyond me. Mixed in with the derelict autos, reflecting the enormous class divide, were the latest Mercedes and other luxury imports outfitted with the latest security protection. That's how the wealthy traveled in town. Apparently, we were in a lawless society where kidnappings were common. Sam and I were lodged in the presidential suite at a five-star hotel with twenty-four-hour armed security guards, plus we were chauffeured in the armored vehicle whenever we wished. Sam was blown away by this VIP treatment.

We figured we would go out, have a drink, and explore the nightlife of the capital. We pulled up at a trendy nightclub in our armored Mercedes. This did not escape notice. We sat down in what was clearly a happening club, crowded with loud music and dancing. I started talking to this beautiful woman, then another approached me, and a third. I figured they must be professionals. But no, not at all. Our car and the pistol-packing guards outside were what had drawn them, and the crowd only increased when word got out that we were from the US and Sam was a Hollywood movie producer.

Sam returned from the dance floor with his partner and told me they were going back to the hotel. We'd only been there an hour. "Okay, bro, but take a taxi," I told him. Right then a stunning woman appeared with her friends; it was her twenty-second birthday, and they were out celebrating. Her name was Tatiana, and her parents were doctors. She told me a bit about herself. We danced and made out a bit. I was smitten. *I'll marry this girl!*

Finally, Tatiana, her birthday entourage, and I piled into the Mercedes and returned to the hotel. We sat in the suite's living room chatting while that devil Sam was noisily doing something in his bedroom. He took a break, looked out into the living room, and saw that the party had moved there. Five minutes later a smiling Sam appeared all dressed up. I told myself, *I'll come back to Colombia for Tatiana*; that's how much I liked her. I had no intention of a one-night stand.

My talk the next day was apparently a success, though the president didn't appear. It was mainly attended by ambassadors and local luminaries. We still seemed to qualify for the VIP treatment until we got on our plane, where we settled back into our seats in economy.

Back in Tinseltown, I stayed in touch with Tatiana. We spoke a lot over the phone and Skype. I even went back to Bogotá to hang out with her. We took some trips; Colombia is spectacularly beautiful. We went river rafting and zip-lining. Once, on an excursion with an important Christian figure in Colombia, we were pulled over by the police. Our friend got out and bribed the officer. Our Christian friend did not want to get that ticket. I'd never seen this in my years in the States, but this was his Colombian reality.

While I enjoyed my relationship with Tatiana, this was during my Hollywood years, which were not conducive to our budding relationship.

BORDER CLASHES

In Asia I had done ayahuasca, a psychoactive brew, some ten times and found it very helpful. My experiences revealed many of the stuck relationships between me and others, notably my family. This amazing plant, when ingested as a tea, helped me move on, encouraging me to let go. My experience was very positive, but I didn't make a religion out of it. A friend of mine proposed we go to Peru and do ayahuasca with an authentic shaman back where it had originated.

We landed in Lima, the capital, and right off it felt wrong to me. Just my first encounter at passport control was disagreeable, with a kind of aggressive interrogation. Then, the little I saw of the gray, foggy, seedy capital city put me off even further. Ayahuasca, for me, had been a sacred and beautiful experience, but what I learned about our prospective ayahuasca expedition came across as shady business with an opportunistic "shaman." I really didn't need to do this anymore.

So, after one dismal day in Peru, I booked the next United flight back north to the US. Arriving at the airport, I headed for the counter to get my boarding pass. Another woman appeared, an officer with the Peruvian Investigative Police (PIP), a plainclothes unit equivalent to the American FBI. She asked me what I was doing there. I said I had come with a friend to explore the country and the culture, but I'd changed my mind, as I was not feeling well and needed to get back home.

"Do you mind coming with me, please?" she asked.

"Why?"

"Just come with me."

We entered a small room. She took my backpack and thoroughly searched it. She thought I was smuggling something. But there was nothing. I was taken to a screen and x-rayed. I had not swallowed something to hide from them. Finally, she shared her suspicion: "You come to Peru; you stay one day; you travel with only a backpack when your application for the visa stated you wanted to stay for three weeks. You fit perfectly the profile of a drug trafficker."

I told her I traveled all over the world this way; traveling light worked best for me. Frustrated at having nothing she could hold me on, she had to let me board my flight. As we took off, looking down at the diminishing city between the Pacific and the Andes, I breathed a sigh of relief that I'd escaped possible real trouble. This was not the familiar War on Terror but the War on Drugs. I did not want to get caught up in that losing war.

My port of entry to the good ol' USA was Houston. Emerging from the tunnel, I was met at the gate. My PIP friend in Lima had called the FBI. Now the real interrogation was to begin. I was taken to some dark hole of the Transportation Security Administration (TSA) and FBI. The first agent dealt with me as a potential drug trafficker. Searching everything, they found nothing. Fortunately, my friend in Lima had decided not to put something in my backpack. Already I'd missed my flight back to LA. Agent number two appeared and pursued the drug possibility, but not only were there no drugs on me, but when he delved into his computer, there was no evidence of my involvement in narcotics. But once they'd gotten into the system, that opened the whole can of worms about terrorism, Hamas, and my father. The whole bullshit began again, questions leading to questions. I repeated the same story over and over. Somehow the facts in the computer weren't enough for them. By now I'd missed my second flight, but that didn't seem so important compared to what I was facing. They didn't know how to deal with me, though I was clearly a suspicious person; the facts in the computer appeared suspicious; maybe my document was not legitimate.

I froze. I had an emotional breakdown. Enough was enough. I said, "Listen, you guys, don't take this as an offense, but I'm not saying another word. Call Washington, Congress, the president. Call whoever you want. I don't know how I got here. I'm legitimate. I just went to Peru for a vacation. I've come back. It's my right to get back into the country. Do whatever you want to do. Keep me out of it, as I have nothing else to say now. I cannot explain my whole fucked-up journey just to satisfy your curiosity."

Next, they left me alone in the room. The state is a blind machine, and here I was again, chewed up in its gears. This was so dumb. After what must have been a couple of hours, they reappeared. "You're free to go. Have a safe flight."

At another time, I decided to fly down to Cancún, rent a Harley-Davidson, and make my way to Chichén Itzá, one of the great Mayan cities. I vroomed off to these fabled ruins where, like so many other vanished civilizations, a society's downfall remains the subject of scholarly speculation. I stayed in a historic hotel with magnificent Mexican architecture right on the site of the pyramids. It was a full moon that night. A ceremony took place at the Kukulcan pyramid. Bathed in moonlight, women performed and sang in a magical ceremony. The Mayan language, the music, the voices, the smoke, all served to transport me for two hours to another world, where I felt this mystical, deep, spiritual connection to the Mayans. I stayed for three days, exploring the site, climbing the ruins with their carved gods and evidence of the celebrated Mayan calendar.

I rushed back to make my flight at the Cancún airport. Speeding along on my motorbike, I was pelted by something flying through the air. Butterflies! Gorgeous monarch butterflies on their September migration, which can take them as far north as Canada. Suddenly the world in my vision was all these colorful butterflies. I couldn't see the road below me. I was effectively blinded as I slowed down to the point where I could still keep the bike balanced upright. I didn't want to kill them. For more than an hour I made my tentative way through this field of butterflies.

What were the chances that I, a solo traveler, would have this mystical experience of one of the greatest ancient civilizations under the light of a full moon, and then be caught up in the migration of the most precious creatures on the globe, representing evolution from the caterpillar to the butterfly? There are no words to describe my feelings as I traveled through this monarch world. It was one of the most beautiful experiences, as though nature were hugging me. Travel helped me accept my aloneness, and experiences like these showed me my unity with the rest of the universe.

I developed my own style of travel, one that suited me well. I preferred to travel alone and travel light, very light. Having only carry-on luggage can be a real plus, like in the China drama when I missed my flight. I am at the opposite end of the spectrum from those who prefer to travel in the safety of groups accompanied by a mountain of suitcases and follow the prescribed route with a guide. I never venture out to explore a new place with a set plan. It is the new, the unexpected, the seeing how people live, the chance encounters with my fellow beings—that is the joy of travel.

Traveling solo has its advantages. Often I'm approached by someone who seems to recognize a kinship with the solo traveler and offers a meal or something without asking for anything in return. As a solo traveler, I never have to wait for anyone, plan with others, negotiate, or compromise. Being alone means you engage with many more people, speak to others, and hear their stories. Also, I have this penchant for taking risks, exploring my own limits—in a sense, my own inner journey. It would have to be the companion I haven't met yet who I could ask to sign up for that.

A good example of this was one day in the jungle east of Chiang Mai in Thailand. Every morning, I would do my yoga practice and my breathing exercises, which charged me with extraordinary energy. On this day I set out to explore some canyons. I came across a narrow one, little more than three feet wide, a dried river channel sculpted out of the land. It appeared to go on to infinity. There was not a sign of another human being, not even a footprint. It was an area of poisonous snakes and wild predators. I could understand why no one would choose to venture into that unknown. It was super hot; I had no water, no food, no cell phone. I didn't want to carry anything. If I was looking for a challenge, the opportunity to face my fear, this was one. I set off, knowing the danger that there would be no rescue if anything went wrong. My attitude was, *If I am bitten by a viper, so be it.* I walked on and on in this deep trench for hours and hours, my eyes blurred with salty sweat, testing what my physical body could endure. The afternoon sun had long left the canyon when I turned around and headed back. The narrow sides of the canyon seemed to keep me from falling as I made my way unsteadily down. I was depending on my breath, my only fuel.

As I made it out of the canyon onto the path, I was surprised by an old woman sitting outside a shack hidden in the jungle. She was also startled to see me, as it must have been a rare person who passed this way, much less an obvious *farang* (foreigner). We looked at each other and quickly realized we did not share a common language. Reminding me of my eighty-year-old grandmother, she was intent on the laborious and nasty task of taking the bright red shells off cashews. Nasty, as cashews have a black shell oil that is a chemical irritant. She was roasting the cashews to burn off the oil. I came closer to her as with her tar-covered hands she patiently uncovered one cashew after another. She neither gave an indication that I should go nor that I should stay. I watched her uncover each precious cashew. This is not a job you would ever want, as it is very time-consuming with only a small result. Most likely she was doing it for herself or her family, not for profit. I was so thirsty and so hungry, sustained only on breath.

She looked up at me as our eyes met. She reached out with a handful of cashews and a tentative smile. I reached out my cupped

hands and she poured her warm gift into them. This simple offering
had nothing to do with a financial exchange. It was so powerful, so
pure. I sat down and ate them. These were the best cashews I'd ever
had in my life. She saw how happy I was. Oh, how I wanted more! But
there was no way in the world I would ever ask that, being a witness
to what it took to give me them and what her gift represented. I stood
up. In that moment she was Mother Nature for me. I gestured my
gratitude with praying hands. She nodded. I continued on my journey, having experienced a moment along the way I will never forget.

CITIZENSHIP?

A few years earlier, my asylum case was granted, so in 2017 it became
possible for me to apply to become an American citizen—to make the
impossible dream possible.

I'd grown up stateless in a violent, corrupt, obscurantist culture,
and now, after this long journey, I had the opportunity to become a citizen of one of the greatest countries and civilizations in history. As I've
mentioned, I've always loved America and its democratic model that I
saw as the polar opposite to the world in which I'd been imprisoned.

America gave me the space to express my true self. I was free to
explore all that was forbidden in my repressive culture, explorations
I've freely reported in these pages. I even appreciated my adversaries
who doubted me, attacked me publicly, and slandered me, because
our differences were expressed in words—words that could get me
deported, yes, but the debate was not carried out with knives and
bullets. America is governed by the rule of law, and because of that I
now stood at the entry door to possible citizenship. I only had a few
more hurdles to clear.

The first step toward citizenship is to fill out the Application for
Naturalization, the N-400. It's very exhaustive, including details
about parents, family members, education, race, and much more. For

race there wasn't a category that fit me, so "white" was the only real option. And then there was that long-familiar questionnaire requiring only yes and no answers unless a question required further explanation. Most candidates could breeze right through, checking nos. But for me, some of these were yeses. I'd come this far sticking to the truth, and indeed, thus far "the truth had set me free."

Right away I was hit with: "Have you ever been a member of, or in any way associated (either directly or indirectly) with: 1. The Communist Party? 2. Any other totalitarian party? 3. A terrorist organization?" Well, that was a yes.

Another question was, "Have you ever been ordered removed, excluded, or deported from the US?" Another yes.

"Have you ever been in prison?" Yes.

There were some relatively easy nos, like, "Are you a habitual drunkard?" I don't remember if I gave that one a thoughtfully considered pause. There were some irrelevant yeses: "Are you willing to give up any titles or ranks of nobility?" Then there was one that I could give an enthusiastic yes to: "Do you support the Constitution and form of government of the US?"

The next step was a face-to-face interview with a United States Citizenship and Immigration Services (USCIS) officer. There was a civics test where we were given in advance one hundred questions and answers in the US Citizenship Naturalization Civics Lessons for the United States Citizenship. The interviewer then asked me a random ten of them, of which correct answers to six out of the ten would be a passing grade. The first one for me was, "What is the supreme law of the land?" *The Constitution.* Another was, "What is the rule of law?" *No one is above the law.*

These were not simple answers to a quiz; these were real and substantial issues, ones that had played key roles in my journey, allowing me to get this far. As to proficiency in speaking and understanding English, the interviewer talking with me recognized I was proficient.

It had been ten years since I'd arrived in the US, and I was now very comfortable with English. In fact, I rarely spoke Arabic these days. Then he perused the application form. He showed no change of expression as his eyes passed over *terrorist, prison, deportee*. I doubt he saw many applications like mine, which appeared to have so many disqualifying answers. Even so, he announced, "Congratulations; you've passed." Twenty minutes and done. *Next*.

Some days later, the ceremony took place in downtown Los Angeles, where some five thousand of us gathered to take the Oath of Allegiance to the United States of America and become full-fledged US citizens. This event was very emotional for me. As I looked around the crowded, expectant room, I again was so impressed with what I appreciated about America—its diversity. This group of human beings looked to have come from all corners of our globe. Each one had a unique story. I was sure some of the other freedom seekers had suffered more than I had. Yet I couldn't help remembering all the ups and downs, the mountains and valleys, of my life of forty years when so much of it had been spent on the precarious cliff edge. How many barriers I'd had to penetrate to get to this point on my chosen journey. Once more I was being given a new life. We were shown some brief videos celebrating the beauty of the land, with the song "America the Beautiful" and the national anthem, "The Star-Spangled Banner." Finally, there was a brief welcoming video from the new president, Donald J. Trump. We then rose to recite the Oath of Allegiance:

> I hereby declare, on oath, that I absolutely and entirely renounce and abjure all allegiance and fidelity to any foreign prince, potentate, state, or sovereignty, of whom or which I have heretofore been a subject or citizen; that I will support and defend the Constitution and laws of the United States of America against all enemies, foreign and domestic; that I will bear true faith and allegiance to the same; that I will bear arms on behalf of the United States when required by the law; that I will perform noncombatant service in

the Armed Forces of the United States when required by the law; that I will perform work of national importance under civilian direction when required by the law; and that I take this obligation freely, without any mental reservation or purpose of evasion; so help me God.

I was then handed my certificate of citizenship. There were smiles all around, families hugging, hands being shaken, slaps on the back. A happy, happy day.

I walked out into the bright Southern California sun as, finally, a citizen. For me, this was the American Dream.

I had picked up a brochure that listed the benefits of citizenship and the responsibilities. As far as I can recall the details, these benefits would make my nomadic life much easier:

1. **US Passport:** Having a US passport brings many advantages including, but not limited to, being able to travel to over one-hundred and seventy-four (174) countries without needing to apply for a visa.

2. **Assistance from US Embassies and Consulates:** When traveling abroad consular officials can provide resources and legal aid. The US Government may even intervene on the person's behalf in the event of incarceration.

3. **Freedom to travel:** US Citizens, unlike Permanent Residents, do not have to maintain a residence in the US, they have the right to travel and stay in a foreign country as long as they wish and return at any given time.

4. **No deportation:** As an American Citizen, you cannot be deported.

This was an important milestone on my journey for which I was deeply grateful, especially to those who supported me and fought for me, people like Sarah Stern, Gonen, my friends, my lawyers, and my fans. I was fortunate, unlike so many sitting alone and defenseless in detention centers, to have platforms from which my voice could be heard.

There was, however, something much more important to me than the certificate that I filed in my backpack, and that was both a sense of vindication and being finally appreciated for who I was and what I had done. We all know what it is like not to be believed when speaking the truth, and, in my case, the stakes were my very life. Once in America, my antagonist was the American government, and the stakes were deportation, which triggered the prospect of decapitation.

As I've said before, dealing with governments is like dealing with a blind machine that registers you as a number on its computers that can crush you in a keystroke. That immigration officer in Anaheim couldn't see me as a human being, one who deserved a chance to live and breathe in freedom. Then there were the immigration court dates and the drumbeat of "You will never be granted asylum; you will never ever become a citizen in this country, along with the liberal media sowing seeds of doubt about my credibility and my being attacked in some evangelical circles. It took years to show those people otherwise and have them overcome their fear, their doubts, their protocols, and acknowledge me for who I truly was. They had to acknowledge my contribution to humanity and bend their rules to make an exception and welcome me without prejudice. Just as AIPAC had let down its shield, the American government finally let down its shield and sheathed its sword and allowed me in. I was finally a United States citizen.

EPILOGUE

This has been an opportunity for me to share some of my forty-year journey with others. The boy from Ramallah made the best out of things, under the circumstances, but that is not for me alone to judge. My challenge these last few years has been to let go, let go of it all—the traumas and the triumphs—to find balance and a measure of closure. Not an easy goal, as these were dense, extreme experiences, some extreme in pain, some in pleasure, leaving indelible marks on my mind and body.

My decision to write these experiences down has been part of the letting-go process, though at times it's felt like blowing on a dying ember that flares up, reliving a painful memory. My quest on this journey to find truth and freedom has been an ambitious and risky one. Everyone has their own idea of what freedom is, and part of my journey has been letting go of the various concepts of freedom, what I might call freedom from freedom, though the goal remains to find true freedom.

My choices and their consequences are what got me here. I went against the flow, against society, and got burned in the fire. I was very lucky to have escaped. It was a miracle, really, though I paid a heavy price. At various points on the way I had identities thrust upon me, identities based on how others viewed me: a trusted son of a Hamas celebrity father, a terrorist to be tortured, a Shin Bet informant to be exploited, a Christian convert to be exploited, a refugee seeking asylum, a deportee to be sent to his death, a media story, a public speaker, a bestselling author, a traitor to be stoned to death, a hero to be given standing ovations from prestigious platforms, a Hollywood producer, a dedicated yoga practitioner, an asylee, an American citizen, a resident of an island quietly minding his own business. I've had to reinvent myself over and over. *Enough already.* When I get up in the morning and look in the mirror, who do I see? I see who I truly am. I've let go of all those other identities, which sought to define who I was. One aspect of freedom is not caring how people label you or what they think of you, or even if they think of you at all.

To find freedom, individual freedom, Asian philosophy offers as good a list as any of the major enemies, those inner monsters we must purge to be truly free: human delusion, desire and lust, hatred, anger, fear, craving. All the monsters I had been seeking to slay.

1. *Human delusion* can be a real spider's web, making it difficult to disentangle ourselves from our conditioning with negative belief systems and start afresh. I was able to escape Ramallah and travel the world, experiencing so many cultures, belief systems, and religions. I could observe diverse religions and cults and know them as creations of the human mind, not a supernatural deity. If I'd only known one sect of a religion, then I might have embraced that belief system and its rules designed to justify my behavior and make me believe I was righteous. But from the get-go, I was rebellious and always questioned what I found illogical. My experience with Shin Bet is related, as they were the masters of creating human delusion to serve their ends—especially in the case of Hamza, whose belief system enabled him to resist torture for six months and buy into the illusion that he was being rewarded with exile in Lebanon.

2. *Desire and lust* are not easy ones. In order to control this part of our animal nature, religions combat these drives with

shame and guilt. These are two corrosive qualities to let go of. Where I live is a mecca for sexual tourism, which I have completely avoided.

3. I was born into a culture of *hatred*. Them and us. As a child, I was taught that Jews drink children's blood and wanted to drink my blood. How could I not hate when I was beaten unconscious in the back of a jeep by Israeli soldiers who took such joy in it, my cries of pain being met by laughter and more blows? They were the ones shooting at us, taking my father away. I realize now adopting "Love your enemy" was not so much about loving my enemy as letting go of my hatred, hatred being one of the inner monsters keeping me from being free. I now seek to look upon my fellow creatures with love and compassion, at the same time keeping my distance, which was one advantage of the pandemic.

4. *Anger* can certainly be justified at times, but not when it is all-consuming. Growing up, I rebelled with anger against the violence and brutality, the corruption, and the senseless loss of life. I challenged the gods, the so-called prophets, and I dared to do what few did. I was bred in a culture of anger and frustration. My father beat me; my mother beat me; so I beat my brother, which I very much regret. Anger, hatred, and frustration permeated our world from the home to the school to the street, where anger expressed through violence was the primary language. I also nursed a bitter anger toward Islam, which I openly expressed in the harshest terms once I was in America, a society that honors freedom of speech yet wrestles with "hate speech." As I've said many times, it's time Islam left the seventh century to join the twenty-first. At some point I gave up my rebelliousness and chronic anger, as I realized those provided no way to achieve peace and tranquility. And I learned that what

we put out into the world is what we get back, be it anger or a smile.

5. I would also add *fear* to the list, as living in fear is no way to be free. Most everyone fears the judgment of society, and underlying our lives is the fear of death. I can honestly say I have no fear of dying, a violent probability I have faced for most of my life. In the war situation Palestinians and Israelis coinhabit, fear is always present.

6. *Craving* can be an endless list with desire for possessions, status, food, relationships, sensual pleasure, success, and on and on. I had that craving for possessions, from the Xbox as a kid to trading in a Ford Mustang for a Porsche as an adult. All those possessions, those toys of the "good life" accumulated in the Hollywood period, I finally gave them all up, stripping down to what would fit in a backpack, letting go, shortening the list of what I wanted to dominate and possess. Relationships can also come under this rubric, especially dependent ones that compromise our freedom. Part of my letting go has been letting go of many relationships. For whatever reason, billionaires for a while valued my company, as I described earlier, and I've let go of those relations in London, New York, Mexico City, and Los Angeles. When money is your master, it's difficult for your conscience to be your guide. Also, when people from my past have contacted me, for the most part I have not replied. I've let them go. I don't have some kind of status that I'm trying to maintain, which limits the freedom of many.

The other side of the freedom coin is responsibility, and the greatest responsibility truly is toward ourselves: to be responsible for the choices we make, and to be responsible for our bodies, which are the vessels that allow us to move through life. Before taking responsibility for others, I first have to heal myself. That is why at this point in life's transit, I'm focusing on myself: to clear out the negative, the past wounds and their scars on body and mind; to reach full potential of beauty and balance. No one is going to come clean my house; that is my job. Socrates, who like many of the great masters paid the final price for his independence of mind, left us with the eternal challenge: "Know thyself."

My view of my fellow human beings, again based on my experience and what I have lived, is not a positive one. Humanity is the most dangerous predator, not to be trusted. It is not simply the traumas of my rape and torture and constantly witnessing extreme violence and brutality, "man's inhumanity to man," but also the selfish nature of humans and their hypocrisy. In the morning a friend, in the evening an enemy; in the morning a hero, in the evening a traitor; in the morning a standing ovation, in the evening left to an angry mob.

We live in our own reality, with our egos and the will to survive. We are animals, after all; there's a reason the lion tamer not only has a whip but carries a pistol. You just never know. Perhaps one of the reasons the story of Jesus Christ has such lasting resonance is because of how it reflects on this aspect of human nature—one week hosannas, the next crucifixion. And for me, there is the father-son part of this eternal story. Jesus' reported last words as he was dying on the cross were, "My God, my God, why hast thou forsaken me?"[18] There are a few avatars, spiritually enlightened individuals, who, like Jesus, have the god within.

One of the choices I have made is to live alone. At this point in my life and with my way of life, I find it suits me very well. I'm not looking for a relationship. I look upon my fellow humans with love and compassion but keep my distance. I don't want to become involved. Part of freedom is not being dependent. Being independent is especially important to my current goal of letting go, releasing the past. This takes considerable discipline and honest self-exploration.

People ask me, "Aren't you lonely?" My true answer is no. If they persist, they say, "But you have no family; they've disowned you." Yes, that is a consequence of my choices, and, yes, in the cultures of the world, family is often ascribed the highest value of all. I sacrificed that.

My father, who I know loves me (and I love my father), declared open season on killing me for my betrayal of him and the cause, a capital offense. From my perspective, I saved his life, and he betrayed me by choosing a corrupt, delusional Hamas belief system over his own son. Who's right and who's wrong is not important. I take responsibility for my choices. Was it worth it? In two words: *damn right.*

Do we become aligned with a universal truth, or do we choose the familiar convenient truth that gives us security and protection along with the absurdity and limitations of a human-made belief system? The mullahs and priests pray for water for a hundred years, and no water arrives. Then someone comes along and simply starts digging and finds water. *Hallelujah.* The holy men say, "He never would have found it if we hadn't prayed all these years." It is what it is. One more on the list to let go.

There is power in letting go and power in adapting. When I walked away from the Hollywood "beautiful life," I wanted to go to a place where no one knew me, where status meant nothing. Where I am now, I found the simple life. The people saw me as a broken man looking for a way out, and they offered compassion and love with no concern about my past. With small adjustments that put me on the path to emancipating myself, I just needed to do the work, the work to find closure and completion to the first half of my life.

While most of my life has been led with purpose, often intense purpose, I live now without big goals or a purpose in life other than letting go. I'm going with the flow, being spontaneous. *What's my plan for today?* I don't know, other than the morning begins like every morning for the last ten years, with my two- to three-hour practice of

Ashtanga yoga. I do it alone here in my home. Physically, mentally, spiritually demanding, and deeply fulfilling. Body. Mind. Breath. Balance. It has made all the difference in my life in terms of my healing and growth.

For what began as an effort to have a better body soon became an adventure in healing mind and body, the continuing effort to achieve a higher level of consciousness—not to mention having inexhaustible energy throughout the day. I have a better understanding of my nervous system and how to manage it. It is all so individual, as fifty people could do the same postures, the same sequences, and get different results. The notion of a practice and discipline was instilled in me early when my father rousted me out of bed to join him in the predawn prayer to please him and a mythical Allah. The road traveled since has taken me light-years from that world where I found neither truth nor freedom. I've been blessed with the opportunity to meet extraordinary people, some of the world's most creative people who have contributed to humanity in every field of existence. I've learned from many masters directly, others through the pages of books and scripture like Jesus, Socrates, and Buddha, all who taught me. Though finally, each of us has to individually do the work to know themselves. That's the truth.

I look out the window of my home at the expanse of sea and distant islands. I might hike barefoot on jungle trails and sit under a soothing tropical waterfall. Or I will go free dive. See if I can go deeper than the sixty-five feet of yesterday, deeper into the beauty and then the blackness of the depths. My nature apparently always seeks to explore the limits of my mind and body, always with the appetite for risk.

But looking further ahead, what's next? I don't know about the future. Will there be a family? Will there be a role to play, perhaps in a form of service, the kind of sacred work where we expect nothing in return? Everything seems possible. Troubled individuals in darkness do come to me for help, and hopefully I'm able to contribute some light. I'm still young, so who knows? But I cannot think about it yet. I'm in a good place right now, despite living without financial security. I'm healthy, which is the true wealth. I'm living amid the magnificence of nature and have managed to achieve a measure of contentment and, yes, finally freedom. I'm content with one healthy meal a day, vegetables and fruits, clean water, and a good night's sleep. To borrow from Descartes, *spiro ergo sum*: "I breathe, therefore I am."

ACKNOWLEDGMENTS

From James Becket

To simply *acknowledge* my dear friend and writing partner Mosab is too feeble a word. I am full of gratitude that some destiny brought us, from totally different backgrounds and life experiences, together. I am in awe of how he not only mastered a second language but also became a very fine writer in English.

There is so much to admire about this brilliant man who has overcome so much adversity in his life, which really is the subject of the book you are reading. His extraordinary discipline is evidenced in his daily practice of the difficult Ashtanga Yoga. He has learned from all the great past masters and explored the depths of mind, including his own. For him it is the examined life. Socrates would approve, and Mosab has of course read his share of Plato. Beyond the spiritual realm, Mosab is a brilliant analyst of today's political reality, which makes him in demand from the media.

And I thank Wes Yoder, Mosab's great friend and agent, who pulled this together. So grateful for that.

And to Jill Smith, fellow writer and editor, with whom I so enjoyed working through the edit of the text. Great to have a real pro. And to the team at Forefront Books who brought all the myriad details together in a creation that sits in the window of a bookstore.

And finally, I must acknowledge modern technology. Here we were, Mosab in Southeast Asia, and I in North America, and we would speak every night and send texts in seconds. I would look forward to those nights—always fascinating—every night I would learn so much. No way we could have done this in the past so quickly. And maybe not at all.

And finally, to my mother, Elise Granbery Becket, no longer with us, who always supported my literary ambitions. She acted as my tireless literary agent and was a co-activist in our political battles. I deeply miss her. To my father who stayed the course even after a dreadful first novel.

NOTES

1. In December 2023, the Central Bureau of Statistics (CBS) of the Israeli Government published data on the country's Christian community. According to the report, approximately 187,900 Christians reside in Israel, which represents 1.9% of the population.
2. Søren Kierkegaard, *Provocations: Spiritual Writings of Kierkegaard,* edited by Charles E. Moore; Plough Publishing, 2014.
3. Seeing my death in his dream, my father was essentially condemning me to death. Had he not, my siblings' lives would have been in danger because, in that culture, if they can't get to the oldest son, they have the right to kill any of the brothers on his behalf. So my father, from his prison cell, was protecting my siblings.
4. John 8:32
5. Catherine Elsworth and Carolynne Wheeler, "Mosab Hassan Yousef, Son of Hamas Leader, Becomes a Christian," August 12, 2008, *The Telegraph,* https://www.telegraph.co.uk/news/worldnews/middleeast /palestinianauthority/2613399/Mosab-Hassan-Yousef-son-of-Hamas -leader-becomes-a-Christian.html.
6. *Escape from Hamas* can be viewed on the Fox Nation streaming platform; https://nation.foxnews.com/escape-from-hamas/.
7. It is difficult to pinpoint precisely where this mission statement is located. I have found it referenced a number of times online, one of which is https://www.icnl.org/resources/research/ijnl/solving-the -necessity-conundrum-what-the-drug-war-can-teach-us-about-due -process-for-u-s-charities-in-the-fight-against-international-terrorist -financing.

8. #07272004: Prepared Remarks of Attorney General John Ashcroft Holy Land Foundation Indictment," n.d. https://www.justice.gov/archive/ag/speeches/2004/72704ag.htm.

9. Benny Hinn Ministries, 2023. "What God Has Begun in You, He Will Finish." Benny Hinn Ministries. December 18, 2023, www.bennyhinn.org/what-god-has-begun-in-you-he-will-finish.

10. Hartford Institute for Religion Research. "Fast Facts about American Religion." n.d. Hirr.hartsem.edu, http://hirr.hartsem.edu/research/fastfacts/fast_facts.html.

11. From the Wikipedia article, "Gilad Shalit prisoner exchange," in the section "The approval of the agreement." Accessed May 6, 2024, https://en.wikipedia.org/wiki/Gilad_Shalit_prisoner_exchange.

12. "Sarah Stern." n.d. EMET | Endowment for Middle East Truth, https://emetonline.org/staff/sarah-stern.

13. "Rays of Light in the Darkness." n.d. EMET | Endowment for Middle East Truth, https://emetonline.org/rays-of-light-in-the-darkness.

14. "Hollywood Tower." n.d. Hollywood Tower, www.thehollywoodtower.com.

15. Found on the business's homepage of their website: www.beverlyhillsmailbox.com.

16. This and more information can be found on Wikipedia's, "AIPAC." Accessed May 6, 2023, https://en.wikipedia.org/wiki/AIPAC.

17. Bykowicz, Julie, and Natalie Andrews. "Pro-Israel Group Lobbies for U.S. Aid, Funds Congressional Trips," *The Wall Street Journal*, February 14, 2019, https://www.wsj.com/articles/pro-israel-group-lobbies-for-u-s-aid-funds-congressional-trips-11550174834.

18. Matthew 27:46 KJV